Banalysis

THE LIE DESTROYING
THE WEST

FRANK HAVILAND

TABLE OF CONTENTS

ACKNOWLEDGEMENTS

I would like to express my very deep thanks to William, Jack, and Katie, without whose efforts this book may never have seen the light of day.

To my darling Emily,

If only you could grow up in a world
where this book was unnecessary.

CHAPTER
1

Rite of Passage

Homo sapiens is a funny old species. The British famously don't like sex, but mysteriously haven't died out. People say 'it's what's on the inside that counts' yet are strangely obsessed with sustaining the appearance of youth. There is nothing so peaceful as religion, until you say something they disapprove of. And, 'money isn't everything' claims a society where the richest 1% own more than the other 99% combined[1]. To say that human beings are economical with the truth would be the understatement of the millennium.

Don't think I'm demeaning the act of lying; on the contrary I have the highest possible respect for it. Of all of man's great discoveries and inventions[2] – the wheel, the telephone, splitting the atom, the theory of evolution by natural selection – none comes close to the beauty and simplicity of the lie.

The idea of recreating reality, of fabricating an entirely new truth to feed to others, for various short or long-term advantages is *the* masterstroke of the human intellect. The intricate pathways of deceit are the finest algorithms ever processed, and humans are exceptionally talented in this department. This book will demonstrate that lying is a highly-evolved, deeply embedded – and deeply troubling foundation of a functioning society.

To look at it slightly more scientifically, consider two very different games: the royal game of chess, and its rather less regal counterpart, poker. Their common core is calculation and deception. As is well known, in poker, this is calculating odds, reading your opponent and bluffing. Whilst in chess, a player needs to calculate variations, and will set traps for his opponent with the hope that the enemy's analysis will not be deep enough to fully understand the strategy.

At the current state of play, computers are now the strongest chess players in the world. Indeed their dominance over human opponents is now so clear that 'odds matches' (ones in which the human has at least one extra pawn) are the only realistic chance for man to beat the machine.

The fact that humans can even compete with their silicone counterparts is remarkable, considering that the machines evaluate hundreds of millions of positions per second. It was always only a matter of time before brute force calculation would defeat us – humans are smart, but not that smart.

Chess however, is a 100% information game, where flawless calculation is crucial. Players always have full access to the facts. Poker on the other hand is not so transparent. You don't know what cards your opponents have, and therefore you don't know if what they're 'telling' you is true. Deception then, is the key factor.

Chess has lessons for life, but does not mirror it; poker does. Poker is akin to real-life lying, and even supercomputers have still not found a way to consistently beat human opposition at no-limit poker.

And that fact is nothing short of astonishing.

Games such as chess barely scratch the surface of man's genius and intellectual endeavour in this department. Who can forget some of history's greatest hits: The sexed-up dossier and weapons of mass destruction that catapulted us into war, Han van Meegeren's forgeries, Bernie Maddofs Ponzi scheme, the shroud of Turin, the Piltdown man, 'Peace for our time', 'I am not a crook', 'I did not have sexual relations with that woman', Enron, Tyco, Adelphia, Barings Bank, Société Générale, and so on.

Of course, these are famous examples where everyone got caught with their hand in the till. The best lies are the ones still in play which no one has yet identified. Indeed, some of the most powerful ideas in society right now are undoubtedly based upon lies. Why not? A lie merely requires imagination and savvy marketing, as opposed to genuine achievement. Why compete fairly, when cheating is so much more efficient? During the course of this book, perhaps we'll identify some grand deceptions together.

And meanwhile, what about all of us in our everyday lives?

Banalysis

Where would we all be without lying? How on earth are you supposed to navigate job interviews, make friends and keep them, or even get your leg over occasionally, if you're not able to lie through your teeth?

This book is about lying. About how, despite what some like to think, it is not a minor foible, engaged in by a decadent few (politicians, used car salesmen, and lawyers being the usual suspects). In fact, lying is essentially everything we do, everything we say and everything we reason. It is the very foundation of society, from norms of behaviour and attitudes, to cornerstones such as religion, current affairs, business, morality and love. It is the underlying unit of human interaction; a currency without which one would be bankrupt in every sense; a compass and passport through the murky waters of relationships; a privacy which none can penetrate.

Sun Zu, in his timeless classic, *The Art of War*, correctly alluded to this. "All warfare is based on deception." I just take issue with the word 'warfare'. It seems arguable that warfare is much more honest than peacetime activities – at least each side knows what game the other side is playing.

The cleverest and most beautiful lies, such as religion (pretending you're on first name terms with the boss), equality (pretending to think other people are equal to you), morality (pretending to be good) and love (pretending humans have the capacity for selfishlessness) are great works of art – they are the poetry of man's evolution. There should be museums dedicated to the glory and majesty of the achievements that this simple skill has created, and continues to create. Perhaps one day there will be.

We ought to start at the very beginning, if only to keep Julie Andrews happy. Fortunately, for most of us this is in the same place. Around the age of two or three, most of us tell our first lie[3]. We've only just become self-aware, and our 'theory of mind' (understanding that other people may think differently from us) is probably not yet in place, so the effort is rather lame.

All over the world, right at this second a toddler is about to have his Eureka moment. Let's call him 'Little Tommy'. Little Tommy is being quizzed re some minor misdemeanour. Mother asks: 'Did you wet the bed? / break the cup? / put the cat in the microwave?' and the genius inside little Tommy says 'no!'

Parents all over the world ought to be cracking open the champagne, stuffing chocolate biscuits and approbation down their offspring's throat, and eyeing exclusive prep schools for their progeny is well on the road to greatness. The research is clear on this issue - all children lie[4]. Indeed early beginnings in deception correspond strongly with success in life and higher IQ[5].

Sadly perhaps, I doubt that this has ever happened. Rather than approval, the poor little tyke is likely to be met with the most awful, hypocritical censure: 'You mustn't tell lies, Tommy!' So the obvious question is, who did the PR for lying?!

Society vs lying

To say that society has a rather fantastically negatively skewed position against lying is putting it mildly. This is consistent historically, with philosophers from St Augustine (5th century) to St Thomas Aquinas (13th century) and Immanuel Kant (18th century) all in agreement in their condemnation. Indeed, all three condemned all lying, though Augustine recognised that never doing so would be hard to live up to, and both he and Aquinas acknowledged that some forms were worse than others. To summarise, their concrete arguments against lying are thus:

1. Lying is a perversion of the natural faculty of speech, the natural end of which is to communicate the thoughts of the speaker.
2. When one lies, one undermines trust in society.

Consulting a dictionary for synonyms for 'dishonest' on the iMac that I am using gives us a plethora of illuminating alternatives: corrupt, cheating, devious, treacherous, dirty, unethical, immoral, unprincipled, amoral, criminal, and illegal. None of these carries any positive overtones, and certainly not exactly character traits that one would aspire to.

Society clearly recognises lying as a dangerous vice which needs to be coaxed out of us, with a good start often made in the home or the classroom. Classic sayings such as the Shakespearian 'honesty is the best policy' or 'the truth will out' demonstrate this.

Not wishing to be left out, God sticks his oar in with a late entry in the Ten Commandments 'Neither shall you bear false witness against your neighbour', more commonly referred to as 'thou shalt not lie', is echoed in all the Abrahamic religions.

In the face of this societal pressure and the concern that one might receive a frosty reception from Saint Peter, lying appears robustly defiant. The Little Tommy scenario plays out in all children, and is consistent throughout the lifespan, because clearly the human mind is predisposed to lying.

Lying is the marketing department's dream, the VHS equivalent of honesty's Betamax. No one has ever needed to be taught the benefits of lying, whilst we have all been lectured on the morality of honesty. Indeed, no matter how much the value of honesty is hammered into Little Tommy it will not necessarily take, for the simple reason that honesty, as a policy, does not pay much of a dividend.

We should perhaps pause here briefly to give a more quantitative look at what is known about human deception, just to see the ridiculousness of the above stigma. *Quirkology* (2008) by Professor Richard Wiseman, chair of the Public Understanding of Psychology at the University of Hertfordshire, makes for some interesting reading on deception. Wiseman's findings include that a third of conversations involve some deception; 90% of lies remain undetected; 80% of people have lied to secure a job, and 60% have cheated on a partner at least once. Interestingly, 8% of people claim never to have lied!

If we look at how information is communicated between people, the results are similarly squarely on the side of lying. Work by Albert Mehrabian in the 1970s gives a rough breakdown of the trust attributed to verbal and non-verbal communication by the receiver. The balance seems to be roughly 10% verbal, 30% tone of voice, 60% body language, that is, people attach much more credibility to the non-verbal channels. This is made more interesting by the fact that the verbal channel is the easier to control, and that many aspects of body language are not under conscious control. Put another way, we seem instinctively predisposed not to trust the data which communicators are able to regulate.

Further research[6] indicates that humans average in the region of 200 lies per day, that the majority of people can't go 10 minutes without lying, and that the rate of successfully detecting a lie is just 54%. This last statistic is perhaps the most pertinent. Humans then are so skilled at lying, they have reduced the competition's detective skills to nothing better than a coin flip

When asked, 'Are you a liar?' 97% of respondents say 'no'[6]. The fact is that we are all lying machines, happy to lynch others for the crime whilst professing our innocence. The gulf between the 3% willing to acknowledge their dishonesty, and the 97% who ought to, underscores just how important a tool lying is for the human race.

Honesty is not the best policy

Examined from a more theoretical perspective, it is easy to see why Tommy and the whole world would choose to invest so much energy in lying. One could very reasonably postulate many different forms and reasons for it. Indeed St Augustine, in his work *On Lying* (*De Mendacio*, 395 CE) proposes eight types, though these distill to a much smaller number. This is partly because of the inclusion of many distinct 'white lies' in Augustine's list, and partly because an exhaustive list is missing the point - the purpose of lying is to serve the speaker.

The slimmed-down version of Augustine is a basic triad: lying essentially serves two honourable purposes. First, self-preservation. Second, leverage against the competition. The third and most important strand is the process by which this is achieved – justification.

In the first instance, self-preservation, the case is as well made by history, as by common sense. As George Bernard Shaw put it: 'If you want to tell people the truth, make them laugh otherwise they'll kill you'. History is not testament to the good humour of man as it is awash with the bodies of those who died for their beliefs: Sir Thomas Moore, Dr Martin Luther King Jr, and Emily Davison being notable examples. How many more millions of lives must have been claimed under religious conquests or persecutions, or before the policy of '*don't* shoot the messenger' became the accepted norm?

In terms of religion alone, the policy of honesty has a lamentable record over the last few thousand years or so. Freely admitting to being a witch, pagan, heretic, infidel, homosexual, Christian, non-Christian, the wrong kind of Christian, a child, bastard, or a Jew at the wrong time, would not necessarily have done wonders for your life expectancy.

In 1937, Dale Carnegie's bestseller, *How to Win Friends and Influence People*, was first published. A reasonable summary is: be nice to people, tell them what they want to hear, and they will like you. Carnegie's point on dishonesty is that it costs you a little, but not much. Closer to home, 'Your bum really does look big in that, honey' is not a great recipe for marital bliss, any more than 'it's a fair cop, guv' should be used in similar clashes with authority.

The only incidences where brute honesty seems to be beneficial for the employer are those in which either the value of the truth is worth more than a lie (eg very close friendships where trust is of the utmost importance, and therefore has a large reciprocal reward), or situations in which the truth is so obvious that deviation from it would be foolish and seriously disadvantageous, (eg in legal settings where the result is clear, and a guilty plea has the advantage of a shorter sentence for not wasting court time).

In Augustine's second case, leverage against the competition, one has a multitude of examples to choose from. In the financial world, positions are leveraged all the time to maximize profit. This is the technique of increasing your exposure (but also your risk) for maximum return. A good example of dishonest leverage is a housing boom, which sees mortgage brokers artificially 'increasing' clients' incomes to enable them to afford more expensive houses. This works fine as long as demand for housing outstrips supply, and mortgage payments can be maintained, but is devastating if something goes wrong. Leverage is a zillionaire 'socialist' politician, calling for a higher tax rate, which he can dodge.

Leverage surrounds us everyday and in every way, we just never think about it: make-up, hair extensions, eye bag reductions, plastic surgery, push-up bras, airbrushed photos, fake Twitter followers, call-screening, CV embellishments, deodorant, perfume, fake tan, height insoles, marketing, advertising, endorsements, and so on. We are rarely brutally honest with the world.

If we consider our poker analogy again, we can see that players 'leverage' by bluffing. That is, they gain an advantage over their opponents by successfully 'lying' about their hands. Substitute poker for business and insider trading, sport and match-fixing, or athletics and banned substances etc.

The returns can be financial, votes, promotion, gold medals, chocolate biscuits, whatever, but the principle is the same: to win, humans need to leverage more successfully more than their cohorts do, and the ticket to doing this is not honesty.

It is worth highlighting that an honest person in the case of leverage is unlikely to finish first. If you are not prepared to leverage your position in a housing boom and others are, you will not get to live in the nice houses and the nice areas. Hence, lying about your income, 'lying' about your cards, etc affords maximum positional leverage over your contemporaries – it gets you ahead of the game. If you are not prepared to leverage, it may cost you.

This, along with self-preservation, is the main reason that honesty does not work. It is too linear to offer enough advantages for the user. As the American humourist Josh Billings put it, 'Honesty is a rare wealth anyone can possess, and yet all the honesty in the world ain't lawful tender for a loaf of bread'.

In terms of the process, justification is where the money truly is. This is by far the most complicated part, and will be covered at length in chapter two. At its most basic, justification is the means to square the impossible circle between honesty and getting what you want. The position is squared by leveraging to the hilt, while maintaining the *appearance* of honesty. Justification is the advertising process whereby we 'sell' leveraged positions (lies) as honest ones, in order to protect ourselves and get ahead of the competition.

For those who prefer maths, we have an equation for success. $S = J - T$, where S = Success (sexual conquests / votes / financial return etc), J = sale of leveraged positions via justification and T = truth one has to include to maintain integrity (ie to be believed). So for instance, a business which wants to maximise its market share and profits (S) may advertise green credentials, ethical business models, investment in the regions it hopes to sell in, rainforest alliances etc

(J). The more effectively its marketing and PR departments can persuade the public of J, the less T it has to admit (which is that profit is the sole motivator), and therefore, the higher its share price will be. Similarly, a politician seeking office will attempt to woo all the demographics in his constituency, feigning interest in all of their concerns despite his own personal beliefs. The more effectively he can do this, the greater his election chances.

As an example, consider the dilemma of the modern car manufacturer. His job is to make products that the public want to buy as cheaply as is appropriate for the model. That's it. However, unlike the good old days when that was the extent of his duties, in modern times he has to contend with an array of auxiliary problems, like pretending to be environmentally friendly or 'green'.

Of course, being green is an anathema to the car manufacturer, just like it is to the oil industry (though, rather ridiculously, even they still feign it). Having to pretend that a car is environmentally friendly is expensive; it costs time, R&D, and more importantly, money. So what is he to do?

Option A (honest and cheap option) is to tell the green lobby to get stuffed, and stick to your guns, with the risk that the public will boycott you. Not many companies are going for this at the moment. Option B (expensive option) is to meet the emissions targets / make hybrid motors / find alternative methods of fuel, and hope that you can beat the competition fair and square.

Wouldn't it be marvellous if you could find a way to combine the two – to get the benefits of B, while basically doing nothing more than A? Volkswagen certainly thought so. Only discovered in late 2015, Volkswagen managed to install a computer program into 11 million diesel cars which was able to cheat emissions tests. When vehicles were inspected, they went into a kind of safety mode, lowering emissions to meet the legal requirements. Post inspection, the cars would then revert to producing 40 times the legal pollution limit.

It's hard not to admire the ingenuity of such lies. Nice too were the slick advertising campaigns, with slogans such as 'Clean Diesel'. Rather below-par in comparison were the words of subsequently-resigning CEO Martin Winterkorn, who claimed he was: *'stunned that misconduct on such a scale was possible.'* or that the defeat devices were the responsibility of *'the grave errors of very few,'* - as if some near-retirement tea lady, in fear of a meagre pension, had sneakily doctored the equipment while the engineers were at lunch.

Make no mistake, Volkswagen are not alone; they may simply have had the misfortune of being the best leveragers, at least until recently that is. In an industry where cheating is commonplace, manufacturers routinely 'facilitate' test conditions by using lighter vehicles, over-inflated tyres, switching off basically everything except the engine, and even testing at altitude. That's why, when independently-tested, vehicles generally are 30% less fuel efficient than the advertising suggests, and between three and five times more polluting.

Even if we assume that Volkswagen was alone (and we'd be fools to), let's turn to an industry where leverage is commonplace. Consider banking. Between 1990 and 2010 the UK's Big 4 banks, RBS, Lloyds, HSBC and Barclays, had a hoot with the PPI scandal.

They sold payment protection insurance on loans or credit cards, often without the customer's consent or knowledge, and often to those such as the elderly or self-employed, who could never have claimed from the policy anyway. Estimates of what they raked in range between £2.2-2.6 billion per annum, until they were found out.

The best feature of this episode, at least for me, is the use of the term 'mis-selling', as if the banks mistakenly gave the customers the wrong product – just like you do when you send your grandmother a Happy Birthday text, but accidentally attach your naked selfie, 45 million times!

If we go back to little Tommy for a moment, we can see that his discovery is of epic proportion. He has outlined what we might call the 'balance sheet model' of human interaction – the compromise between lying as successfully as he can and maintaining an image of integrity. I suspect that there is an optimal ratio for this equation, ie a minimum element of truth to maintain credibility, though it may vary from industry to industry or scenario to scenario. It is likely, for instance, that a great poker player knows precisely just how often to bluff, and then does not deviate far from that ratio.

Of course, there are naturally many settings where people are unlikely to lie. When asked, 'Would you like a cup of tea?', it would seem a reasonable assumption that people reveal their true intentions. There is no value in lying, and potentially something to be lost – ie getting the wrong drink, or none at all. In comparison, when escorting a beautiful date home at 2am, and being asked, 'Would you like to come in for a coffee?' a man would be well-advised to say 'yes' automatically, even if he's watching his caffeine intake.

The principle of leverage is a fascinating eye-opener in terms of human behaviour. We do not like others to even contemplate using it, because it dilutes our own potency. If we reuse the poker analogy, we can see that the optimal position would be a game where no one else is allowed to bluff in any way, thus maximising our deceptive edge. Of all the commodities you could have a monopoly over, lying would be the gold standard. This perfectly explains society's (at least vocal) antipathy towards it.

Lying in the leveraged sense is therefore an effective nuclear arms race amongst the population. The desire to lie is kept somewhat in check by the destruction which would result from everyone lying all the time.

In many ways, the balance sheet model (S=J-T), is merely an extension of Darwinian natural selection, except that whilst the rest of the animal kingdom is playing an honest game of survival of the fittest, man's edition incorporates an extra element, so that evolutionary success is measured by the ability to sell lies as truth. Or, 'survival of the Arthur Daleys'[7].

Good Acts

If the notion of leverage has any validity, then a good place to start looking for it will be in 'good acts'. This is because a nominally good act affords the employer the maximum amount of leverage over his contemporaries, and therefore would be something that people would want to do.

When we say 'good', implicitly we accept that we are talking about a deviation from the norm. I am using the term to encapsulate the idea of virtuous, morally admirable, upright behaviour. When we talk about good actions, we mean ones which do not directly benefit the actor, but someone else.

We also know that logically, and in the Darwinian sense, those who perform genuine good acts – which cost the individual more than he recoups – are unlikely to thrive, because they are too expensive in evolutionary terms. What makes sense therefore is that 'good' acts will only be old versions of self-interest, with some PR and spin to market them as philanthropic[8].

In the animal kingdom for instance, scientists have often claimed the existence of altruism (this helps if you are trying to prove it exists in humans), though it always turns out under closer inspection to be a fallacy, or at least misunderstood. The meerkat model is a good example of this. Whilst feeding, meerkats can be reliably observed with a single 'sentry' standing guard in an exposed position, waiting to sound the alarm should a hawk be seen, so that the feasting group can escape. What transpires, however, is that the sentry is always well-fed beforehand and is the first to dash for cover once the alarm is sounded[9], so being 'good' is worth it.

Other examples of alleged altruism are kin selection (favouring closest family members, and therefore those who share your genes) or quid pro quos (grooming behaviour, food sharing), you scratch my back and I'll scratch yours, in the animal kingdom, literally. These are no more altruistic than the bank paying you an interest rate on your savings.

In terms of humans, the example which is generally wheeled out to save our honour is charity. And it does seem to be a hard thing to dismiss, since charitable donations genuinely do disadvantage the donor financially.

On closer inspection, the case is not so clear. Donations can often be written off against tax; bolster one's self esteem; ingratiate the recipients; and boost one's public profile. This is illustrated by the fact that only one per cent of donations are made anonymously; we really do feel good about ourselves when we give, and people will work twice as hard to make charitable donations when the results are made public[10].

Moreover, the cited incidences of goodness suffer from 'localisation'. An experiment into tolerance to pain for financial reward found that participants were able to hold out much longer if close family members rather than strangers were rewarded. In other words, people are willing to suffer more for those with the best chance and reason for reciprocity[11]. According to the Center on Philanthropy at Indiana University in 2004, 80% of American giving goes to the local community, with only one per cent going to international aid. Indeed, even in the most generous countries, combined governmental and individual charitable donations do not top one per cent of GDP.

In 2009, with a major world recession, Bill Gates and Warren Buffet founded 'The Giving Pledge'. This is a philanthropic movement to get other billionaires to give up at least half of their wealth to charitable causes, either alive or posthumously. This sounds great, but should we really be impressed by this?

Recent research on happiness[12] indicates that a salary increase does increase happiness, but only up to a reasonably low point (equivalent to a UK salary of £40,000 pa), at which point it levels off. Beyond a certain point then, money will not make you happier. Perhaps this is where philanthropy becomes more attractive?

Here is the billionaire, Warren Buffet, explaining his motivation for giving:

> This pledge will leave my lifestyle untouched and that of my children as well. They have already received significant sums for their personal use and will receive more in the future. They live comfortable and productive lives. And I will continue to live in a manner that gives me everything that I could possibly want in life.
>
> Some material things make my life more enjoyable; many, however, would not. I like having an expensive private plane, but owning a half-dozen homes would be a burden. Too often, a vast collection of possessions ends up possessing its owner. The asset I most value, aside from health, is interesting, diverse, and long-standing friends.

In other words, only when I have everything I want, to the extent that more would be a burden, do I give. Altruism indeed! Clearly therefore, there is a strong leverage element to charity. Appearing to be doing good things is a strong motivator. Are there any additional benefits to good acts?

When it comes to giving, a good motivation is what is in it for us. For instance, despite the fact that women score higher on empathy measures[13], it is often men who are most willing to lend their assistance. When giving money to beggars, men give more to females than to males[14]. When stopping for broken down female drivers, men are more likely to stop for a woman, and more likely still if she is attractive[15].

Let's consider a more recent example, which will be familiar to most of us. In mid-2014 the 'Ice Bucket Challenge' went viral. Millions of people, including celebrities, posted videos pouring ice water over themselves to Facebook and YouTube. The 'challenge' also involved a donation to charity, and the ability to nominate subsequent participants.

The act of participating therefore is incredibly public, so the potential for leverage is great. What about the cost to the individual? According to the Charities Aid Foundation[16], one in 6 people in the UK have participated in the challenge, yet only 10% of the participants have donated.

That would suggest that the desire to leverage and to be considered 'good' is 10 times as strong as the desire to actually be good.

The value of the victim

It follows then that not only the mere action of pretending to be good is important, but so too is the brand of victim you choose to assist, of pivotal importance to the leverager. Consider the woeful plight of do-gooders across the globe, staring forlornly at the impoverished surrounding them. Who wants to help an old granny across the road or give some dirty homeless guy a bit of loose change, when those individuals are doing nothing to boost your public profile; they probably don't even have Instagram accounts to thank you on. Wherever can you find a decent victim, who can maximise your leverage?

Finally, the Syrian refugee crisis hit Europe in 2015. It must have felt like Christmas, the Oscars, and a never-ending line of celebrity charity events all rolled into one. At last, here was a campaign you could really get behind and prove just how much you cared.

The bidding was started with Labour politician, Yvette Cooper, who volunteered to take in a refugee family to her London home while running for the Party leadership. Scotland's first minister, Nicola Sturgeon, soon followed suit, and the hashtag *#refugeeswelcome* was rushed out rather prematurely into the world, before it was confidently on solids.

The bandwagon snowballed on, as the charlatans tried to outbid each other, in ever-flashier gestures of moral indignation. The actress Emma Thompson (worth a mere $45 million) tried the race card:

> The idea of 3,000 people in Calais who have been through unspeakable things makes me feel very ashamed.... I think it's got a lot to do with racism. If these people were white, European...I think we would feel quite differently about it.

The considerably wealthier ($150 million) Bob Geldof said he felt *'profound shame'* at the growing refugee crisis, and offered to share some of his property (notably, for a limited period)

> Let's put our money where our mouth is. I'll start. I'm lucky. I have a place in Kent. I will take three Syrian families into my place in the country and one family into my flat in London. They can stay there until they get set up here and get going by themselves. Anyone else? Any takers?

The actor Benedict Cumberbatch compensated for his paltry personal fortune of $15 million, by stating that the UK should take in an unlimited number of migrants, as he lambasted the British Government at the end of a performance of Hamlet.

The UK could not monopolise the grief however, as German Chancellor Angela Merkel pulled out all the stops to unleash a national 'all refugees welcome' policy.

Meanwhile, across the UK the hundreds of thousands of homeless children, disabled war veterans, mental patients, cancer, aids and multiple sclerosis sufferers, drug addicts, and the deaf and blind, were kicking themselves that they had picked the wrong kind of victimhood to work with.

The human need to be considered a good person is extremely strong. I doubt whether even Hitler got up, sipped a cup of finest Gestapo Grey, looked himself squarely in the mirror and, while combing his moustache thought to himself: 'I'm going to be a real shit today!'

But the fact is that we are not good. From the cradle to the grave, we're all doing the same thing all the time – trying to leverage our positions. The baby in the high chair is exactly the same as the President being impeached – one didn't eat all the chocolate biscuits, the other definitely did not have sexual relations with that woman. Each is guilty of the same crime, getting caught doing what everyone else is doing.

Leverage is everything, everywhere, and every one. We all know this intuitively. We also know how to spot the obvious stuff. When we read online: 'Single mum earns $6,000 per day at home using this simple trick', we don't click on the link, because we are leveraging experts, and we know when we are being oversold. How do we know? We know because the leverage is too high, too thinly disguised.

In many ways, life is just one extended game of no-limit poker. We have to perfect our own bluffs, but we also have to beware that others may bluff too. Justification is the process by which we sell those bluffs.

CHAPTER
2

Justification

Recognising leverage

It is important to always be on the lookout for other people's leverage hanging around delinquently on street corners, waiting for the chance to mug us. I remind myself of this when my barber tells me soothingly that I am not going bald, my tailor insists that I look good in my new suit, and my wife affirms that I am a very sexy man. I'm sure they're telling me the truth. At least they're better than the people at work, always joking around saying things like 'lazy bastard'.

Spotting the leverage is difficult, not least of which because of its ubiquity. Fortunately, however, there are certain clues which can help us to make a correct diagnosis. The first is that leveraged positions (lies) generally need to be sold (justified) to the listener.

'Truth never needs to justify itself' as the saying goes, and the point is a valid one. Lies, on the other hand, do require a little more work, since the chance that someone else will stumble upon your particular version of events without encouragement, is very slim indeed.

Research on the linguistic analysis of deception reveals that when lying, our workload is increased, and consequently we need more time to come up with our answers. For instance, liars speak more slowly than those telling the truth[17], write significantly longer emails to convince the reader[18], take significantly longer to send dishonest chat messages[19], as well as significantly longer to identify true/false statements[20].

Time and length of utterance are not the only distinguishing features of a lie. Liars are aware of their dishonesty, and the need to persuade the listener[21]. Therefore, rather ironically, the justifier is doing you a massive favour. Not only does he highlight the probability that he is lying, but he also provides you with a code which can be decrypted. He says: 'Here I am presenting to you the facts. However, I may have embellished a little. I may have reshuffled the components. I have certainly added my commission. My commission might be a 5% lie (you look nice in that dress darling) or a 100% lie (I'd never sleep with your sister).' Can you crack the code?

Absolutely everything anyone ever justifies to you of importance may fit this description, and is deceptive in some way. It is trying to influence you, to sell you a position, or to get you on side. If not to get your bra off, at least to loosen the straps. What it is almost certainly not doing is merely trying to give you the truth. If a situation is worth leveraging, people invariably do.

The code of language

This is where the romantic, philosophical position on lying as 'a perversion of the natural faculty of speech, the natural end of which is to communicate the thoughts of the speaker' is shown to be insanely naïve. Like claiming that men ply women with drinks in a bar, due to concerns about the chronic dangers of dehydration. Rather than clarity, the purpose of speech is to *serve* the speaker.

As translators of code, there are a number of tools at our disposal, as well as obstacles to negotiate. On the plus side of ledger, is the fact that words have concrete meanings, and that, despite what people may say or like to think, yes means yes. Moreover, because of the rather binary nature and inherent honesty (meaning) of language, the lying process is refutable by the fact that somewhere in the overall message an inconsistency is being conveyed.

On the minus side is the fact that indulging in semantics, increasingly relativistic approaches to truth, and political correctness all foster an environment whereby chicanery is a perennial problem, and words are robbed, or at least diluted of their implicit value, so that yes means yes in all cases, apart from when it means no.

At its most fundamental, lying is simply an inversion of reality. The startled child who shouts instantly 'wasn't scared!' or the hapless Romeo who claims 'She's a lesbian,' are using 100% deception. They simply inverted the truth to protect themselves. Usually though, the process is more complex, with justifiers injecting lies sporadically onto an otherwise pure canvass.

To recall the Balance Sheet Model for a moment, success is achieved by the sale of leveraged positions as true ones. The process works by taking an aim, converting it into a lie, and selling via justification. Importantly, this is often under the aegis of rectitude, so that A is achieved and B is the accepted explanation.

Hence A, aim (having an affair) = B, leveraged position (not having an affair) sold via C, justification (I was working late at the office, dear). When listening to justification therefore, we must always ask ourselves what are we being sold and why?

Inversion: the first port of call

When trying to decipher what people are really saying to us, a good place to start (and with some people a good place to remain indefinitely) is this crude inversion technique. When politicians, for example, claim that they want to 'serve the public' no doubt many of us have an eye-rolling-induced filter mechanism which translates it to something like: 'I'm not remotely interested in serving anyone but myself: I want to climb the greasy pole, make a name for myself, wield as much power as possible, finish off with a few salacious affairs, and retire to the Country with a Knighthood.' Sounds pretty good to me; someone on that ticket would get my vote at least.

By contrast, a sales job is much harder to leverage, because there is basically only one component: sell lots of units and you get lots of money, don't and you're out of a job. Unlike his political counterparts therefore, the salesman has a harder time trying to convince you that he has socially acceptable motivation for selling his wares. What he would dearly love to sell to you is the notion that he is not trying to sell anything, and indeed that the unspoken commission is an anathema to him. He is simply so enamoured with his product that he just has to share the information with you.

This was obviously picked up on recently by sales companies, which is why you have presumably had a phone call of this nature:

> Salesperson: Good morning, how are you today?
> You: Fine thanks
> Salesperson: The first thing to say is that this is not a sales call
> You: *hangs self with phone cord*

Here are some more Selling strategies:

> Limited offer (offer completely unlimited)
> Last chance to act now! (we need money quickly, so please act now)
> Last flat in block! (we haven't sold anything yet)

What is really occurring here is the need to sell, inverted and translated into urgency for the customer rather than the salesman. *Last Flat in Block* for instance. Has anyone ever seen a new development which didn't have only one more unit to sell? Moreover, if there really is only one more unit / stock / item etc, is advertising this paucity really necessary or efficient for the seller?

A hilarious recent version of this was one company trying to get their share of the PPI commission in 2017, following a Government ruling that there would be a cut-off deadline for claimants. The radio advert opened like this: 'To those of you worried about the deadline for PPI...' Yes, the PPI company is concerned about *you* missing out on your money!

The inversion technique is good, but rather crude – the blustery John Wayne of deception. Despite that, it is always a good first port of call. For those who are not John Wayne fans, leverage has spawned a multitude of variations. Like genetic mutations in a strand of DNA, so lies also evolve and grow in complexity. Ingenious leveragers keep developing new ways to conceal their deception, as in the following examples:

Force Majeure

As an atheist, and firm proponent of evolution, the idea of maintaining the existence of a God in the absence of any evidence, is absurd to me. Yet personal beliefs are not the issue. The point is, organised religions have succeeded in ensuring billions of followers essentially 'take their word for it'; whatever the truth may actually be.

While it may appear to be a cop-out on my part, I believe the exploration of religion as the greatest lie in history requires a book in itself. For the sake of brevity, I hope you will forgive my merely stating that I consider religion to be the ultimate blueprint for leverage. It is for this reason I feel it deserves great respect, whatever else one may think about it.

In terms of this book, perhaps the greatest asset that God brings to the table is a divine *force majeure* (a legal term meaning unforeseen circumstances which exonerate contractual obligations, such as war or earthquakes). This force provides multiple advantages to the adherents of religion: justifying the unjustifiable, explaining the inexplicable, and exonerating us from responsibility because it's 'God's will'.

Force majeure arguments are often employed outside of the religious framework too. The simplest perhaps being the child's version. Realising that 'Screw you, teacher!' might not cut it when caught without homework, the child throws his four-legged friend under the bus with 'The dog ate my homework, Sir.'

As an interesting aside, *force majeure* subjects appear to come from a very narrow pool, as though there is a certain degree of 'acceptability' in the leverage chosen. In addition, these pools may be age, industry, or culture specific. When I was at school you were most likely to hear 'we had a power cut', which has subsequently morphed into 'our Wi-Fi was down'. By contrast, the rail industry seems to suffer rather predictably from 'leaves on the line' every autumn, and 'the tracks being too cold' in winter.

In Asia however, it's a different story. Having taught university English in South Korea for many years, I could always guarantee that selfish grandparents would hold out on death until the end of term exam. It was the long night before the test itself however, which proved too much for them; necessitating that their hapless grandchildren could not attend the following day. In some classes, as many as 50% of the students would be affected in this way. Given that testing was a bi-annual event, it was often possible to wipe out entire generations in a single year – Hiroshima and Nagasaki eat your heart out!

Force majeure may also be used to avoid facing reality, a sort of intellectually-dishonest comfort blanket. In effect, it is a way of controlling that which we cannot control. The individual can gain great comfort from the notion of a grand plan of which he is an integral part. God, Astrology, Tarot, Palm-readings, Psychics, Fate, Karma and Destiny all have a part to play; it's a big market.

If we consider the following expressions straight from the sophist's Bible, we can see that this dishonesty is endemic in the language:

If you can't beat them, join them. (Pretend you at least made the decision, so you're in control.)

Que sera sera. (We can't influence anything, so actions are unnecessary.)

It's for the best. (It's doubtless not for the best, but what's done is done.)

It has also been invoked in literary form on several occasions, for instance Voltaire's 'Dr Panglos', or Eleanor H Porter's 'Pollyanna'.

The most powerful abdication of responsibility is when you call God to the witness box himself. After all, omniscient, omnipotent entities are quite hard to argue with. Here is former US President George W Bush (according to Nabil Shaath, the Palestinian Foreign Minister) explaining in 2003 how God told him to invade Iraq: 'I'm driven with a mission from God. God would tell me, "George, go and fight those terrorists in Afghanistan." And I did, and then God would tell me, "George, go and end the tyranny in Iraq." And I did.'

Good News / Bad News

God is a good seller, but so too is the salesman who manages to convince you that he is doing you a favour; he has done everything he needs to do. L'Oréal tried to achieve this with their 'because you're worth it' slogan. L'Oréal however, is of course wrong – you're probably not worth it, but either way beautification is a decision for your wallet, rather than your character.

In Hans Christian Anderson's *The Emperor's New Clothes*, the naked Emperor is told that he looks 'Magnificent!', 'Splendid!', 'Regal!' etc, which just goes to show you cannot trust people who tell you what you want to hear, especially when they're staring at your dick.

A better example would be 'Peace for our time' where Neville Chamberlain was duped by Hitler into reassuring the British public that Germany had no intention of entering into a second world war. Though often criticised for this, Chamberlain was in fact merely the victim of Hitler's good news leverage tactic – good news that the country so desperately wanted. Hitler's great coup was that he managed to get Chamberlain to do the selling for him!

Sometimes of course, good news does not work or is inappropriate. Bad news then might be a viable alternative. If you are a software company and someone is making pirated copies of your product, thereby denying you revenue, how can you effectively persuade them not to do so? Microsoft tried: 'If this software was not purchased for corporate or institutional use, it may be counterfeit. Using counterfeit software exposes your computer and data to increased security risks, including viruses.'

Aha! You thought you were saving money by ripping us off, but in fact you are damaging yourself. Notice how the company does not mention the lost revenue, its only concern apparently is the data loss of criminals.

Compartmentalisation

In this scenario actions are not defended as such, but rather are suggested to belong to discrete categories which in themselves carry different rules, and are therefore used to justify actions which would otherwise not be permissible. The most famous example of this is 'befehl ist befehl' (orders are orders), also known as the Nuremberg Defence employed by many Nazi's at the Nuremberg Trials of 1945-46. The defence is not restricted to war crimes however, and is popular in many guises:

> *Business is business.*
> *All's fair in love and war.*

Alternatively, compartmentalisation is used as a get-out-of-jail-free card when faced with an uncomfortable question. The leverager merely points out how the question does not pertain to himself, or that it belongs to a field which is not the topic of discussion in an attempt to avoid answering it.

Evasion

The tactic employed here can be quite entertaining. The evader pretends to mishear the question, pretends that he doesn't understand the question, and/or simply answers a question he preferred to answer in the first place. It's a tactic that any effective politician must know. Perhaps the best example of this is the now infamous Jeremy Paxman interview with former Conservative Party leader Michael Howard, back in 1997. Howard was asked whether he had threatened to overrule the Head of the Prison Service, Derek Lewis, over the dismissal of the Governor of Parkhurst Prison, John Marriot.

Not only did Howard manage to ignore the 'threaten' part of the question 12 times, but by the end was actually conducting the interview himself, explaining what the correct question should have been.

Diffusion

Humour has often been a great foil, cleverly sneaking in a guilty plea under the radar by making others laugh. 'Many a true word spoken in jest' as we all know. Here is Boris Johnson, former Mayor of London, and longtime contender for leader of the Conservative Party, who has essentially made a career out of this, 'I'm backing David Cameron's campaign out of pure, cynical self-interest.'

Having been accused by George Galloway of being a 'drink-sodden, ex-Trotskyist popinjay' meanwhile, the late and razor-witted Christopher Hitchens quipped, 'only some of which is true.'

Displacement

Displacement is, once again not denying the action itself, but merely the reason for doing so. At some level displacement is key to all leverage as it is simply finding a more convenient way to frame an action.

In February 2011, British Prime Minister David Cameron was on a tour to promote 'democracy' in the Middle East. To illustrate his commitment to the cause, he brought with him a group of senior defence manufacturers to promote the British arms industry to the region. Cameron must have been studying the Al Capone guide to democracy: you can get much further with a kind word and a gun than you can with a kind word alone.

Sensing that some misguided onlookers might detect a slight incongruence between the simultaneous promotion of democracy and armaments, Cameron's justification was:

The idea that we should expect small and democratic countries like Kuwait to be able to manufacture all their means of defence seems to me completely at odds with reality.

In other words, the role of the British Arms industry is to address bomb inequality. The displacement technique is a fantastically rich field for leveragers. If you can convincingly pretend that you're not after money but instead have a higher moral purpose, then the possibilities for leverage are limitless.

Let's take the art world. For centuries, artists struggled for years over one single painting, lived in abject poverty and merrily cut bits off themselves, secure in the minute possibility that they would be famous long after their death. How lucky they were. Pity the modern or contemporary artist. They lament that 'everything in art has been done already.' Cue Damien Hirst, the world's richest modern artist (estimated to be a billionaire), and quite possibly the only man in history with less artistic talent than myself. His career consists of dead animals in formaldehyde, boxes of pills placed on medicine cabinets, and a production team who produce paint coloured dots on plain canvas for a mere million dollars a throw. Or how about Piero Manzoni, famous for his excrement in a tin. What are we to make of that?

Susie Hodge, British artist and author explains in her book, *Why your 5 year old could not have done that*[22], that to appreciate modern art you have to understand it. Re Manzoni, she explains, 'Manzoni intended to parody the heady valuations attached to art and put a spin on 1960's consumerism.'

But Susie Hodge is wrong. When the Prince Art Gallery in Soho, New York displayed modern art paintings by pre-schoolers, the audience gushed and fawned as usual, unaware that they were being duped[23]. Even in properly controlled psychology experiments, when famous modern artists' work was showcased along with children's and even animal's work, the fake modern art was preferred 30-40 % of the time[24].

Freddie Linksky, a toddler of 2 meanwhile has fooled the art world into buying his tomato ketchup works. His mother, claiming her son was an art critic, posted his works on collector Charles Saatchi's online gallery. Here is Freddie's mother's caption on one of his paintings:

The striking use of oriental calligraphy has the kanji-like characters stampeding from the page, showing the new ascent of the East. It is one of Linsky's most experimental works.

Little wonder that a gallery in Berlin emailed to request an exhibition, saying, 'Freddie's work was of a high standard and (it) would like him to participate.'

The genius (if we can call it that) of modern art is to invert (leverage) the responsibility of who precisely is doing the work. Former wallies like Rembrandt and Picasso thought that the responsibility lay with *them*, whereas the modern artist knows that under the right circumstances, a good soupcon of piss on a canvas is enough to make the right punter struggle to find meaning where none exists.

Here's Damien Hirst again, when asked by Jeremy Paxman whether he cares more about money than art: 'Money's not real and art is'. At other times, Hirst has been seemingly more open about his motivations. 'What I really like is minimum effort for maximum effect.' Alternatively, 'The spot paintings, the spin paintings, they're all a mechanical way to avoid the actual guy in a room, myself, with a blank canvas.' Or, my personal favourite, 'I do believe still that art is the most powerful currency in the world, and that's why people pay a lot of money for it.'

Willful Incoherence

Modern art's trump card is that it compels the viewer to do the work of discerning a meaning. Some people manage to forge a career similarly, by calling upon others to find meaning in their incoherent babbling.

British comedian Russell Brand falls rather heavily, headlong into this category. Brand, continually repackaging himself from junkie to political commentator, has recently become a sort of modern day messiah to his fans, touring with a show of the same name. In his book *Revolution*,[25] he advises the electorate not to vote, and calls for 'massive redistribution of wealth'.

Brand does not appear to grasp that it's a bit rich lecturing on equality when you're an unashamed multi-millionaire, bourgeois hedonist. Lest we get carried away with the name-calling, let's consider some of his erudition. The following are two of the more readable excerpts from his magnum opus:

This attitude of churlish indifference seems like nerdish deference contrasted with the belligerent antipathy of the indigenous farm folk, who regard the hippie-dippie interlopers, the denizens of the shimmering tit temples, as one fey step away from transvestites.

Or, in more scientific mood:

If we consider humanity to be not a disparate and separate conglomeration of individuals but the temporary physical manifestation and expression of a subtler electromagnetic, microcosmic realm (thy will be done, on earth as it is in heaven), like in Campbell's lightbulb allegory, then all resultant phenomena emanated from a single source, so we are all jointly responsible.

Makes you feel better about your own education though, doesn't he? Brand's esoteric gambit here appears to be to stick a few intellectual-sounding long words together in a grammatically-incoherent mush, and then to lob the literary grenade as far away as possible, leaving it for someone else to clean up.

To be fair to Brand he is not a man of letters, so let's jump to Deepak Chopra. Chopra is a different kettle of fish. He has a thorough grounding in science, having obtained a medical degree in India and then specializing in endocrinology. At some point in his career, he seems to have realized that science is a damned hard game. There are so many things which get in the way, trivial things like empirical rigour, peer review, evidence. What he really needed was a niche market where his talents could be a given a free, less regulated reign.

In the 1990s, he gained a cult following thanks to his promotion on The Oprah Winfrey Show, and has since morphed into possibly the wealthiest and most famous New Age guru in the world[26]. Like Brand, but with more polish, Chopra has made a career out of being so esoteric that he is effectively beyond criticism or contradiction. After all, how can you contradict nothing?

Here is Chopra being typically lucid: 'Spirituality is the experience of that domain of awareness where we experience our universality.' Or:

I think I'm going to have to say that science is now in a process of overthrowing the climactic overthrow of the superstition of materialism. That everything that can be called matter comes from something that is not material, that the essential nature of the physical world, is that it's not physical.

Many allege that Brand is sincere. No such support however can be made for Chopra. He knows all too well that his estimated $80 million bank balance relies heavily on his incoherence. To test that, take a look at Wisdomofchopra.com, a website which matches genuine quotes from the great man with quotes 'generated from a list of words that can be found in Deepak Chopra's Twitter stream randomly stuck together in a sentence.'

The results are astonishing. Thirty-five per cent of participants cannot tell a genuine Chopra quote from a randomly-generated series of nonsense words, which tells you just about all you need to know. Chopra is no fool. While being essentially incomprehensible, he manages to slip in just enough good news sporadically for his followers to lap up, as in: 'Ageing is simply learned behaviour that can be slowed or prevented.'

Semantics

Even when you're being nailed to the floor, and the evidence is overwhelming, you can sometimes still put up a good fight. Semantics is the panicked, often last resort where the exponent doesn't fight the accusation so much as the meaning of the words used. Here's Bill Clinton when questioned about his relationship with Monika Lewinsky, famously trying to work out the meaning of the word 'is':

> Ken Starr: That statement is a completely false statement. Whether or not Mr. Bennett knew of your relationship with Ms Lewinsky, the statement that there was "no sex of any kind in any manner, shape or form, with President Clinton," was an utterly false statement. Is that correct?
> Bill Clinton: It depends on what the meaning of the word "is" is. If the. If he. If "is" means is and never has been, that is not, that is one thing. If it means there is none, that was a completely true statement.

Euphemisms

Sometimes, danger can be averted by deliberately misnaming something, either so as not to cause offence, or, the more likely case, to avoid people correctly interpreting what you are saying. In the UK in 2014, it came to light that 1,400 children had been sexually abused over a period of 16 years in the town of Rotherham. The crime was exacerbated by the fact that the police and officials turned a blind eye, not wanting to be classed as 'racist'. The crimes, perpetrated by mostly Muslim men, were euphemistically reported in the media as committed by 'Asians'.

Rectitude

Of all the leveraging attempts that we can discuss, the most flagrant example must be that of invoking rectitude. When a speaker has to resort to the charade of 'it's the right thing to do', you know he is really scraping the bottom of the barrel. In fact, he may as well erect a 50ft high neon sign screaming: 'Leverage Alert!'

Appearing on Radio 4 in July 2010, Foreign Secretary David Miliband was asked whether he regretted not stepping down at the same time as Work and Pensions Secretary James Purnell in June 2009. This was at the height of a potential coup to oust Prime Minister Gordon Brown. The loss of such a senior cabinet member would undoubtedly have led to a leadership challenge, which, in the end, Miliband was unsure he would win:

I could've resigned with him and then we would have had two people out of the Cabinet. That would've meant more damage to the Government, more damage to the party and, since we would have lost the Foreign Secretary, more damage to the country as well.

There is an interesting element of seepage involved here. While focusing on the major lie (the inversion of disloyalty to the justification of loyalty to the party and the leader), Miliband neglects to control the rest of his statement with quite the same fervour. 'Damage to the country' comes almost as an afterthought to bolster the position that challenging for the leadership was a bad option, when politicians will always insist that the country, rather than the party or government, comes first.

David did get his chance to run for the leadership, once Labour had lost the election. Keeping it in the family, younger brother, Ed, decided to run against his brother, a race David was almost certain to win. Indeed, Ed only managed the narrowest of wins (50.5%) resulting in David (the more accomplished and experienced politician by far) withdrawing from professional politics, and his ambition to lead the party. Ed's comment in 2010: 'Because what is happening in politics, what really counts is my family and I think it is very, very important to realise that and hold onto that.' Ed wants to have his stab-big-brother-in-the-back and eat it too, but the attempt to leverage that as 'what really counts is my family' is wholly insulting.

So remember, the next time someone in authority sincerely claims, 'We're only concerned with your welfare', you can be sure that's the very last thing they are concerned about.

Invalidation

If you're starting to run out of ideas, and none of the above will save you, you can always resort to one of the most popular modern brands of deceit – invalidation. Claiming that your opponent is an unworthy man appears magically to exonerate you from having to deal with his accusation. The tactic of invalidation works by discrediting the speaker, in an attempt to colour the conclusions arrived at (tarring each side of the equation with the same brush). Hence the syllogism:

> X is an imbecile and X makes a statement = therefore, the statement is imbecilic
> This twisting of logic is nicely exposed by Joseph Heller in *Catch 22*. 'Just because you're paranoid, doesn't mean they aren't after you.'

Politics is a good arena for invalidation. The slightest stain on a person's character can be enough to ruin their political career, even when the accusation may be unfounded, or seemingly has little bearing upon their ability to do the job. Former Conservative minister, Ann Widdecombe, for example, is famously considered to be responsible for ruining Michael Howard's 1997 leadership election chances when she remarked, 'there is something of the night about him.' Howard was thereafter frequently satirised as a vampire, and went on to come last in the poll. A similar phenomenon befell 2001 Conservative leadership hopeful Michael Portillo. At the outset, Portillo held a six percent first ballot lead, which was still a considerable five percent after the second ballot. According to eventual runner-up Kenneth Clarke, Portillo's chances were damaged by press stories, in particular those about his homosexual past[27], which resulted in him finishing a disappointing third.

Offence

In the current climate, the most popular choice of the invalidation technique is that of 'playing the victim card' by claiming that you have been offended. Not for these poor souls the starving of Africa, the massive problems caused by wealth inequality, murder, rape and torture – those issues are so yesterday. Pity the guy with hurt feelings; his problems definitely need attending to.

In the summer of 2015, with thousands of illegal migrants stationed at Calais, trying to break into the UK, David Cameron received criticism for commenting thus: 'This is very testing, I accept that, because you have got a swarm of people coming across the Mediterranean, seeking a better life.'

This was immediately leapt upon by senior opposition figures, intent on making political capital. Labour's Harriet Harman essayed, 'He should remember he's talking about people not insects...just using inflammatory language is not going to help.'

Liberal Democrat leader Tim Farron opined,

> By blaming "immigrant swarms" for the current crisis in Calais, David Cameron risks dehumanising some of the world's most desperate people. We are talking about human beings here, not insects.

Labour leadership hopeful, Andy Burnham commented,

> 'Cameron calling Calais migrants a "swarm" is nothing short of disgraceful. Confirms there's no dog-whistle these Bullingdon Boys won't blow.'

Labour here highlighted the self-evident fact that some immigrants' feelings might have been hurt, but conveniently failed to notice other facts. The first was the actual meaning of the word 'swarm' which can refer to a throng or mass, as well as insects, or the fact that Cameron used the word 'people', and acknowledged their reasons for migrating. Labour also failed to acknowledge how the immigrant problem was largely its fault, being responsible for the exponential increase in migrant numbers coming to the UK post 1997, not least of which was (according to former Labour adviser Andrew Neather) to 'rub the right's nose in diversity, and render their arguments out of date', with the added bonus that it added to the Labour vote. Nor did Labour recognise the steps that Cameron had already taken (ie working with the French police, calling in the army, etc.), in a tricky situation, not least of which because of EU free movement laws, and the minor detail that Calais is in fact on French soil. Nor was Labour interested about the deaths of migrants attempting to enter the UK, nor the potential Islamist threat, nor the economic implications. No, the key thing to notice, above all else, was the potential offence which the comment might have caused.

The importance of Risk

This list is not intended to be exhaustive, but rather to illustrate the smorgasbord of continually evolving means the leverager has at his disposal to trip us up. It is important to consider that these elements are not isolated, but rather they are the connected strands of the same policy – that is to promote the individual in any way possible.

Finally in this chapter, we need to briefly mention the concept of risk. The potential for risk in what someone says is of great importance, because it markedly increases the probability that they genuinely mean what they say. Risk might express itself in different ways: it might equate to increased expense, for example paying more tax to help the poor; or social alienation, for example, offending people who don't agree with your position; or otherwise disadvantaging the speaker. The extent to which someone is prepared to accommodate risk in what he says is directly proportionate to the honesty of his statement.

If we take for instance, the ubiquitous bromides which litter our political discourse, we can see that the speakers risk nothing at all; in effect then, they are saying nothing. If it is self-evidently the case that 'diversity is our strength', that 'it's what's on the inside that counts', and that 'everyone is equal', why then are we compelled to keep stating the obvious?

CHAPTER
3

The Majesty of Variation

Variation matters

As this book is concerned with lying in general, let's consider for a moment that which is not lying – the normal distribution, or as it is more commonly known the bell-shaped curve. This is the graphical representation of a simple variable across a population, perhaps the test scores of a class.

As is common, the variable being measured (in this case, test scores) will be plotted on the x or horizontal axis usually from 0-100%, while the frequency (number of students obtaining that score) will be plotted on the y or vertical axis.

Frequency

Score

It really is a thing of beauty. Drink it in, consider it for a moment. All human attributes can be represented within its simple boundaries: Height, weight, IQ, 100M sprint times, drinking habits, shoe size, sex appeal etc. all fit neatly inside it, with the more extreme points at the edges (asymptotes), and most of us clustered rather nondescript, somewhere around the middle.

Depending on the variable that you want to measure, the shape of the distribution may be somewhat compromised, but in essence, the above is what we are talking about when we are talking about people. Necrophiliac tendencies for example, may not yield the same graph as Radio 4 listeners (then again), however the point is this – there is variation within populations.

In terms of the individual, all we are seeking to do is to tweak the circumstances in our favour, so that we appear to be present in the right section – i.e. not too weird, being interesting or sexy enough, paying lip service to rules and laws and so on. Hence, the individual game of leverage is merely a repackaging of the true variance.

Tax avoidance leverage, for instance, might look like this:

Frequency

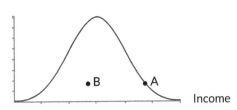

A = true position
B = leveraged position

The leverage might be achieved via taking work 'cash-in-hand', offshore banking, or tax loopholes. Conversely, sex appeal leverage (achieved by make-up, working out, borrowing your mate's flash new car, etc.), might look more like this:

Frequency

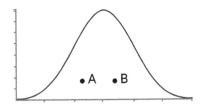

A = true position
B = leveraged position

Whatever form it takes, individual leverage isn't that much of a problem, at least any more than it has always been. It's a sort of upgraded Musketeers motto: All for one, and every man for himself. Essentially, the problem of individual leveraging is kept in check by the presence of millions of other leveragers. That's to say, the market regulates itself. Those who exploit their leverage too much, run the risk of being found out and exposed, eg Robert Maxwell, Johnathen Aitken, Nick Leeson, Grigori Rasputin, Judas Iscariot etc.

You can get away with a reasonable amount of leverage that fits in with the general population (eg you photo-shopped your pictures):

Frequency

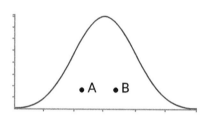

A = true position
B = leveraged position

Go too far however, and you might get caught (eg you used your model friend's photos and your date was disappointed):

Frequency

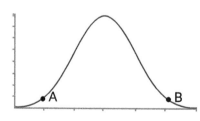

A = true position
B = leveraged position

Collective Lies

A self-regulating market is a fine and healthy thing. The problems start, however, when a lie becomes so successful that a larger audience adopts it. In effect, it goes viral, and its adherents forget, or never knew that it was a lie in the first place. We might consider that these lies hold a special status as 'collective lies'.

Consider religion again for a moment. At the individual level, this is not too big a deal. Some guy worked out a nice con on afterlife insurance, but you could take it or leave it. Alternatively, you could dodge the copyright and invent your own brand. However, once the state got hold of it, you'd better start paying your tithes, get your arse to church on Sundays, and pretend you believe in the right franchise, or the penalties could be severe.

Collective lies are infinitely more sinister than their individual counterparts, for two reasons: firstly, they do not have the 'honour' of the individual lie, which is at least open to scrutiny and falsification (and demands a high price from the individual leverager, should he be caught – perhaps in the form of jail time or opprobrium). Secondly, they are often given ill-deserved endorsement from the majority, the state, or the zeitgeist more generally. That means that the individual not only has to work out that it is a lie in the first place (much harder to do with large numbers of supporters behind it), but then has to work out whether it is safe to criticize it. A double-whammy.

Consider perhaps, the notion of the gender pay gap, relentlessly promoted by feminists and those wishing to appear on the right side of things. In principle, this is something that we should be concerned about. The idea that women earn a mere 78 cents on the dollar earned by their male counterparts (as it is usually represented) is something that deserves investigation. The problem is that the 78 cents statistic is completely fraudulent. Factually, women's unequal pay is due to the career choices they make, the shorter hours they work, and the time they take off for having children. It is not due to discrimination.

But we don't even need facts for this. Logic tells us that, were it the case that a woman was performing an equal task to a man, but paid only 78% of the salary, the offices of every company would be crammed to the rafters with such employees, with their expensive male-counterparts out on their ears. There is also the minor point that such pay discrimination is illegal.

The 78 cents statistics is merely a facile comparison of median salaries of all workers. When you control for women who leave work to raise families (that's their choice, right?), the pay gap vanishes. In fact the data shows that full-time women now earn more in their twenties and early thirties than their male colleagues[28]. Where's the feminist outcry?

Many supporters of the gender pay gap myth, are clearly not aware of these findings, and can be hard to convince even when presented with the facts. All the same, many other supporters really do know that it is a lie, but persist with it nonetheless. Perhaps this is because claiming an aggrieved or victim status affords a fair amount of general leverage over your fellow man. What is the individual to do up against such a lie? Does he accurately debunk it and risk being labelled a misogynist, a male-chauvinist or a callous individual?

Consider alternatively, the Black Lives Matter movement, started in the USA and spreading to other western nations. This group claims to be aggrieved by the disproportionate targeting of blacks by police. Again, a very serious problem if true. Again, completely at odds with the facts.

A cursory analysis of FBI statistics does seem to indicate that black people are overrepresented in police homicides. According to Criminologist Dr Richard Johnson[29] from the University of Toledo, 61% of those killed by police are white, with only 32% being black. Seeing as black people comprise around 13% of the US population this does appear to be over-representation. However, the Department of Justice[30] also reveals that blacks account for 62% of robberies, 57% of murders and 45% of assaults. Any reasonable analysis of the data on police shootings which takes this disproportionality into account, entirely contradicts the police brutality narrative.

Digging a little deeper, the facts are surprising. For instance, a 2015 study of the Philadelphia Police Department revealed that black and Hispanic officers were more likely to shoot unarmed blacks than their white colleagues[31]. A 2016 New York Police Department study meanwhile found that black officers were 3.3 times more likely to shoot than white officers[32]. In addition, a 2016 empirical analysis of racial differences in police use of force found that police officers in Houston were 24% less likely to shoot blacks than whites[33]. The police often demonstrate 'reverse racism' to blacks, which is no wonder when you consider the impending backlash they will knowingly receive.

According to the *Washington Post's* database of fatal police shootings[34], 12% of white and Hispanic homicide victims died at the hands of police in 2015. The comparable black victim rate was just 4%. Far from police brutality, it's actually police officers who should worry, being as they are almost 19 times more likely to be killed by a black assailant than the other way around.

If you want cast-iron victim status, how about Islamophobia? It suggests that the real sufferers of suicide bombings across the west are the innocent Muslims, who will subsequently feel the heat from an anti-Muslim backlash. Again, hard evidence shows that this does not exist. The FBI's Uniform Crime Reporting Program investigating hate crimes in America in 2017, shows that 16.1 % of anti-religious hate crimes were committed against Muslims[35]. The figure committed against Jews was a whopping 56.8%. These findings are echoed across Europe; anti-Semitism is a serious problem, Islamophobia not so much.

The Equality Lie

Perhaps the most popular collective lie on the market today is that of equality: the idea that people are all intrinsically worth the same, despite race, creed or gender. At face value this does appear to have the wind of moral rectitude in its sails. Instantly, that should worry attentive readers, because as we know rectitude is a good seller of leverage.

If we were to have an Olympic Games for the stupidest collective lie of all time, equality would be a shoo-in for the gold medal in any discipline, with a perfect start, and a headwind in lane four.

Let us say for argument's sake that equality is a laudable pursuit, how exactly would that work amongst the human race? Take for example, very important, and (even *I* would argue) noble principles: equality of opportunity and equality before the law. They are both completely overridden by the human variable of attractiveness.

There is a myriad of reliable, peer-reviewed research which demonstrates irrefutably that more attractive individuals have enormous advantages in all spheres of life: whether it is obtaining substantially shorter prison sentences for the same crime[36], receiving higher marks for the same piece of work[37], or getting faster promotions and higher pay throughout one's career[38].

In fact, there seem to be precious few arenas in which attractiveness is not a major asset. In the 1970's an interesting Psychology paper titled 'What is beautiful is good' was written[39], which summarised beauty as a 'halo effect', leading to almost limitless positive evaluations. Physically attractive people are judged to be more intelligent[40], more altruistic[41], more hireable, more competent, and more likely to succeed[42]. They are also actually healthier, have fewer mental health issues, and are more likely to be chosen as a business partner[38].

This is just a small illustration of the simple fact that people come at a premium. Furthermore, that however desirable or moral it might be to claim the virtues of equality, to all intents and purposes in a human society, these virtues are unworkable.

What about the caring individual, who claims not to judge people on their appearance, might equality not work for them? Not a snowball's chance. Physiognomy, the ancient science of interpreting someone's character from the dimensions of his face, largely discredited and ignored in recent times, actually turns out to have a bit of bite to it. For instance, first impressions, sightings of an unfamiliar face for a mere tenth of a second, are enough to make a lasting impression of a person's character: his competence, trustworthiness, aggressiveness and so on. What is more noteworthy is that different people come to much the same conclusions when viewing the same face. Perhaps the most interesting finding was that there is even some validity in the conclusions reached[43].

One of the reasons that equality gets such an easy ride is

that (quite understandably) few individuals want to run the risk of challenging it. In the first place, the concept of equality is neat and tidy, requiring no cognitive effort. Secondly, challenging equality doesn't allow you to leverage or virtue-signal. In fact, the exact opposite is true: by definition, arguing against equality means that the 'victims' of your analysis are going to be minorities or women, those whom most people like to defend. No matter how right you are, questioning the validity of equality exposes you to other people's leverage; this is why there are almost no politicians who will ever do so.

Even in terms of science, we can observe this clearly in society's reaction to it. Any evidence which does not confirm the egalitarian results that society has come to count on, is likely to receive a very negative response. In today's world, it is just about acceptable to state that men and women vary physically. Rephrase that and claim that men are physically superior, and you've already lost a sizeable chunk of your audience.

The data

It's not hard to see therefore that the social sciences are becoming discouraged from pursuing avenues that clearly identify variance amongst the population (as though there were any better jobs for it to be getting on with). Nowhere is this more prevalent than the issue of IQ. It's plainly obvious that weightier intellects bring more to the table, and that therefore marked variations across variables such as race or gender are going to insert a substantial nail in the equality coffin. Unfortunately, for the proponents of equality, if we genuinely consult the data variation is all we find.

Let's start with a review of the world literature on brain size and IQ[44] by Professor John Phillipe Rushton, formally of the University of Western Ontario. Rushton found that average cranial capacity varied significantly by race. While those of African descent averaged 1267 cm3, Europeans averaged 1347 cm3, with East Asians topping the table at 1364 cm3. Rushton concluded that these brain size differences underlie the consistent racial disparities on IQ tests, with Blacks scoring an average of 85, Whites

100 and East Asians 106. If these findings are valid, then it should be fairly easy for us to predict which countries have the highest and lowest average IQs. Professors Richard Lynn and Tatu Vanhanen conducted extensive research from 2002[45] to 2006[46], measuring the average IQs of over 100 countries, and extrapolating the rest. The results are spectacularly in line with Rushton's conclusions. Hong Kong and Singapore top the table at 108, with South Korea (106) slightly ahead of Japan and China (105) and Taiwan not far off the mark at (104). The Europeans then come in at around (100), with African countries completely dominating the lower half of the table, ranging from Nigeria (84) to Equatorial Guinea (59).

Lynn and Vanhanen also examined the possibility of a correlation between a country's average IQ and its GDP. They found a substantial positive correlation between IQ and per capita income: the higher the IQ the higher the mean income.

It is important naturally to note that IQ is not the only factor in town, and that environmental issues play an important role in these complicated pictures. However, many advocates of equality believe that all variation is due solely to inequality, and they are quite wrong to think so.

Rushton examined some interesting data of children who were raised by foster parents (thereby controlling the environmental element to a large extent). All the children were raised in white, middle-class homes. The results across race make for interesting reading: children of black biological parents raised in white, middle-class homes had an average IQ of 93; those of mixed-race parents averaged 104; those with white biological parents averaged 109, but Asians again topped the table with 112. Clearly then, environment plays a crucial role. But it is interesting to note that the gap, and racial order by IQ has been consistently replicated.

In *A Troublesome Inheritance: Genes, Race and Human History*[47], Nicholas Wade considers the same issue of variance across race in terms of SAT scores and income. Again, he found the same pattern. Whether incomes are $10k per annum or over $70k per annum, the gaps remain. Asians outscore whites, who outscore blacks. The data starts to get a little harder to refute, when you consider that the poorest white students outperform black students from very wealthy families, where access to education and tuition is obviously not an issue.

In terms of gender, IQ is hardly an issue of equality either. Most of us 'know', or have the conception that female and male IQs are exactly equal, averaging out to the standard score of 100. However, that is not quite the same thing as saying that male and female IQs are equal. For a start, IQ tests are standardized so that any question favouring one gender is removed from the tests.

Secondly, there is a proliferation of research indicating that male brains are not only larger in general[48], but larger in proportion to their bodies[49]. Furthermore, while IQ tests are standardized to avoid gender differences, males often outscore their female counterparts on various non-standardised tests. Researchers at Erasmus University, Rotterdam[50] for instance recently found that male brains are on average 14% larger than female brains, with males scoring on average 3.75 IQ points higher on intelligence tests. Similarly, a 2004 meta-analysis by Richard Lynn and Paul Irwing[51] found that men's mean IQ exceeded that of women by up to 5 points.

While the debate on IQ flits back and forth between males having a slight edge, and the edge being non-significant, I think the bigger point is this: the variation of IQ according to gender is an issue that has pertinence for society. Male IQ scores vary significantly more than female scores[52], which means that there are a lot more male dunces floating about, but also a lot more male geniuses to contend with.

According to Dr Irwing[51], at the IQ level of 120-plus there are twice as many men as women; at 145-plus the ratio is 8:1, and at 170-plus there are 30 men for every woman. That's not fair, it's certainly not egalitarian, but that's reality.

The reason that this is so pertinent is that the upper end of the market is what everyone is fighting over. While the equality advocate usually stops short of trying to break the male hegemony in important professions such as refuse collection or sewer workers, there are naturally clamours for women to take their 'fair share' of the top jobs. Females desiring equality here have a problem: their underrepresentation at the elite end of the market dictates a certain degree of acceptance of their relatively lower IQ, or a great deal of fudging to try to hide it.

This means that, however fair or unfair a society might be, the best people in almost any field are going to be men. In 2014, when Oxford University released their distribution of first class degrees for the previous year, there was an uproar because men were substantially overrepresented, outscoring women in 26 out of 38 schools. In chemistry for instance, 52% of males were awarded a first class degree, compared to 30% of females. The furore was so marked that the university announced it would 'take steps' to rectify the situation. They're going to need the female equivalent of Neil Armstrong: one small step for woman, one giant leap for womankind.

In 2016, the annual *Le Chef* list of the 100 best chefs in the world was released. The list is compiled in secret, by asking two and three-starred Michelin chefs to provide a list of five names that they think best represent the cooking profession, and highlighting which one they believe is the best. There are precisely two females on this list, Anne-Sophie Pic coming in at number 29 and Nadia Santini at 58. Surely, no one is arguing that women are discouraged from spending time in the kitchen?

Since 1901, there have been 825 male winners of the Nobel Prize, but just 47 female winners. In 2014, a Fields medal was finally awarded to a female mathematician after having been previously awarded to 50 consecutive males. No patriarchy worth its salt would push its luck that far, unless something else was at play.

If you forget politics and wish-thinking for a moment, it is not difficult to concede that men represent the variation in society. While females are the selection gates through which evolution functions, males are facing an ever more stringent set of hoops to jump through, as the female shopping list of requirements for a mate expands.

The mild sexual dimorphism witnessed in humans (that males are on average 12% larger than females), is one such example of this. Intelligence is another. It is no coincidence that words such as 'nerd', 'geek' or 'dweeb' invariably refer to highly intellectual, but otherwise socially awkward males rather than females. Intellect, just as stupidity, is a man's game.

The fraudulence of equality lies in its ideological lust for everything to be the same. From this stance it is easy to grasp that any conflicting data (the overwhelming majority) is simply wrong. What equality really needed was a systematic and pervasive bias, upon which to blame the variation. Why do you think feminists invented the 'patriarchy'?

Predictive validity

As unpleasant as one may find the data, it is surprisingly effective at making predictions. Consider the world of international chess, a cerebral game if ever there was one. If what we have just read has any validity, we should see the game's elite players comprised of Asians and Caucasians, with men vastly outnumbering women, and a dearth of black players.

While this sort of comparison is imperfect (for instance, chess is not very big in Asia, with many countries having their own form of chess such as Changi), nonetheless, the results are not that far off what one might expect. As of October 2017, the world's top 20 elite players are comprised of four Chinese players, and one Indian, with the rest white Europeans, Russians or Americans (one of whom is half Japanese). Of the 1,570 Grandmasters in the world (the highest title that a chess player can receive), only 35 are women (that's 2%). There have only ever been 3 black Grandmasters.

While it's always easy to criticise conclusions drawn directly from sport, and indeed while many sports are open to corruption, chess goes a long way towards being the ultimate meritocracy. There are no judges to bribe, or who may make a bad decision on your behalf. There are no performance-enhancing drugs (at least as far as I know). There are just good moves.

There are also no large costs involved, at least at the outset for a player. A chess set costs practically nothing, and indeed the chess computers or programs that players use to study require a one-time fee or are indeed freely available online.

The world's elite players are masters when still at primary school, and often before they have come into contact with any sort of chess coaching. The late, great Bobby Fischer, still considered by many to be the greatest player of all time, was raised in impoverished circumstances and had no opportunity to play other children after his sister lost interest in the game. He circumvented this problem by playing against himself. Chess is truly an egalitarian sport, but the results that come from it are anything but.

Caveats to the caveats

To be fair, it should be noted that one needs to tread carefully with any kind of assertion of reliable differences, as mistakes can easily be made. The environmentalists have indeed got a point, but they do not have the only point. The distinction can be clearly seen in a sport such as tennis. A mere cursory inspection of the numbers might lead one to conclude that white people have some kind of genetic advantage in terms of this game. If you examine the Roll of Honour at Wimbledon throughout most of its history, you could certainly be forgiven for that conclusion.

This kind of argument might once have held water, until the advent of the Williams sisters. Venus and Serena are two of the most powerful and most dominant female tennis players of all time, so it seems clear that cultural and economic factors are likely to explain the dominance of white people in the sport.

But change that to heavyweight boxing, or basketball, and you start making the case a little harder to proceed with. Where exactly are the white people? Surely, no one is going to argue that white people are discouraged from participating in these sports? According to the Institute for Diversity and Ethics in Sport, the NBA was 74.3% black during the 2015-16 season, bear in mind again that the black population of America is around 13%. Since the 1980s, there have been 86 boxers to hold some form of the world heavyweight title. A meagre 18 of whom have been white.

It is not for want of trying. Great champions aside, there is a reason why the term 'great white hope' is well-known in heavyweight boxing, but 'great black hope' has never been heard.

What do you do with the information?

This book sadly has limited space to address multiple issues, and the illustration of variance in the data is one that unfortunately requires brevity. I hope, however, that it can be plainly seen that the data indicates variance, whole variance, and nothing but variance. One of the rather bizarre attacks usually foisted upon anyone claiming that genuine variance exists is that its adherents must be advocating some sinister or malicious conclusion, using the data as justification. I don't believe that that is in any way inferred from the data, nor would I advocate any such position.

If asked, I would argue that people ought to be treated as individuals, rather than as belonging merely to groups. Having said that, it is no good sticking our heads in the sand and pretending that the data leads us in another direction. Group differences matter, and, rather than expecting reality to conform to the social mores that we would prefer, it would be much healthier to embrace reality for what it is.

One should not be required to undergo a sex change in order to make the point that males are definitely superior to females at the upper ends of most disciplines, nor that there are persistent racial differences which are much better explained by nature rather than nurture. If society is not adult enough to speak the truth without first calculating all the possible ramifications, then that is something which ought to be stated openly and plainly. I have never heard anyone advocating such a position.

What kind of equality do you want?

Homo sapiens does not do equality; it naturally establishes hierarchies given the slightest chance. But what if it didn't? What if equality could be achieved or enforced, what exactly would that look like? For a start, we could forget any scientific breakthroughs – why on earth would those at the forefront of science (or any discipline for that matter) bother? Funding presumably would be scant or non-existent – why privilege one field over another? In fact, scientists probably wouldn't even be allowed to research, selfish as they are for making those at the bottom end of the scale feel bad by their achievements.

Education generally would be finished; we would have to hold all those bright students back, those who selfishly leave behind their 'thicko' colleagues in a despicable search for dominance. Basically, you can forget medicine, progress, transport, knowledge, art, literature, architecture, music, technology – you name it, it's gone. Equality would be the worst kind of 'regression to the mean', where the bone-idle would be praised over their heretical hard-working cohorts.

Perhaps it's just as well that it's an unworkable dream, one which in practice has never managed to flourish. The tragic demise of Venezuela right now ought to serve as a reminder to equality advocates such as Jeremy Corbyn and Alexandria Ocasio-Cortez, that you cannot gain prosperity by punishing success.

Humans as a whole do not seek equality. Some members of the public would of course be better served by it, namely those on the bottom. Given the choice, what do you think they would choose – poverty for all, or merely to replace those at the top? Historically we have seen more of an appetite for revolutions than egalitarian mushes. Meanwhile, those in the middle devote their time to getting near the upper end of the market, and those at the upper end of the market, who have the power to change the system, or at least redistribute the wealth, have absolutely zero intention of doing so.

It seems unthinkable that equality will ever be achieved, indeed the notion that people are or could ever be considered the same on any measure, requires self-deception of the absolute highest order. It would also violate the fundamental principle of life, to compete and win, or to die trying.

For equality to have a shot, it would require rather drastic intervention. For one thing, it would require that something other than women be placed in-charge of evolution. Women, despite their many virtues, do seem rather consistent in their short-sighted selection of large, handsome, strong, intelligent males to copulate with. This confers an unfair and, presumably pointless advantage over the next generation, and ensures that equality has no chance of getting out of the starting blocks. It might be worth pointing this out to the next feminist who complains about inequality. You can of course lay the blame, quite literally, at their door.

The bell-shaped curve rather nicely and incontrovertibly puts the lie to equality, as it accurately reflects the spectacularly hierarchical nature of the human race. Because of variation in populations, the general outranks the private, the father is head of the family, the matron runs the hospital ward, the CEO turns up to work when he feels like it, the star striker gets more tabloid inches than his substitute colleagues, while the toilet cleaner gets rather less inches than her supermodel counterparts, the prefect gives lines to the younger boys, the Prime Minister gets a good seat at PMQs, and the big dogs shit where they like. Don't like it? Fine, it's still true.

The 24th chromosome

It's nice to pretend that you care about equality, and even promote it. The leverage dividend can be high, provided you're selling to the right market, and that you have enough people listening to you.

The slight downside is that people are betrayed by their 24th chromosome, that is, their wealth. We might as well consider money to be a biological unit, as it seems to work similarly (old money especially), whereby the wealth advantage is passed along the blood line, and is so strong that it can compensate for almost limitless deficiencies elsewhere in the phenotype's make-up. What was it, for example, that first attracted 26-year old Playboy Playmate of the Year, Ann Nicole Smith, to the 88 year-old billionaire oil magnate, James Howard Marshall II?

The problem with money is that it's quite hard to pretend that you don't have any. You can take steps to hide your dealings in a variety of ways: you can live modestly; you can espouse all the correct views on the evils of capitalism, and so on. But the trappings of wealth are hard to conceal completely, even if you hire professionals to help you. That doesn't stop people trying, especially those who wish to parade their equality credentials.

Unfortunately for the equality mongers, they often get caught with their pants down.

If you fancy a little bedtime reading, have a look at the Panama Papers; a modest 11.5 million documents detailing the tax avoidance of celebrities, heads of state, Prime Ministers, and members of various royal families – you know, the kind of people who lecture us about wealth inequality, and being 'all in this together'. The Panama Papers set out exactly how much these upright citizens and leaders had hidden from the taxman with the assistance of the world's fourth largest offshore law firm, Mossack Fonseca.

Closer to home, Labour Party leader Jeremy Corbyn obviously values the need to appeal to the average Labour voter, so he tried the following: 'I don't consider myself wealthy'. Corbyn has been an MP for 33 years, and earns a salary of £137,000 per annum. Similarly afflicted, actress Keira Knightley, star of the Pirates of the Caribbean trilogy, wailed in 2004, 'I still live at home with my parents. I can't afford to move out, let alone buy a house. You can't buy a house in London. It's impossible now. No one can afford it.' Knightley, whose wealth was at the time estimated at a paltry 1.75 million pounds, must have grown up playing with an odd monopoly set, as she subsequently bought her first home in Mayfair.

All of us in our daily lives understand implicitly the realities of inequality: the moment you have anything non-essential to your life, you know that the money could have been better used by some needy individual. In fact, the moment you *have* anything, a spare pound, a spare room, clothes you do not wear, excess food or weight, you know that you are allowing starving children across the globe to die. Indeed, even reading this book puts you instantly ahead of the 17% global illiterate population, let alone having the money needed to buy it in the first place.

The essence of a hierarchical, unfair, (ie completely natural) society is thus: if you claim to care about equality, you need to start paying voluntary tax and giving your things away before you can be taken seriously. Or, slightly easier on the palate, you need to find an easy way to leverage your private love of inequality, whilst professing your hatred of it. In short, you need to lie.

The nobility of variance

The world can be criticised for many things, but being fair is not one of them. Indeed, anyone claiming to want this should immediately have their bank accounts and assets checked, just to see how egalitarian-minded they are on a voluntary basis when there is nobody there to 'like' their status.

Despite the world's unfairness, there is a majesty and an honour in its hierarchy. And this is not something to be dismissed without thought. Although the hierarchy can be easily compromised at the level of the individual, it is staggeringly robust at the level of society. Your brother's successfulness, for instance, can readily be stymied by killing him, in much the same way that Cinderella's ugly sisters can be made instantly more favourable with a daub of rouge, and a surprise $100 million inheritance. The big picture however, remains much the same:

- The best person will usually win at anything
- Good ideas beat bad ideas
- A Ferrari is better than a Lada
- Someone with a higher IQ will do better than someone without
- The CEO probably does know more than the toilet cleaner
- Real beauty, intelligence, charm, sophistication, talent etc do not need advertising campaigns.

The values of people compared to others and the abilities they possess are the fruit of hundreds of thousands of years of evolution. The persistent value of beauty, and the disparities in intellect are the shared musings of millions of females selecting their mates throughout the centuries, coupled with the differing environmental constraints that *homo sapiens* has faced.

To override this as wrong or immoral, or to claim that it does not exist at all, is to commit a crime of supreme intellectual dishonesty and should not be allowed to go unchallenged. When the Lada comes a distant second to the Ferrari, do you blame the Ferrari for having privilege and standardize its score, or do you grudgingly concede that the Lada is an inferior car?

CHAPTER
4

Banalysis: The Massacre of Variance

Banalysis

Equality certainly has appeal. Equal societies are happier[53] and safer[54] places to live. Differences meanwhile, in whatever guise they come, create conflict and hostility. Progressives wishing to claim universal equality exists however, have created a problem for themselves. In simultaneously stating that 'diversity is our strength' and that 'everyone is equal', the left has given itself an impossible square to circle. Their solution appears to be the destruction of variance.

Over the last few decades, this war (there is no other word for it) against variation has escalated. The inception of political correctness, multiculturalism, affirmative action, relativism and all the many facets of liberal progressivism are part of a broader narrative. Increasingly (whilst never openly stated), variance has become the 'problem' that western liberalism feels compelled to solve.

The advocates for equality (usually acting under the soubriquets of 'social justice warriors' or 'feminists'), appear to believe that society must be perfectly homogenised. They perceive variance to be not only an inherent evil, but moreover, flatly wrong: everyone *must* be equal, and therefore anything that deviates from perfect homogeneity is clearly the result of sinister forces, such as the patriarchy.

Banalysis (banal analysis) is what we may collectively name their campaign: the destruction of all vestiges of variance in society. In short, the denial of reality. Banalysis is the insistence that there is no meaningful variation amongst individuals, the sexes, groups, populations or even things generally. Such a position is not only a crime against science, but a crime against intelligence. Correctly identifying differing patterns of behaviour is not discrimination, but accuracy: rich people are more educated than poor people, women talk more than men, boys play sport, and girls like dolls. Variance deniers want to pretend that this is not the case, and that they most certainly do not think this way. They are lying. Not being able to discriminate effectively would make life impossible.

Banalysis is a puritanical, linear representation of reality. Instead of embracing the grace and integrity of the bell curve, it is the dismantling of it. The beautiful contours of variation in our species, which have taken 200,000 years of evolution to shape, are cruelly stamped on until they can no longer offend.

Banalysis is pretending the truth is what you want it to be to appease and placate. It is bending the data to fit social mores and collective lies. In short, an egalitarian fantasy. It means nothing can be better or worse than anything else, and that everyone can be whatever they claim to be without criticism. Success therefore must be punished for offending failure, just as straight, white males may identify as non-binary, black lesbians (I hope you didn't bat an eyelid at that, that would be offensive to the palpebrally-challenged after all).

Everywhere you look, you are now confronted with insane statements, presented as though they were undeniable facts. Elizabeth King for Brit & Co tried, 'Women are stronger than men and even science says so.' The Huffington Post's Gabby Aossey suggested, 'Muslims are the true feminists'. The Pope, meanwhile, had a stab with, 'It's wrong to identify Islam with violence'.

Banalysis means rights over duties, victimhood over self-sufficiency, and the perversion of reality over truth. If you refuse to accept that Caitlin Jenner is a woman or that Shaun King is black, then you are unfit to be welcomed into decent society.

Under the microscope, reality looks nothing like equality: $x \neq y$ (don't like it, tough – it's still true). For example:

- The best people in almost any discipline will invariably be men.
- Islamic terrorism is a larger problem than Jewish terrorism.

- All cultures are not equal.

Banalysis rewrites the reality equation thus:
$$x = y$$

- Men and women are equal, and must be seen to be in every way.
- All religions are equally good / bad, and no one may suggest otherwise.
- All cultures are, of course, equal, you xenophobe!

Here are the reasons, which might compel one to hold such a view:

- I like equality and I want it to be true.
- It serves me in terms of leverage (eg virtue signaling).
- If I say this, people will not attack me.
- $x \neq y$ is messy, I want a tidy answer to everything.
- If x is not equal to y, some people might be offended, and the truth ought to be flexible enough to change, should the situation call for it.
- I can't handle the reality of life, so I will change my response to it and hopefully reality will go away.
- Claiming this means that I don't actually have to know or think about anything.

Here are some popular current examples of banalysis:

- Gender and race are social constructs.
- Winning doesn't matter.
- Looks don't matter.
- All rape is the same.
- Transgender women are women.
- There is no such thing as good weather or bad weather, there is just weather and your attitude to it.

By contrast, consider how much the following true statements offend you:

- Beauty is *not* in the eye of the beholder[55].
- Men are more promiscuous than women[56].
- Men are better at parking than women[57].

Why are you offended by them? Are you already finding 'solutions' to these problems?

Refusal to accept banalysis is a dangerous game, one which can lead to public embarrassment, dismissal, or even jail time. Again I shall attempt to keep it brief; here are just a few of the wide-ranging examples of banalysis:

Isms

If you should be incautious in your critique of something non-white and or non-male these days, you are almost certain to be accused of an -ism. The lexicon has had a bit of an upgrade recently, so while you may have your defences ready for accusations of racism or sexism, did you prepare against ageism? Ok, how about fattism, classism, able-bodyism, heterosexism, cissexism, lookism or mentalism? They'll get you one way or another.

Genuine maltreatment of individuals based on nothing but race or gender is I believe morally quite wrong. Mere dislike on the other hand, however bigoted, ought to remain the sovereign territory of the individual, and not be something which society seeks to control.

Consider the 90-year old lady on her last legs who is consistently mugged 6 times per year on her way to the post office to cash her pension. If she is sharp enough to notice that these attacks are all conducted by similar young men, do you really want to label her with an –ism, because she accurately classifies precisely what she is a victim of?

Identity politics is a dangerous game. We must all be free to criticise each other, no matter how non-white and how non-male we are. As a case in point, consider Barrack Obama, America's first Black President. A guy everyone wanted to like. Obama cornered diversity; he was the original banalysis President. He garnered the black vote and the white vote simultaneously.

Before his inauguration, you couldn't move for people who'd

never seen him or heard him do anything, lecture on how wonderful he was. For months on end, any media you couldn't plug-up was submerged with those on the verge of orgasm, extolling the virtues of a man whose greatest talent appears to be the inability to read a teleprompter.

The intense desire to approve of an untested Obama created a problem, whereby the man was beyond reproach before he had achieved anything. Any subsequent valid criticism of the Obama presidency was written off as racism, which ironically will have harmed his legacy.

Fancy criticizing the IRS under Obama? No you can't you're a racist. 'Republicans are using (the IRS scandal) as their latest weapon in the war against the black man. "IRS" is the new 'nigger',' said Martin Bashir.

Didn't predict the future, and coincidentally scheduled a Republican convention at the same time that a hurricane hits? (Hurricane Isaac), then you're racist too. 'They are happy to have a party with black people drowning,' Yahoo news chief, David Chalian.

Think Obama is angry? Think that adjective is in the public domain? Better think again. 'That really bothered me. You notice (Romney) said anger twice. He's really trying to use racial coding and access some really deep stereotypes about the angry black man,' said Touré

Don't conform to liking Obama personally, that's outrageous and probably we can stick an -ism on the end of it. 'I think an overwhelming portion of the intensely demonstrated animosity toward President Barrack Obama is based on the fact that he is a black man, that he's African-American,' said President Jimmy Carter.

Don't like Obama interfering in your own internal politics? Are you white? Then we can ring that bell! Former London Mayor, Boris Johnson, was roundly criticised for racism and 'dog-whistling' when he reacted to Obama's unwelcome interference in the British decision whether or not to remain in the EU. Johnson's crime? Calling Obama a 'part-Kenyan President', and pointing out that because of this, he had an 'ancestral dislike' of the UK.

The Obama presidency can be described as a litany of failure. From the nightmare and inefficiency of Obamacare, to the failure to close Guantanamo Bay. From the stimulus package to the near $20 trillion national debt, more debt than all other 43 presidents combined. Obama was at war for longer than any president in history, and is the first president never to preside over one single year of 3% GDP growth. Despite this, he received an eyebrow-raising Nobel Peace prize for not being George W Bush.

The question of whether Obama is the worst or the greatest president in America's history is beside the point. The more pertinent fact is that holding one of those viewpoints will inevitably get your motives called into question. This should not be the case.

Sport

Tennis world no.1 Novak Djokovic managed to ring the outrage bell in 2016 by suggesting that men should receive more pay than women, because they attract more viewers. In other words, he wouldn't pretend to believe that women justified equal salaries to men. 'I think that our men's tennis world, ATP world, should fight for more because the stats are showing that we have much more spectators on the men's tennis matches.' The powder keg had already been lit by Indian Wells chief executive, Raymond Moore, who had commented that the Women's Tennis Association was a 'lucky organisation' which 'rides on the coattails' of the men.

Of course this is true. Sport, a genuine meritocracy, is based on who is the best, and on how much people are prepared to pay to watch it. Viewing figures for the men's ATP tour in 2015 were 973 million, compared to the women's 395 million. To pretend that the average spectator is as interested in female tennis, or female football, or female boxing is nonsense.

Despite this, women now receive equal pay to that of men in all major tennis tournaments, irrespective of the fact that they generate substantially less interest (and consequently less advertising revenue), play only 3 sets to the men's 5, and that the skill level of their game is inferior.

Perhaps you'd feel like that was enough, but no. Dissent from the idea that women deserve the same pay as men must also be banned. That it where Djokovic made his mistake. Within

24 hours, Djokovic had presumably been taken off for a little light electroshock treatment and reprogramming, because he came back singing from the equality handbook.

> As you all know, I care deeply about the future of the game and all of the players. Tennis helped me so much in my life and being where I am today, I felt the need to speak about the fairer and better distribution of funds across the board – this was meant for both men and women. We all have to fight for what we deserve... This was never meant to be made into a fight between genders and differences in pay, but in the way all players are rewarded for their play and effort. Tennis is a sport that I love and that gave me the opportunity to help others who still have a long way to go to achieve their dreams. This was my view all along and I want to apologise to anyone who has taken this the wrong way.

I have no idea who wrote this for Djokovic, but it's arrant nonsense. Djokovic is not remotely concerned about all players as they are his competitors; caring about them would instantly render him unable to thrash them as he so consistently does. Moreover, this is exactly a fight between genders and pay – that's the only thing it is!

In another sport, Formula 1 chief executive, Bernie Ecclestone, caused controversy, but with a nice twist, which presumably left him in post. Ecclestone commented that, 'I don't know whether a woman would physically be able to drive an F1 car quickly, and they wouldn't be taken seriously.' In other words, Ecclestone refused to pretend that gender meant nothing. Ecclestone was naturally roundly criticised for his comments on variance, and this was quickly backed up by pointing to other things he had said which do not align with typically politically correct views re Hitler, Putin, the EU and migrants.

However, the interesting twist came when Ecclestone shared his opinion that he thought more women would reach top jobs such as his, because 'Women are more competent, and they don't have massive egos.' Unsurprisingly, that bit of sexism did not ruffle any feathers.

Advertising

Kevin Roberts, Executive Chairman of Saatchi & Saatchi, was forced to resign in 2016 for denying that sexism was an issue in the advertising world (ie contravening the accepted line). In an interview for *Business Insider*, Roberts 'provoked fury' by claiming that women in the industry 'lacked ambition' and favoured happiness over their career.

> We have a bunch of talented, creative females, but they reach a certain point in their careers ... 10 years of experience, when we are ready to make them a creative director of a big piece of business, and I think we fail in two out of three of those choices because the executive involved said, 'I don't want to manage a piece of business and people, I want to keep doing the work'.

Roberts, unlike many leaders in the advertising industry, doesn't necessarily consider this a failure, just a difference.

> If you think about those Darwinian urges of wealth, power, and fame — they are not terribly effective in today's world for a millennial because they want connectivity and collaboration. They feel like they can get that without managing and leading, so maybe we have got the definition wrong.

Roberts was of course speedily told to recant, and offered the following: 'My miscommunication on a number of points has caused upset and offence, and for this I am sorry.' Incidentally, Roberts has nothing to apologise for. He's quite right; women *are* less driven than men[58], but you can't expect the truth to be any sort of defence these days.

Science

Cut to science, which in the modern era is becoming as hazardous to your career as it was for Galileo. Dr Matt Taylor, chief scientist on the Rosetta Mission (resulting in the ground-breaking landing of a rocket on a comet), sparked controversy by his choice of gentleman's apparel. Taylor appeared at the launch in a 'sexist shirt', featuring scantily clad women, the sort of thing you'd expect a geeky scientist to wear. Actually, it was a shirt made by a friend, Elly Prizeman, featuring cartoon women with firearms. It didn't take long for the condemnation to begin, as some people saw it as a reflection of a culture where women are unwelcome in scientific fields. 'I don't care what scientists wear,' lied Katie Mack, an astrophysicist, 'but a shirt featuring women in lingerie isn't appropriate for a broadcast if you care about women in STEM (science, technology, engineering and mathematics).'

Not the fact that kids could be watching, or that the shirt was, in a stretching of Mary Whitehouse-esque prudery, in vaguely bad taste. No, on the most jubilant day of his career, Taylor should be most concerned about promoting women in the field, and quite possibly berating himself for stealing the place of some, more-deserving female on the team.

Taylor, who was so upset he was reduced to tears in his humiliating public apology opted for, 'The shirt I wore this week – I made a big mistake, and I offended many people. And I'm very sorry about this.'

Taylor was so sincere in his apology that he managed to keep his job.

Things

Popular British politician, Ken Clarke, avoided the problems of talking about non-white or non-male things, but he slipped up by talking about things generally. Clarke got himself hauled over the coals in 2011 when he made the mistake of suggesting that rapes differ, and should therefore be treated differently. In other words, he set out his stall as being an advocate of variance.

Clarke had been planning to introduce shorter sentences for those who admitted their guilt early (a key issue for many in terms of rape, where the conviction rate is around 6%). The headline figure had been five years, meaning that those convicted might only spend 15 months in prison. In a radio interview, Clarke defended the government's position thus: 'That includes...17 year-olds having intercourse with 15 year-olds,' and 'A serious rape with violence and an unwilling woman – the tariff is longer than that.'

He was immediately challenged by Victoria Derbyshire, who commented, 'Rape is rape, with respect.'

Clarke responded, 'No, it's not, if an 18 year-old has sex with a 15 year-old and she's perfectly willing, that is rape. Because she is under age, she can't consent... What you and I are talking about is we are talking about a man forcibly having sex with a woman and she doesn't want to – a serious crime.'

Clarke's point (a perfectly valid one, surely) is that it is important to distinguish between different degrees of the same crime. There is, for instance, considerable difference between a husband unsympathetic to his wife's predictable 9pm headache, and forced, violent rape from a complete stranger.

Clarke's own example – of a 15 and 18 year old girlfriend and boyfriend, where the sex may even be (perish the thought) instigated by the female – whilst technically rape is about as far from the actual crime as it is possible to be.

The anti-variance campaigner seemingly has a great deal of trouble with this distinction, but the issue of variance aside, what is the genuine complaint supposed to be? That differentiating somehow trivializes or encourages rape? If that's the case, then we'd better ban Cluedo pretty sharpish – all those characters running amok with the lead piping, it's enough to give you ideas.

Fortunately for Clarke, he has long been a highly charismatic and popular figure with the public, and he did not have to resign. He was however, forced to tour the television studios and explain that he regards 'all rape as a serious crime' 'I have always believed that rape is extremely serious, and must be treated as such.'

Jokes

Serious topics are dangerous, but so too are jokes. Former UKIP MEP Godfrey Bloom soon discovered this, when he addressed party activists at a UKIP conference in September 2013. Bloom made the mistake of jokingly referring to women who do not clean behind their fridges as 'sluts'. He ought to have been lying low, since he'd already caused a stir a few days previously by stating that 'Britain should not be sending aid to Bongo Bongo Land'. Unfortunately for Bloom, his words were interpreted as meaning sexually promiscuous instead of slovenly, and he subsequently had the party whip removed.

Also under fire from the joke police was noted scientist, Sir Tim Hunt, Biochemist, Molecular Physiologist and Fellow of the Royal Society. Hunt was awarded the Nobel Prize in Physiology or Medicine in 2001. On 8th June 2015 at a lunch for female scientists as part of a conference for Science Journalists in Seoul, Hunt was asked to give an impromptu toast. Hunt obliged with the following outrageous piece of variance propaganda:

> It's strange that such a chauvinist monster like me has been asked to speak to women scientists. Let me tell you about my trouble with girls. Three things happen when they are in the lab: you fall in love with them, they fall in love with you, and when you criticise them they cry. Perhaps we should make separate labs for boys and girls?... Now, seriously, I'm impressed by the economic development of Korea, and women scientists played, without doubt an important role in it. Science needs women, and you should do science, despite all the obstacles, and despite monsters like me.

Hunt's remarks were met with laughs and applause, but that did not save him. The Royal Society wasted no time making it clear how anti-variance they were, by formally distancing themselves from Hunt, doing so on the same day and emphasizing their commitment to equality in the sciences.

Two days later Hunt followed suit, formally distancing himself from himself on Radio 4. Unfortunately he was not nearly contrite enough. Hunt apologized, claiming he had made 'light-hearted ironic remarks.' The trouble is, he made the *faux pas* of stating that he 'did mean the part about having trouble with girls', noting that if somebody 'bursts into tears, it means that you tend to hold back from getting at the absolute truth' (which is kind of the point of science).

On the same day, Hunt was forced to resign his honorary post at UCL where he had been for 20 years, as well as his position on the board of the European Research Council (a council he had helped to set up). Not wishing to deny Hunt the hat trick, the Royal Society couldn't resist letting him go too.

How can it be that such an eminent man is dismissed so readily for so minor an infraction (assuming you consider it to be one at all)? Hunt is merely voicing his opinion, which he was asked for. I do not know if any data exists on gender disparities in the acceptance of criticism, it might make an interesting research topic. But he's either correct – females handle criticism worse than their male colleagues, or he's wrong – perhaps his experience represents a biased sample.

Examining his actual words however, he has nothing but praise for women in general. His harsh criticism is actually reserved for himself. The fact that the penalties for voicing an opinion were so extreme, suggests that the only opinions you are entitled to hold are those which have been pre-approved. Who gets to decide which opinions are valid?

Identity

Identity is a key player in terms of banalysis because it's one of the most obvious ways to refute the lie of equality, and therefore requires maximum policing. People do not look the same, and those differences often actually represent genuine underlying distinctions, rather than merely visual ones. Because of this, the hysteria over identity is rarely out of the news. Even the skin colour of fictional characters can cause controversy. Author JK Rowling claimed that people who criticised the casting of a black actress to play Hermione Granger in the latest instalment to the Potter saga, 'Harry Potter and the Cursed Child', which opened in London's Palace Theatre in June 2016, were 'a bunch of racists'.

Rowling stated that she had 'a great deal of difficulty' with the insistence that the character 'must be a white woman', claiming that black actress, Noma Dumezweni, 'was the best actress for the job'.

Rowling then lied that Hermione's ethnicity was 'never specified'.

Purists often get annoyed about very minor plot or dialogue alterations, because naturally they find it affects their interpretation of a work that they already admire. Similarly in music, a bad cover version of your favourite song can have much the same effect. It's odd to see Rowling so confused about this. In the first place, if Hermione's ethnicity was not specified, why would there be such an uproar? OK, so the character was played by Emma Watson in the film version. However, it is perfectly untrue to say that Hermione's ethnicity is unspecified. For a start, the black characters in the Harry Potter books are all very clearly designated as such. Kingsley Shacklebolt is described as ' a tall, bald black wizard ', Angelina Johnson, 'a pretty black girl with long black hair', and Lee Jordan, ' a black boy with black hair and dreadlocks'.

Hermione, on the other hand, is described as having 'lots of bushy brown hair, and very large front teeth.' In the second book, she is holidaying in the south of France and comes back looking 'very brown' meaning tanned, not something you usually associate with black people. Furthermore, the illustrated editions of the Potter books (illustrations by Jim Kay) all show Hermione as white, something you think would have been noticed. But the casting nail in the coffin, is Rowling's own sketch of the characters from 1999, which makes it pretty hard to claim that Hermione's race is up for debate.

Yet again, the idea that wanting a character to actually look like they are portrayed in the book can only be explained by racism, not by purism, fanaticism or anything else, is spectacularly lazy. The very real damage caused by indiscriminate accusations of racism ought to behove a little more caution from the mudslingers.

Want your characters a bit more butch? Consider James Bond, the cornerstone of masculinity originally portrayed by Sean Connery. The minutiae of what constitutes a suitable 007 is something that shakes the vodka martini of the mildest Bond fan. Even Daniel Craig, perhaps the most accomplished actor to inhabit the role, was initially lambasted for the crime of being blond! Indeed, a whole campaign was launched to prevent this desecration of the role, calling for a boycott of Craig's first outing in Casino Royale.

So it is little surprising that the rumoured casting of Idris Elba as the next 007 has raised a Roger Moore-esque eyebrow or two. A black Bond is newsworthy, and those who wish to dismiss the race issue as somehow irreverent are being rather economical with the truth. Invariably when asked for their opinion, anyone of note has felt the need to either enthuse a little too zealously about the prospect, or have pooh-poohed it while making it quite clear that race is a non-issue – it is of course, little else.

When rumours first emerged of Elba playing the part of Bond in 2015, post-Fleming Bond author Anthony Horowitz expressed concerns about his suitability. 'For me, Idris Elba is a bit too rough to play the part. It's not a colour issue. I think he is probably a bit too 'street' for Bond. Is it a question of being suave? Yeah.'

Naturally in these politically correct times, Horowitz was instantly forced to recant, and the issue went away as Daniel Craig agreed to stay on for the latest instalment, Bond 25. With Craig finally bowing out in 2019 however, the issue of a non-white Bond is firmly back in the frame.

Another getting their knickers in a twist over the miscasting of Elba was Joanna Lumley, who recently commented,

> Idris Elba is stunning – and was incidentally in Absolutely Fabulous – but I don't think he is right for Bond, who is quite clearly described in the book. I'm colour-blind when it comes to acting, but Idris Elba is just a zonking great star anyway.

So there you have it – Elba doesn't match the book description, but it's not a race issue. While no one wishes to fall foul of the race card, James Bond's bio leaves little to work with in terms of diversity. Born in 1920 or 1921 (depending on which source you trust), Bond is the Eton and Geneva-educated, multilingual son of a Swiss mother and a father from the Scottish Highlands. Trying to extract Sadiq Khan-approved vibrant diversity from that, would leave Harry Houdini in chains.

Why stop with skin colour? A campaign was soon started for a female successor to the quintessentially male role. Can you imagine the intro? 'The name's Bond, Jane Bond.' An aging, feminist cougar perhaps? Or is that too politically incorrect? How about Jane Bond, a teetotal, reformed gambling, asexual, gay feminist representative for the Women's Institute? The gay part at least is not without its advocates. Former Bond, Pierce Brosnan certainly thinks it's a possibility. 'Actually, I don't know how it would work. I don't think Barbara (Broccoli) would allow a gay Bond to happen in her lifetime. But it would make for interesting viewing.'

Being afraid

Everyone seems to be nursing a secret fear these days, whether it's not wishing to get blown up on your way to work or not wanting to bake a cake for gay people, we've all got a dirty little secret. Germaine Greer opted for transphobia. The famously outspoken feminist ignited a firestorm in 2016 when she stated that men who undergo gender reassignment are not women. Greer's comments were prompted by Glamour Magazine's nomination of Caitlyn Jenner as 'Woman of the Year'. Here's Greer explaining her views on the BBC's Newsnight program: 'I'm not saying that people should not be allowed to go through that [gender reassignment] procedure. What I'm saying is that it doesn't make them a woman. It happens to be an opinion. It's not a prohibition.'

Perhaps unsurprisingly, Greer was widely criticized as being transphobic, misogynistic, and accused of committing hate crimes. A petition was then raised, calling for her to be no-platformed at a planned lecture on 'Women and Power' at Cardiff University. When subsequently interviewed on the radio, Greer was equally unequivocal, and refused to change her mind.

> Just because you lop off your dick and then wear a dress doesn't make you a fucking woman. I've asked my doctor to give me long ears and liver spots and I'm going to wear a brown coat but that won't turn me into a fucking cocker spaniel.

The sanctions didn't stop at no-platforming. According to Greer, her own college (Newnham College, Cambridge), refused to grant her a honourary degree because of her comments. Meanwhile, transgender comedienne and actress Rebecca Root (who clearly outranks Greer on the box-ticking victim hierarchy) described Greeʌr's remarks as 'absurd' and 'grossly offensive', adding:

> This is something that I would equate with the worst of the gutter press, not from somebody of such an academic standing; a woman who should know better... On the one hand it's tempting to ignore her, and not to give her a greater platform, but at the same time if we didn't stand up to bullies then they would just continue bullying. [...] [Her comments are] grossly offensive, quite ludicrous and very very out of date.

The rather sinister implication here is that Greer ought to understand the modern lie regarding variance, and that this is not something to question. By voicing a simple and logical opinion, that biology cannot be circumvented by a mere operation, Greer was apparently bullying.

The adjectives too are terribly revealing. *Offensive*, which has no bearing on the truth of an assertion. *Ludicrous*, some truths are hard to believe, or counter-intuitive. *Out-of-date*, the truth has been around for a long time, it does not always require modernizing. Greer is actually not bullying at all, but merely voicing an opinion on variance. She believes that gender is a discrete category, and that popping out for a quick pint and a penectomy simply doesn't cut it.

In summary, we can see a clear pattern developing here. First, there is the consistent notion of a 'correct' opinion – not correct in the sense of scientific fact, but 'correct' in terms of having been successfully vetted and mandated by the liberal mainstream. That opinion derives from an ideology that presupposes variance to be dangerous, and something which therefore has been outlawed. To all intents and purposes then, everything is (and must be considered to be) the same.

In practice what this means is that any statement or opinion which violates this rule, is something which could be construed as offensive. Such offence – the embrace of variance and therefore reality, is liable to face a varying range of censure from individuals, groups or authorities, regardless of whether or not it is true.

In seeking to promote cohesion and unity (which one can only assume is the noble pursuit of such policies) banalysis is likely to backfire. One of the essential ingredients of democracy is freedom of speech, and by definition that demands that truth, offence and even foolishness be tolerated. Revoke that civil right and the heretic is left no room for manoeuvre. He must then either be cowed into submission, or seek more radical avenues to communicate through.

CHAPTER
5

Enforcement

The Conversation

The history of man is a celebration of variance. From Sunday League to Premiership football, playground punch-ups to World Wars, spelling bees to Nobel Prizes - the best has always been glorified. This is simply the most natural face of evolution in motion. Reality does not reward failure, and survival of the shittest never quite took off. The conversation we are currently having seeks to disavow this.

Those ideologically opposed to variance have a major problem when confronted with it; what are they to do? 'No black scientist has ever won a Nobel - that's bad for science and for society' bemoans Phys.org:

> Many in the scientific world are celebrating the fact that two women received this year's Nobel prizes in physics and chemistry. Donna Strickland and Frances Arnold are only the 20th and 21st female scientists to be recognised by the Nobel Committee. Yet in over 100 years, we have never seen a black scientist become a Nobel laureate.
> Every year, the annual October Nobel Prize announcements coincide with Black History Month, which is a painful reminder that of the more than 900 Nobel laureates, only 14 have been black and none in science...
> By contrast, there have been over 70 Asian laureates, the majority in the sciences, and since 2000 that number has significantly increased.

To those accepting of variance, this is an interesting statistic; to those opposed to it, it is a crime. It's what Alexandria Ocasio-Cortez means when she says, 'There's a lot of people more concerned about being precisely, factually, and semantically correct than about being morally right', and what Slate Magazine means when it publishes, 'It's time to give up on facts, or at least to temporarily lay them down in favour of a more useful weapon: emotions.' For the variance denier something has to be done; something is being done.

Variance statements are now being monitored and prosecuted by our legal system (under the guise of offensiveness naturally), using the labels 'hate speech', 'hate crime' and (rather bizarrely) 'hate incident.' At the same time, the realms of what constitutes offensiveness are being evermore expanded by those with the thinnest skins. These two prongs are working together highly effectively, to render our speech and our thoughts either meaningless, or criminal.

Here are just a few examples of how our language is now being policed:

Cambridge University Lecturer, Lucy Delap, recently told examiners not to use words such as 'flair', 'brilliance' or 'genius' when assessing students' works, because such words 'carry assumptions of gender inequality'. The *Huffington Post* proclaims, 'It should be illegal to call somebody fat', while the *Guardian* goes for, 'Why we need to lose biased words like 'mistress' for good'.

Cardiff Metropolitan University revised its code of practice in 2017, and identified 34 words and phrases which would be banned on campus. The list includes items such as 'mankind', 'sportsmanship' and 'housewife'. According to the University's code: 'students should not allow their 'cultural background' to affect their choice of words on campus', and warned that 'students and staff could face disciplinary procedures if they failed to adhere to the language policy'.

Jokes are also no laughing matter. Jutta B, a 62-year old female resident of Berlin was arrested in 2017, had her house raided, and was forced to pay a fine of 1,350 Euros for sharing this gag on Facebook: 'Do you have anything against refugees?' 'Yes, machine guns and hand grenades'.

Robbie Travers was investigated by Edinburgh University, when he mocked ISIS on Facebook in 2017, 'Excellent news that the US administration and Trump ordered an accurate strike on an IS network of tunnels in Afghanistan. I'm glad we could bring these barbarians a step closer to collecting their 72 virgins'.

Way back in 2006, Codie Stott, 14, was arrested for the hate crime of wanting her classmates to be able to speak English. During a science class, the teenage girl had been placed in a group of five Asian pupils, only one of whom spoke English. When she asked the teacher if she could change groups, she was placed in isolation for the rest of the day, and then a week later was taken to the local police station and placed under arrest.

However thinly-stretched the UK police's resources may appear, they are increasingly finding time to police citizens tweets and blog posts. Within the space of a fortnight in early 2019, they managed to subject Harry Miller to a 34-minute telephone interrogation to 'check his thinking' after he retweeted a 'transphobic' limerick. They also gave 74-year-old Margaret Nelson a rather nasty morning call, telling her to 'tone down' her blog posts and tweets. They then went all-in by arresting, and locking up Kate Scottow, for 'misgendering' a transwoman on Twitter.

Then there is the case of 7-year old Elliott Dearlove, who was accused of the hate crime of racism back in 2012, and was subject to an inquiry after he asked a friend at school, 'Are you brown because you come from Africa?' This insanity was perhaps only eclipsed in 2016 by the case of Stacy Dos Santos's 9 year-old son, who had a fully-armed policeman arrive at his New Jersey school to quiz him over the accusation of racism, after he was overheard referring to his brownie snack as – wait for it – a brownie.

Serious crime aside, here is the Crown Prosecution Service's definition of a 'hate incident':

> A Hate Incident is any incident which the victim, or anyone else, thinks is based on someone's prejudice towards them because of their race, religion, sexual orientation, disability or because they are transgender... If you, or anyone you know, has been called names, been bullied

or had anything happen to them that you think may be because of one of these factors, then you should report this as a hate incident. Even if you don't want the incident to be investigated, it is important that the police know about it, so that they can build up a picture of how many incidents are happening and where. This information can help police investigating other hate incidents.. Not all hate incidents will amount to criminal offences, but those that do become hate crimes.

The prioritisation of police manpower for mean words, is like having the emergency services show up to the sinking of the Titanic, and watching them arrest the conductor for not having his top button done up.

The Correct Opinion

It's not only the police that are policing; we're all doing it. Across the west, there is now the very open sentiment that there are acceptable and unacceptable opinions. Whether it is politicians of every hue bizarrely declaring whether or not voters' concerns are 'legitimate', whether it is Hilary Clinton's calling Trump supporters a 'basket of deplorables' during the 2016 presidential election campaign, or Mark Rutte, Prime Minister of the Netherlands who classified 2017 election runner-up Geert Wilders as voicing the 'wrong kind of populism'. The politicking is clear: liberal opinions are fine, conservative ones are not.

To illustrate just how widely 'correct' opinions are being enforced, consider the landmark case of James Damore. Damore was fired by Google in August 2017, because of a leaked internal memo he wrote, *Google's Ideological Echo Chamber, how bias clouds our thinking about diversity and inclusion.*

Damore is no mug. He is a former child chess champion and FIDE Master, a former researcher at Princeton, Harvard and MIT, and has pursued a PhD in Systems Biology from Harvard University. Damore basically states that Google is so focused on increasing diversity, in particular, employing and promoting more women, that they are lowering their standards to do so. He argues that undeniable biological gender differences clearly explain men's suitability and preference for tech roles, and that that should be something to be embraced, rather than controlled against.

Damore's piece is extremely well-written, factually grounded and well-referenced. He goes to great lengths to cite his own biases and to explain that he is fully in favour of inclusion:

> I hope it's clear that I'm not saying that diversity is bad, that Google or society is 100% fair, that we shouldn't try to correct for existing biases, or that minorities have the same experience of those in the majority. My larger point is that we have an intolerance for ideas and evidence that don't fit a certain ideology. I'm also not saying that we should restrict people to certain gender roles; I'm advocating for quite the opposite: treat people as individuals, not as just another member of their group (tribalism).

In conclusion, Damore again tries to explain his motives sincerely:

> I value diversity and inclusion, am not denying that sexism exists, and don't endorse using stereotypes. When addressing the gap in representation in the population, we need to look at population level differences in distributions. If we can't have an honest discussion about this, then we can never truly solve the problem. Psychological safety is built on mutual respect and acceptance, but unfortunately our culture of shaming and misrepresentation is disrespectful and unaccepting of anyone outside its echo chamber. Despite what the public response seems to have been, I've gotten many personal messages from fellow Googlers expressing their gratitude for bringing up these very important issues which they agree with but would never have the courage to say or defend because of our shaming culture and the possibility of being fired. This needs to change.

Some in the scientific community came out in support of Damore's scientific claims, for example Dr Debra Soh, a Canadian science journalist who confirmed the manifesto was scientifically accurate: 'As a woman who's worked in academia and within STEM, I didn't find the memo offensive or sexist in the least.'

The vast majority however, felt that Damore had violated the sacred rules of homogeneity, as he had clearly forgotten to believe that everyone was the same, and that of course women were just as suited to any job as a man.

Google CEO Sundar Pichai explained the dismissal thus: parts of the memo 'violate our Code of Conduct and cross the line by advancing harmful gender stereotypes'. He went on to say, 'To suggest a group of our colleagues have traits that make them less biologically suited to that work is offensive and not OK.'

So there you have it. Nothing about inaccuracy, nothing contradicting the papers Damore cited, nothing about the criticisms of current Google policies, in fact nothing about anything. For a tech company (whose job surely should be to question everything?), Google's position appears breathtakingly non-technical: diversity is great; you have dared to question diversity, ergo we cannot listen to you. Nothing disproves a heretic quite like cutting out his tongue.

Like Google, the European Commission are in the vanguard in the enforcement of correct opinions. Here is one of the Commission's recent (February 2019), scary tweets on their commitment to policing, 'Companies are now assessing 89% of flagged content within 24 hours, and promptly act to remove it when necessary, while respecting freedom of expression.' You've got that right? You can say whatever you like, as long as it passes the censors.

The idea that there is now a marked disconnect between the opinion setters and opinion followers is not a new one, and indeed this book is of course not the first to sense that something is in the air. Already the monikers of 'Liberal Elite', 'Global elite', 'Mainstream Media', 'Westminster Bubble', and even 'Fake News' have all entered the vernacular, usually via conservatives who are concerned that their voices are not being heard, and with the direction that society is taking.

In addition, there is now some recent evidence to suggest that, despite their claimed love of diversity, Liberals are in fact much more conformist and less politically diverse than their Conservative counterparts[59]. Moreover, another recent study[60] found that Democrats were almost three times more likely than Republicans to block or unfriend people on social media for holding views that they did not agree with. Diversity is great, as long as it's the right kind.

Artificial Intelligence is not much better

Humans clearly cannot be trusted to think correctly, but taking them out of the equation altogether does not necessarily aid the egalitarian cause. Blind recruitment is one such modern attempt to diversify the workplace more, and to employ fewer white males. In fact, it has the opposite effect, as Harvard academic, Dr Michael Hiscox, was disappointed to conclude. Overseeing a recent blind recruitment trial in Australia[61], Hiscox had to resign himself to the following:

> We anticipated this would have a positive impact on diversity — making it more likely that female candidates and those from ethnic minorities are selected for the shortlist. We found the opposite, that de-identifying candidates reduced the likelihood of women being selected for the shortlist.

When assigning male names to a candidate's CV it made them 3.2% less likely to get a job interview, compared to the positive increase that a woman's name had (2.9% more likely to get one). In other words, far from the claimed 'patriarchy', employment is already rigged in favour of women.

If you are hoping to eliminate humans from the workforce altogether, and employ robots instead, you still might not get what you hoped for. Beauty contests judged by AI are anything but egalitarian. In 2016, a team at the Russia and Hong Kong based Youth Laboratories asked individuals from around the world to download their application, and to submit selfies of themselves. The Beauty.AI bot then used algorithms to judge the contestants on facial symmetry, youthfulness, skin quality, appearance and many other parameters.

The results were similarly not in line with egalitarian ideals. In total, 6,000 people submitted photos, from more than 100 countries. Of the 44 winners, almost all were white with a few Asians and only one winner with dark skin. The bot has since, naturally, been accused of racism.

Perhaps you are concerned about inequality in the criminal justice system? How about designing a computer to predict criminals for you, thereby eradicating racism altogether? Former police officer, Brett Goldstein founded CivicScape in 2017, a technology company that sells crime-predicting software to police departments in the United States. In an attempt at transparency, Goldstein has even published his algorithms. The trouble is the software keeps accurately predicting crimes in black neighbourhoods, which is a result many people find uncomfortable.

Controlling the reaction

A more creative way to control for variance is not to go after the variance at all, but to control the reaction to it. If no reaction is permitted, then the variance essentially disappears, right?

Andy Burnham, current Mayor of Manchester, took this line recently when he criticized a demonstration against terrorism organized by 'UK Against Hate'. The demonstration took place in Manchester June 11, 2017, just three weeks after the terrorist Salman Abedi carried out a suicide bombing at the Ariana Grande concert, killing 22 and injuring 116. Bizarrely, rather than support the protest, Burnham decided to protest the protest itself, with tweets such as, '@gmpolice are stretched to limit & in middle of on-going investigation. These EDL-types who came today need to have a look at themselves.'

When it was pointed out to the Mayor that in fact the marchers were not EDL-types, simply protestors fed up with seeing their family's blown apart in compensation for the Muslim vote, he added, 'To those saying they weren't EDL - I honestly don't care. They still need to take a long, hard look at themselves. @gmpolice deserve better. I care about our Police being unnecessarily distracted when they are worn out & still working hard to investigate a major incident.'

Meanwhile, across the northern towns of England, hundreds of young, vulnerable white girls have been systematically raped by Muslim men over the span of decades. The grooming gang scandal has been an enormous problem to the authorities. Here was the deliberate targeting and gang rape of innocent girls by one community – the Muslim community. What were the authorities to do? If they accepted that it was happening, they would have to deal with the immense variance on parade. They would also run the risk of being called racist or islamophobic. So the girls were sacrificed on the altar of multiculturalism – the idea that cultures have equivalent moral value. This conveniently avoided the acknowledgement of division, in short, the acknowledgement of reality.

When, on the rare occasions someone did speak out about the rapes, they were swiftly taken away for diversity training[62]. The most chilling aspect of these cases, is that the girls were targeted *because* they were white, non-Muslims, and were therefore perceived as worthless. This had already been alluded to by former Home Secretary, Jack Straw in 2011 when he said, 'There's a particular problem involving Pakistani heritage men who target young, vulnerable, white English girls'(and consider them) 'easy meat.' It was confirmed by Badrul Hussain, one of an 18-strong convicted grooming gang in Newcastle, who commented, 'All white women are good for one thing, for men like me to fuck and use as trash, that is all women like you are worth.'

This inability to charge Muslims with crimes because of fears of racism or Islamophobia has not abated. In 2017, the Labour Party once again found itself at the centre of chastising the reaction rather than the cause. MP Sarah Champion was forced to resign because she spoke out about Pakistani grooming gangs:

> Britain has a problem with British Pakistani men raping and exploiting white girls. There. I said it. Does that make me a racist? Or am I just prepared to call out this horrifying problem for what it is?

Upon reflection, Labour decided that it very much did mean she was a racist. Champion was roundly criticized by, amongst others, Corbyn ally, MP Naz Shah. Shah is a colourful character, having herself already been stripped of the Labour whip, and having undergone an investigation in 2016 for anti-Semitism. But in this case, she was in her element. According to Shah, Champion's comments were nothing more than 'blanket, racialised loaded statements' which stigmatized the Pakistani community. Furthermore, they were 'Irresponsible' and setting a 'dangerous precedent'. Labour leader Corbyn opted to accuse Champion of using 'Nazi-like terminology about a minority community.'

Interestingly, Shah was in the headlines again just days later, this time for apparently accidentally 'liking' and 'retweeting'. Shah retweeted a parody account of the prominent left-wing figure, Owen Jones, which read, 'Those abused girls in Rotherham and elsewhere just need to shut their mouths. For the good of #diversity.' Not only was Shah not disciplined, she was subsequently promoted to Shadow Minister of State for Women and Equalities.

Europe has a much more benign approach to rape these days – it has to as the crime is so prolific. Barbro Sörman, a left-wing, Swedish politician aptly highlighted this, when she tweeted in 2016 that migrant rape isn't as bad as when Swedes do it, 'The Swedish men who rape do it despite the growing gender equality. They make an active choice. It's worse.'

Education too is all about trying to change attitudes to crime, rather than address crime itself. Finnish Police Chief Jari Taponen suggested in 2017 that terrorists in schools might be a good idea. 'It might widen views and expand tolerance!' Meanwhile in the UK, school children are being taught to respect terrorists. A new teaching aid, the book *Talking about terrorism*[63], recommends children as young as seven 'write a letter to a terrorist'. It explains that terrorists kill people because they believe they are being treated 'unfairly and not shown respect', and gives examples of other 'terrorists' who were subsequently vindicated – you know, those famous suffragette terrorists.

Crime is bad of course, but nowhere near as bad as those who do not possess the good taste to ignore it. Why can't we all just get along and kill each other in peace?

Conspiracies abound

It is worth mentioning here briefly, that there are other possible motives for the war on variance. Because it is totally illogical to deny the existence and the importance of variance in society, some have come to the conclusion that there must be a sinister all-encompassing reason behind it. Maybe there is.

Jordan Peterson believes it is Marxists and Postmodernists (though I am not sure whether he would agree a war on variance is taking place per se). Some believe that western nations are attempting to atone for previous atrocities via a form of 'white guilt'. Others still, believe that white genocide is taking place. One in four French people, for instance, believes that elite Europeans are attempting to replace their own populations as a means to global governance[64].

On the issue of a conspiracy or grand plan, it is obviously the case that these things genuinely occur from time to time. My problem is firstly, I have not found the evidence to be compelling (which is not the same as saying that compelling evidence does not exist), and secondly, that conspiracies usually suffer from being overly-simplistic, by failing to account for the complexity of the interacting factors. Having said that, present me with conclusive evidence, and I'm happy to believe anything.

Perhaps more importantly, the truth of conspiracy theories is often largely irrelevant in the sense that bad decisions made in good faith are more than capable of yielding bad results, irrespective of the true intentions of the actors. I doubt whether most newlyweds in Luxembourg have a 'divorce conspiracy', though with an astonishing divorce rate of 87%, it's the safest bet you can place on the outcome of anyone walking up the aisle in Luxembourg City.

Consequently, I prefer to illustrate the fact that a war on variance is taking place, without muddying the waters further. Besides the reasons already outlined in the previous chapter about why society is issuing a war on variance, it is unclear to me whether there is a broader pattern. A plan behind the madness is unclear.

That madness is occurring is not.

Sadly, I fear we have not got anywhere near the bottom of the rabbit hole yet. As the parameters of 'acceptable' discourse are evermore reduced, a large swathe of society appears hell-bent on finding offence in everything. We are now entering the realms of zero tolerance.

CHAPTER
6

Zero Tolerance

Most of us lead lives of barely tolerable misery. We wake up in our rather nondescript houses, eat a dull breakfast and grate the nerves of our immediate family with impressive regularity. We then trudge meekly to the office to do a job we hate in order to sustain a life just about worthy of complaint. On the occasions that we have time off or a weekend to enjoy, we are then in the enviable position to pursue whatever hobbies or diversions we actually want to spend our time on. We don't know how lucky we are.

The variance denier, or, as the vernacular has it the social justice warrior, has no such luck. His life is never dull, no matter how much he might like it to be. He is going to have his hands full from Monday to Sunday, come rain or shine. His is a battle not for the fainthearted. Refusing to accept that anything varies, or that things will affect people disproportionately, necessitates an eternal struggle.

He can in fact (assuming we haven't violated his correct pronoun choice), scarcely open his eyes without some form of offensive variance striking him. Breakfast tends to be a tricky affair. The obligatory morning cuppa is now cultural appropriation[65]. Coffee is not much better, especially if you like the full white supremacist shade of milk[66]. The full English, meanwhile, is fraught with the dangers of bacon misuse, and could even be flagged up as latent Islamophobia, should any unfortunate Muslim be within earshot.

He might try skipping breakfast, probable vegan that he is, but that still leaves the problem of leaving the house. He can't open the front door for fear that the sun[67] (racism embodied) might be shining. If he happens to live in the British Isles where the sun is not much of an issue, he'll still find it spectacularly hard to get to work. And of course, his white privilege is just itching to betray him at any moment.

He'll need to make use of the backstreets to get around, the main thoroughfares being naturally too dangerous as bumping into people[68] may well now be interpreted as racism. He'll have to take care where he is looking – staring at people[69] is now a racist's domain, and he could get done for stare rape into the bargain. Staring at his feet won't help much either, as not looking at people[70] is now quite rightly, also considered racist.

Assuming he can make it onto public transport, his woes are likely to multiply. Naturally, he'll have the good taste to avoid manspreading – regardless of how much my sexist spellchecker doesn't recognise that as a word, it is now considered a criminal offence[71] in some places.

If he's in London taking the tube, his day might be slightly brightened by the reduced risk of getting triggered by ridiculously gender-rigid announcements such as 'Ladies and Gentlemen'. Who can say how many poor souls have been injured over the years, until Transport for London decided to implement the more gender-neutral, 'Good morning everyone'?

That amelioration may be short-lived as he'll need every ounce of his strength to combat the latent racism to which he is no doubt prone. Much as he might relish the task, avoiding being racist now is pretty much a 24/7 occupation, with new varieties being added to the charge sheet on a daily basis.

'Racism' has been a good seller. There's pretty much nothing left in the universe that can confidently claim not to be racist, and more conveniently still, the accuser is usually considered to be judge and jury on the matter.

Our SJW hero will need to definitely avoid sandwiches[72], classical music[73], maths[74], punctuality[75], dating sites[76], the climate[77], science[78], Dr Seuss books[79], being white[80], having a white family[81], disliking foreign food[82], liking foreign food[83], paying for ketchup[84], the Oscars[85], all white people[86], wearing 'streetwear', or worse still saying it[87], the English language itself[88], and of course, not being racist[89], which is the worst racism of all.

The crusader against variance is never at rest. He is in a constant struggle to seek out and destroy variance, and in this cause he will find himself in a perpetual win-win situation. The triviality of the matter he pursues is actually inversely proportionate to the zeal with which he fights the campaign. Should the struggle not be won or taken seriously, he claims victory, for he is a victim being oppressed. Should he be awarded some concession from society, fantastic, and of course, there are always more dragons to slay.

Ever-decreasing minutiae

Variance is such a dangerous commodity, that it needs to be kept under lock and key. Zero tolerance can be had on any forms of variance, because you never know when this stuff will get out of hand. There'd be chaos everywhere. Hairdressers and beauty parlours would market their wares ineffectively to women, wrongly supposing that they would be more likely to part with their hard-earned 78 cents than their overpaid male colleagues.

It is no longer possible to even parody this, because the reality of what provokes the variance hunter's ire is always more extreme than anything you could come up with yourself. It's their job to find the smallest non-issue to campaign for – how can you compete with that? There's even a name for this now: 'Poe's Law', the inability to create a parody extreme enough that some people will not believe it to be genuine.

There are many periodicals, television channels and websites which can keep you abreast of what you should be most offended by at any given time. The liberal media rarely does anything but report variance issues to which you should take offence.

So, in no particular order, here are ten of the stupidest assaults on variance that I have come across. These are the minutiae that supposedly should occupy your rage.

1. On violence:

Back in 2011, as a mere MP, Justin Trudeau blasted the Conservative government for its use of variance language in the *Discover Canada* guide[90]. The Conservatives had used the word 'barbaric' to describe honour killings, to which Trudeau took issue. 'There's nothing that the word "barbaric" achieves, that the words 'absolutely unacceptable' would not have achieved.' So honour killings should not be called 'barbaric.'

To see what Trudeau does not think justifies the variance word 'barbaric', here is the Human Rights Watch 'World Report on Women's Rights', 2001[91]:

> Honor killings are acts of vengeance, usually death, committed by male family members against female family members, who are held to have brought dishonor upon the family. A woman can be targeted by (individuals within) her family for a variety of reasons, including: refusing to enter into an arranged marriage, being the victim of a sexual assault, seeking a divorce—even from an abusive husband—or (allegedly) committing adultery. The mere perception that a woman has behaved in a way that "dishonors" her family is sufficient to trigger an attack on her life.

While to naïve outsiders the punishments may appear a little harsh (breast ironing, acid attacks, FGM, beating, stabbing, beheading, hanging, throat slashing, strangulation, burning, lethal acid attacks, shooting and other culturally diverse practices), it is important to bear in mind that the women may have committed extreme acts such as seeking divorce, or complaining about rape.

It is also important to note that the murders are highly inclusive, often being performed in public to warn other individuals within the community of the possible consequences of engaging in what is deemed illicit behaviour. So Trudeau is right, the acts are not very nice perhaps, but definitely not worthy of discriminatory language such as 'barbaric'.

He supplemented this analysis of violence with military *nous* that would make Sun Tzu jealous, 'If you kill your enemies, they win'

2. Tampons are not only for women

Tampons have an unhappy life at the best of times, but usually come under scrutiny because of the VAT (luxury goods tax), which some feel they do not warrant. They have been under the spotlight a little more recently however, because some people fear that menstruation is not inclusive enough. University of Wisconsin-Madison has dealt with this by providing menstrual products in all bathrooms in designated buildings across the campus. As University spokesman Steve Wagner explained, 'Menstrual products will be available in all of the bathrooms of the Red Gym so that they are available to any student who might need them'. The University magazine, The Badger Herald, came under fire and had to correct itself when it mistakenly referred to the products as 'women's hygiene' in an article. Meanwhile in the UK, the same red-hot issue was being singlehandedly dealt with by Sergeant Peter Allen, a hate crime officer who takes his hygiene products seriously. In August 2016, he took the trouble to photograph supermarkets that had unthinkingly placed the products under variance labels such as 'feminine hygiene', and then tweeted the stores asking them to change this. As he explained to Sainsbury's, 'It's an issue of gender identity. Men may use the products.'

3. Juries have no place at rape trials

Crime and punishment is a tricky business. Testimonies are often flawed, people are prejudiced and that's before you even start taking account of lying. According to Julie Bindel of the *Guardian* however, rape is a special case in this regard whereby trial by jury should be suspended. This is because victims deserve unprejudiced justice, and you can't get more victim than women. What Bindel really means is that women must be believed no matter the facts because they are society's perpetual victims, and men are at fault even when they are not.

The small matter she fails to note is that some accusations of rape are false. Even if you take conservative estimates of false accusations of rape (the FBI has it that 8% of rape allegations are found to be false through investigation[92]), that still leaves you with the incarceration of a large number of innocent men. For Bindel perhaps a new take on the old presumption of innocence before guilt would look like this, 'It is better that ten innocent men suffer than that one guilty man escape.'

4. Egalitarian principles are much more important than becoming infected with HIV

From January 2018, it will no longer be a felony in California to knowingly expose a sexual partner to HIV without disclosing the infection. Instead, this will now be classified as a misdemeanour. This is progressive as Scott Wiener, one of the Democrats behind the amended bill, explained, 'The most effective way to reduce HIV infections is to destigmatise HIV.'

Now I'm no expert on this subject, but I would have naïvely thought that the most effective way to reduce HIV infections would be give people as much opportunity as possible to not become infected in the first place, stigma or not.

Of course, nothing stigmatises people like accurately identifying who has a given condition, and this has been genuinely celebrated as a progressive victory. Rick Zbur, director of Equality California, said that he was 'elated' about the bill, and the updating of the state's 'archaic laws'. 'This is an important bill that modernizes California's HIV laws. It will really advance public health and reduce stigma and discrimination that people living with HIV have suffered.'

Zbur's sentiments were echoed by The Los Angeles LGBT Center, which also supported the bill. Aaron Fox, director of government relations, said the new law would see HIV-positive people 'treated fairly under California law.'

Being treated fairly is not always appropriate, especially when it means that your friendly blood donor is less concerned about disclosing his HIV positive status to you. Presumably, the ideal scenario would be for the entire population to just hurry up and get HIV, at which stage it would no longer be an epidemic, and just part and parcel of the human condition. What would the stygmatisers do then?

5.Time to stamp out charisma before it outshines us all

Joel Golby (yet again of the *Guardian*) is not going to take charisma lying down. Golby's refutation of charisma is that, according to science, it merely stems from being quicker, or more able to think on your feet than others, and so is not worth anything. I wish I'd got in there sooner, but unfortunately I've had a charisma bypass.

> Finally, researchers have figured out the deep truth of what charisma is, and it's basically "just being quick"... According to a University of Queensland study, the ability to think and act quickly is a key column around which the most intangible of personality traits is built. They backed up their findings with a do-it-as-quick-as-you-can general knowledge quiz, and found that those who completed it quickly were viewed as more charismatic by their friends... The study also looked at the most likeable musicians, leaders and celebrities. "When we looked at charismatic leaders, musicians and other public figures, one thing that stood out is that they are quick on their feet," research leader William von Hippel said. "Our findings show that social intelligence is more than just knowing the right thing to do. Social intelligence also requires an ability to execute, and the quickness of our mind is an important component of that ability.

The problem with charisma of course is nothing to do with charisma itself, but rather that we are not all equally-endowed with it. Evolution and science are true enemies of variance haters as they simply will not conform to their wishes. It's a small consolation, but charisma, or specifically the lack of it, does seem to explain *Guardian* appointments rather well.

6. A third of Britain's Rio medallists went to private schools

Throughout the 2016 Rio Olympics, most British media sources contented themselves with celebrating the UK's record medal tally, and the nation's most successful away games in history.

The *Guardian*, however, was more fixated on the quotas for medal winners. Of course, it ought to have been clearly mandated to the schools in advance, that it would be helpful if their subsequent medal winners would conform to some sort of egalitarian pattern. Nonetheless, the headline is a rather strange way of reporting that two-thirds of Britain's Rio medallists *didn't* go to private schools, but I suppose the Guardian's reader base might not have gone for that.

7. The question not to pop this Christmas: 'Can I marry your daughter?'

Have you been dating your girlfriend for a while and still very much in love? Thinking about popping that all-important question, but respectfully want to ask her father's permission beforehand? Think again!

According to Rhiannon Lucy Cosslett, *Guardian* and Vagenda columnist (look it up, but yes it means what you think), who's obviously led a rough life in the inner cities, nicely shoots down your respectful proposal plans thus:

> Asking your partner's father for permission to propose is an outdated sexist convention rooted in a time when women were regarded as property – and there are far more modern alternatives.

She continues introspectively:

> I don't know if it's because the relationship I have with my dad is more chummy than most father-daughter relationships (he's more of a smoking buddy than a patriarch), but the idea of a man asking my feminist dad for my hand in marriage makes me want to lie down on the floor. I also doubt my father would react well. If anything, it would be a warning sign. I imagine he would be tempted to withdraw permission on the very basis of the guy asking. Except he wouldn't be able to, because he doesn't own me.

I'm not sure if anyone has had the temerity to pop the question to Cosslett's feminist father, but for anyone who should take the job on, you might want to get your ticker checked - those family Christmas parties are going to be a hoot.

8. Not enough women edit Wikipedia

Sadiq Khan is a man of special talents. As the incumbent Mayor of London, he has presided over the unprecedented transformation of London from a reasonably safe city to one of nightly stabbings, rapes, acid attacks, and almost daily murders. The crime figures are currently so bad that London eclipsed New York's murder rate in February 2018 – the first time this has occurred in history.

You might be forgiven then for thinking that our wonderful Mayor would devote the entirety of his energy to resolving this crisis, but you would be deceived. Have a quick browse through the Mayor's Twitter feed (he's big on social media), and you will notice gems such as this from June 2018:

> *The vast majority of Wikipedia editors are men - and just 17% of its biographies are of women. We're calling on Londoners to help us redress this gender imbalance and ensure women's stories are fully represented online.*

Just to be clear, he's campaigning against the additional volunteer work of men. Of all the inequalities he could be fighting – particularly how many men got stabbed last night – he still manages to find a cause of scant importance.

9. Sex offenders, including paedophiles should be allowed to adopt

This spectacularly anti-variance headline was the reporting in the British press of an article in the respected *Child and Family Law Quarterly*. In 2010, Helen Reece, a reader in law at the London School of Economics, called upon Theresa May, then Home Secretary, to relax the rules which automatically ban sex offenders from caring for children, claiming that this could breach their human rights.

In her article, Reece argued that reoffending rates were not that high among sex criminals, 'Despite growing public concern over paedophilia, the numbers of child sex murders are very low.'

This level of variance denial is bordering on mental illness. Are there really any adults in the world so bereft of parental instinct that they would willingly allow children to be adopted by those with a history of child-abuse? Perhaps there are, but why should the child have to pay the price for this insanity?

10. Tinder needs to stop acting like there are only 2 genders in the world

There are few people more offended in the world than *Guardian* journalists, and on this particular occasion they do not disappoint. For our last entry, Zach Stafford explains that Tinder really needs to get with the program, and embrace the multitude of genders that so many other applications are going for.

Having decided that indeed there were more than two genders, Stafford decided to get offended by the fact that other Tinder users would react differently to him if he set his profile to female (for research purposes naturally). He was right. Rather shockingly, the less enlightened male users thought that gender meant a little more than Stafford did.

> Lazy men swiped right – and were then offended that we had been matched. But most men whom I matched with while using Tinder as female would just not engage me or message me and suggest a glitch happened but wishing me luck on the app.

Gender is actually a good place to pause on this whistle-stop tour of bizarre anti-variance campaigns, as it now actively finds itself at the vanguard of the defence of normal society, and we need to examine why.

Primary Targets

The Holy Grail for the variance denier is to now force the submission of either gender or race to the equality template. The reason is clear: nothing screams variance quite like the diametric opposition of male and female, nor does anything put the sword to equality like the irrefutable markers of race. Liberals have put all their money on the notion that gender and race are social constructs, and it's a good line. After all, no one can be superior if gender and race don't mean anything, can they?

The question of race is now so sensitive that most white people will back down before the race card is even deployed; gender on the other hand, has put up a stiffer resistance. In attempting to dismantle biology, Liberals have shifted their attack ever so slightly to the number of genders. The number two is much too binary, and therefore the number needed to be raised, and raised quickly. While good enough for the animal kingdom, and the past 200,000 years of evolution, Liberals are now no longer content with a paltry 2 genders. Indeed, woke statuses are directly correlated with how many genders you believe in.

The bidding was started fairly conservatively, with people suggesting 'intersex' or 'third gender'. Then the LGBTQwerty brigade started testing how many keys they could type on the keyboard before someone called them out. Once social media outlets joined the game, it turned into a farce. Someone mythically pulled the number 53 out of the air, I suspect the same lawyers who campaigned for 72 virgins as part of ISIS's benefits package.

Once Facebook got involved, the results got silly. Fifty-six became fifty-eight, but Zuckerberg soon found himself under attack from those who felt that the numbers just weren't enough. People were still complaining about being 'pigeon-holed', and I must confess that 'polygender' doesn't cut it for me either.

Facebook finally got it right in the end. To complement their current, minimal set of 71 genders, they now allow you to fully customise your own, in short to make your own (potentially infinite) gender. According to Facebook Diversity:

> Now, if you do not identify with the pre-populated list of gender identities, you are able to add your own. As before, you can add up to ten gender terms and also have the ability to control

the audience with whom you would like to share your custom gender. We recognize that some people face challenges sharing their true gender identity with others, and this setting gives people the ability to express themselves in an authentic way.

From social media all the way up to government, the normalization continues. In October 2017, the Office for National Statistics revealed that it will make the sex question on the next census (scheduled for 2021) voluntary, after protests that it discriminates against transgender and non-binary people.

Despite the slight problem that this will leave the British government without an accurate figure for the number of men and women residing in the country (borderline relevant for a census, you'd think), the ONS explained that the question was '*considered to be irrelevant, unacceptable and intrusive, particularly to trans participants, due to asking about sex rather than gender.*'

The assault on gender shows how pitifully we are doing in the defence of variance, and just how far our enemies have come. The absolute beauty and grace of the feminine lady and the rugged handsomeness of her protective beau have been brutally assailed.

It's a mistake however, to think that Liberals don't know what they're doing. Of course gender is a social construct, and there are infinite varieties; except that is, when you need someone to pick up the tab.

CHAPTER
7

War on the Y chromosome

Not content with having infinite genders, Liberals have decided to confuse us further by getting us playing genital Top Trumps in the same toilets. They have their work cut out for them nonetheless. It was always going to be a Herculean task to claim that males and females were one and the same. The rather obvious reason being, that males do not remotely conform to the homogeneity script. Not only do they largely represent variation in our species, but they flaunt it with such gay abandon in evermore excessive displays to attract those variance-loving females. For progressives, the answer is simple – genuine masculinity needs to be annihilated.

In all walks of life, unabashed masculinity is now under fire. Men with their charm, their wit, their charisma, their intelligence, their bravery, their strength, their protectiveness, their creativity, their daring, and their do-or-die attempts to get into the enemy's knickers, are now largely despised. In short, all the things that females have ever so carefully selected and insisted upon from men, are now open to ridicule, considered inappropriate, or downright criminalised.

Society is increasingly a realm where the male is not welcome – the merest whiff of his toxic masculinity being enough to debar him, and something for which he will need to apologise eternally. In the modern world there is effectively no malaise that cannot be successfully blamed on the Y chromosome.

The Matriarchy

The war on males begins early on. Expulsion from the womb leaves many men typecast for the remainder of their time outside it. This is not the fault of men, but the failings of a drastically over-feminised society, that places such little value on what boys bring to the table. Instead of traditional masculine traits of protectiveness, individualism, competitiveness, leadership and assertiveness[93], our boys are being forced to learn early on that feelings matter more than truth, that safety is an imperative which should never be overridden by risk, and that winning is a sin, unless of course it's a woman doing it. Boy, are they learning!

According to the Department for Education, in 2016 just 26% of teachers in the UK were men. That's 38% of secondary school teachers and a paltry 15% at primary level. It's hard to blame men for this. In an age when setting 'Lolita' as a text would probably get you up on a rape charge, and when praising a female student but forgetting that she was pretending to be a boy on that particular day, gets you suspended[94], it is no wonder that most men seem to think the risk just isn't worth the reward.

Still, this does nothing to help the boys learn how to become men, nor to help them keep up with the girls, for whom education is increasingly solely run. The pervasive opinion of our time is the prevalence of male privilege, and that girls and women are disadvantaged in society. Not only is this not true, but in terms of education this is a bad joke. While historically boys have outshone girls in the classroom[95], that is no longer the case. Girls are now outperforming boys on almost every metric. Only in science and maths[96] are boys still holding their heads above the water.

For example, at GCSE level in 2016, 71.3% of girls scored at least a C grade, compared to 62.4% of boys. At A-level, the gap is lower but still favours girls. In 2017 however, when boys marginally outperformed girls for the first time in years, there was an outcry from critics[97] that the assessment of grades was favouring boys. Girls are now supposed to do well; boys ought to know their place.

Far from courses being designed to help boys, the exact opposite is true. In recent years, examinations have been increasingly designed to favour the ladies. By 2000, modular courses (which reward girls' slow, methodical, consistent approach) had been brought in, as opposed to the end of year exam in which boys excel[98]. Set texts for English Literature are increasingly geared towards girls, which is not surprising since girls outnumber boys 3:1 at English A-level[99]. Oxford University have pushed the boat out even further, intending to change their final exam to a take home paper, in order to boost female scores in history[100].

According to the Higher Education Statistics Authority, the number of women gaining firsts at University has trebled over the last decade, meaning that even in tertiary education, the women are finally outscoring the men. While it is nice to think that women have suddenly trebled their collective intellect over a short period of time, it is more likely to be the consequence of the complete feminisation of education generally.

We should of course be cautious in our panic here, because of what we know about the intelligence ranges according to gender. It should not surprise us that girls are slightly outperforming males on average at the university level, because of the fact that males are significantly overrepresented at both extremes of the IQ scale, and that therefore, there are fewer men going to university in the first place. While it appears everything is being done to assist girls so that they could 'match' their male counterparts at the top end of the market, little to nothing is being done to help the boys at the less politicised, lower end of the scale.

Boys are often seen as problematic from an educational point of view. They exhibit many traits which teachers find difficult to deal with. This begins with basic things like sitting still or neat handwriting, to more complicated behavioural problems. Since the 1970s, it has been widely accepted that more than five times as many boys as girls will be diagnosed with behavioural disorders such as ADHD[101]. A large proportion of those boys are then prescribed controversial drugs such as Ritalin, and are even threatened with expulsion if they do not take it.

As if that wasn't enough, teachers are consistently biased against boys, rewarding girls with higher marks for the same quality of work. According to Andreas Schleicher, education director at the OECD (Organisation for Economic Co-operation and Development), this is because girls are more 'school friendly'. In other words, they are rewarded for better behaviour and attention in class, rather than academic merit.

In short, boys are up against the odds from day one. In addition, they are three times more likely to be expelled[102], or to simply dropout of education altogether. There are now 35% more female graduates per year in the UK[103], and the gap is widening. Decades ago, when boys were outperforming girls, this was a chronic problem which needed to be addressed. Now that the opposite has been enforced, the silence is deafening.

In every sphere where gender is concerned, male domination is a sin which must be rectified while female domination is welcome - a hearty kick in the balls, if you will. As an example, there is seemingly no end to the resources available to encourage women to have a go at the 'men's' jobs. Despite the comparative lack of female inclination for STEM careers (women prefer working with people, men prefer working with things)[104], there is no end of support for them to give it a go anyway.

In 2014 for instance, Google announced a $50 Million fund to motivate women into coding. The UK taxpayer meanwhile can't throw enough money into persuading women to become engineers. In 2013 for instance, David Willetts, Minister for Universities and Science, unveiled a £400 million cash injection in the field, with the expressed aim of encouraging women.

> *The proportion of engineers who are women is one of the lowest in Europe and we've got to raise our game. That is why we support the ambition to double the proportion of engineering degrees taken by women.*

You might think that women would be appreciative of the encouragement, but there appears to be a lot of hostility from the gentler sex on this one. Rather than working harmoniously alongside the men, aggression is widespread on the part of feminists, reflected by such headlines as: '*How can men help women in STEM: shut up, sit back and listen[105].*' This aggression is misplaced. Women are now in fact overrepresented in STEM, and hired at an astonishing 2:1 ratio over identically qualified males at faculty level[106]. Who's sticking up for the boys?

Listening to the media meanwhile, you'd be confident that

males are guarding the corridors of power, but that ain't necessarily so. Take a quick glance around the UK, and you'll see that more than a few positions of authority are devoid of the requisite penis. Four of the top five jobs are now filled by women: The Queen is still apparently indifferent to calls for a sex change, and is matched in her antipathy by Prime Minister Theresa May, Chief Commissioner of the Metropolitan Police Cressida Dick, and Nicola Sturgeon as First Minister of Scotland.

At Westminster too, despite the historic dearth of female MPs, the situation has never looked brighter. Leader of her Majesty's loyal opposition, Jeremy Corbyn, must be pleased to preside over a Labour Party, 44% of whose MPs are unprecedentedly female. Of course he would have liked to do better, but he was stymied somewhat by the demands of the ballot box. Not to worry though, his shadow cabinet is exemplary in its makeup, being as it is perfectly-balanced with 16 men and 16 women.

Naturally, he had to cut a few corners to achieve this, and the women are not exactly what you would call first team material. Emily Thornberry as Shadow Home Secretary is a consummate professional who knows the answer to absolutely any question, provided it is not asked by a man. Diane Abbott, Shadow Defence Secretary, is blessed with the kind of numerical understanding that would embarrass out-takes of Sesame Street. Rounding them off is shadow Attorney General, Shami Chakrabarti, whose MP status must have got lost in the mail as she was delivered rather circuitously via the backdoor of the House of Lords. Chakrabarti was a tough signing for Corbyn, as she had already been earmarked for a lucrative career with Dulux as chief whitewash inspector.

As we examined previously, not only does the 'gender pay gap' not exist for men, but it actually exists for women under the age of 35[28]. Finances aside, the workplace is also increasingly hazardous for the average male: men are 45% more likely than women to be made redundant[107]. Men also constitute an astonishing 96% of workplace casualties[108], partially because men undertake the most dangerous jobs. Sewage plants, mines, roofs, oil rigs et al are all monopolised by the patriarchy. Try as they might, women have been spectacularly unsuccessful at breaking through any of these grime-ridden glass floors. Even in industries where they are now welcomed with open arms, such as the military, women still cannot get anywhere near the action. In the UK women currently constitute 10% of the armed forces, yet it is men who hog 99% of injuries and deaths[109].

On Civvy Street, life is not much better. According to the Office for National Statistics[110], men are almost twice as likely to be the victims of violence (2.4%) compared to women (1.3%), and make up the lion's share of murder victims (68%).

Safe spaces

When he's not shanting it up in the sewers or down the mines, there are increasingly few places for the sullen male to retreat to should he be desirous of isolation, or the company of his own. If he is fortunate enough to find such a place, modern man is fully aware of the ridicule he must endure for doing so. While it is considered perfectly normal for women to spend time alone in any part of the house, a man doing the same is retreating to his 'man cave'. The wife may enjoy herself in the garden, hubby must content himself with 'the shed'. She's off to her sister's, he's off 'down the pub'.

Not only does the practicing of masculinity necessarily involve the ignominy of pejorative overtones, it is also becoming something of an endangered pursuit. Perhaps the feminists think men will start getting ideas if left alone or allowed to congregate too often. In any case, men's clubs are now under increasing pressure to accept female members. So much so that only a handful of the most stoic gentlemen's clubs in London, such as the Garrick Club, has not relented. Conversely, women's clubs are under absolutely no pressure to admit men (no doubt, they would not be inundated with requests to join if they did). Younger males face a similar double-standard, as their girl-free zones such as the Scouts have long since admitted girls, while the Girl Guides steadfastly refuses to return the favour. A woman wishing to be alone or with the sisterhood is 'empowered', a man wishing to do the same is invariably seen as a 'misogynist'.

Men are, therefore, continually forced to come up with more and more ingenious ways to avoid the Matriarchy. One such male holiday camp is prison, which is essentially Center Parcs without the bikes. Women have been a bit slow on this one. In 2016, only 4.5% of the UK prison population was female[111]. You'd think that woke feminists would be kicking up more of a fuss over the inequality. The problem is that women just can't get through the vetting procedures, try as they might. Despite committing their fair share of crime, women suffer greatly in terms of incarceration rates. They are significantly more likely than men to avoid charges or convictions entirely, and twice as likely to avoid jail time, even when convicted of a crime. In addition, men also receive a bonus 63% longer sentence on average for committing the same crime[112].

As if that were not good enough, it's now been declared that prisons favour men – they are simply not feminine enough. Here's the *Washington Post* with the attention-grabbing headline: 'We should stop putting women in jail. For anything.'[113] Its spiel continues:

> The argument is actually quite straightforward: There are far fewer women in prison than men to start with — women make up just 7 percent of the prison population. This means that these women are disproportionately affected by a system designed for men.

In a similar vein, men have long since refused to share the best-kept secret of cheap accommodation and al fresco dining, or as it is sometimes referred to, homelessness. Sadly, women have finally caught us out on this one. To bemoan the fact that women make up one in four of the homeless population[114] (a rather insincere way of reporting that men make up the other three), the *Guardian* ran a typically balanced article entitled, 'Why homeless services are failing women'[115]. Presumably if homelessness was made more female-friendly, then more women would be able to enjoy its benefits:

> *Women make up 26% of people who accessed homelessness services in 2013. Homeless services are predominantly developed by and for men, because they make up the majority*

of clients {interesting word}... Our research has also found that women do not generally like being in a minority in mixed hostels or housing projects as they can feel unsafe in male-dominated environments.

As is so often the way, not content with joining the party late, the girls have to start changing the rules, and spoiling things for everyone else. To avoid the Matriarchy altogether therefore, men are left essentially with two choices at this stage of the game: a man of sufficient means may get himself a rod and line, and trek out into the river for a spot of fishing. Those for whom the licence fee is a little steep, will have to make do with the line on its own, and try his hand at the world's fastest growing male sport, suicide. Men are becoming surprisingly good at this, with UK males now outperforming their female counterparts four to one[116]. If only the feminists genuinely cared about equality.

Men are oppressors, women are victims

Despite the feminist clamour for equality, any reasonable examination of the data would lead you to conclude that it was in fact men getting a raw deal on most things. This mistaken impression can be easily clarified however, by understanding the greatest coup of feminism: women are victims, men are oppressors. No matter the circumstances, men are at fault. Indeed, any man who politely challenges this concept instantly makes a rod for his own back. In attempting to take away their victim status, he is oppressing women further. Civilised societies have long since decided that females are preferable to males.

What are little boys made of? Frogs and snails and puppy dogs tails. What are little girls made of? Sugar and spice and all things nice.

If there's anything going free, it's always ladies who ought to at least get first refusal, with men a very distant second.

If you have no daughters, give them to your sons. One a penny, two a penny, hot trust funds!

Indeed, there is less than nothing a man can do to upgrade his second-class ticket. Even if he should make the ultimate sacrifice and lay down his life for his family or country, he will still not be exonerated from the narrative of oppression. As the old Hilary Clinton line famously has it: Women have always been the primary victims of war. Women lose their husbands, their fathers, their sons in combat.

That's right, even being machine-gunned into oblivion, men are just off on a jolly with the lads, and to hell with the consequences!

Don't get me wrong, of course men love to oppress women. The trouble is that the latter-day pansy is not quite up to the task. Even in traditionally male-dominated fields like wife-beating, the modern man has met his match. In terms of domestic abuse, husband-bashing is now as popular as the former. Wives are now just as likely to attack their husbands as to be the victims[117]. The gender difference lies not so much in the level of abuse meted out, but in the lack of public knowledge and more importantly lack of public sympathy to which a male victim would be entitled. Indeed, many men admit not reporting abuse out of shame or embarrassment, and when they do are often not taken seriously, or simply laughed at by the authorities[118]. Provision for such abuse is also woefully skewed in favour of women. According to Parity, which campaigns for men's rights in the UK, there are currently 7,500 refuge places available for women nationally, compared to just 60 for men.

Sexual abuse is also a realm where the feminists are gravely misleading us. The shrill and incessant cries about 'rape culture' across UK university campuses are simply not true. Sexual assault and rape does occur of course, but the true picture is not consonant with the stereotype that it is always males as the perpetrator.

The genders are yet again, fairly evenly matched in many aspects of sexual abuse[119]. Women coerce or force men into having sex just as often as the reverse is true[120]. The rape of boys is committed by women around 50% of the time[121]. Amongst the prison population, the majority of men serving sentences for sexual assault against women were abused by women in their childhood[122]. In female prisons, inmates are significantly more likely to be sexually abused by fellow inmates or female staff, rather than male staff[123].

Again, the disparity lies not so much in the figures, but in the readiness with which society is prepared to assign blame to the Y chromosome. The consensus seems to be men always want sex[124], or that no harm is done if men are raped[125], and that therefore they ought to be grateful. This stigmatisation of males is so marked, that UK law still does not recognize women as potential rapists. In English Law, rape is defined as non-consensual penetration with a penis – a task which women (at least in the old-fashioned sense) are unable to perform.

In short, society is simply not interested in seeing women as anything other than victims. The judicial system compounds this. In the UK, women make up less than 2% of convicted sex offenders[126].

Besides physical methods of abuse, there are many other strings to the misogynists bow. One of the more aggressive ways that the patriarchy likes to assert itself is by selfishly picking up the tab for everything, and this is a department in which women's generosity seems to know no bounds. Recent research[127] indicates that while women are estimated to outspend men by roughly four-to-one, they contribute little financially themselves in the way of taxation. Apart from a small window between the ages of 45-59, women are a net burden on society – which means men are paying all the tax. Men meanwhile, are net contributors between the ages of 23 to 65. While the gender pay gap is a myth, the gender tax gap is real, with men paying roughly twice as much tax as women.

Another arena that the toxic male likes to display his wealth is the divorce court. Women initiate divorce at least 70% of the time in the UK[128], and it's not hard to see why. Divorcing mothers win sole or main custody of their children in at least 80% of cases[109], often qualifying for legal aid while the enemy bolsters his macho image at the expense of his pocket book. He will then end up either paying child support or even lifetime settlements, which he himself is exceptionally unlikely to receive should he be less wealthy than his soon to be ex-wife (according to the 2013 US Census, only 3% of divorcing men are in receipt of alimony payments for example[129]).

In the workplace, the macho man loves to oppress women with his hard work. Until recently in the UK, women had to endure the ignominy of mandatory retirement at 60, bolstering the notion that women are not up to the job. Men could go on until the ripe old age of 65, just to prove their superiority.

Furthermore, men cement their egos with a complete lack of regard for their health – it's almost like some of them want to die. In the UK, both prostate and breast cancer are major killers, each taking over 11,000 lives per year in 2014. Despite the relative equality in the figures, prostate cancer has received £227 million of government and charity funds since 2002, less than half the £529 million invested in breast cancer. The gender health gap is consistent globally, and while the gap varies, the disparities are shocking. In Australia for instance, from 2003-2014 women's health research received more than $833 million from the National Health and Medical Research Council compared to less than $200 million for men.

Their poor health results in men dying on average 4.5 years earlier than their spouses[130]. This is yet another cruel form of oppression, deliberately designed to ensure that women are lumbered with funeral arrangements, not to mention the irritating bureaucracy that inheritances bestow.

Not so toxic masculinity

For all the talk of toxic masculinity, modern man is woefully under-qualified for such a prestigious title. While previous generations had men whose toxicity you could really aspire to, there are precious few around now who could raise a semi, let alone a modicum of testosterone. According to YouGov[131], just 2% of today's young men (aged 18-24) report feeling 'completely masculine', compared to a sturdy 56% of men over the age of 65. Furthermore, in contrast to most women and older men who view masculinity as a generally positive thing, young men are so confused about their role that half of them consider it a dirty word.

Masculinity is in such decline that men now need re-educating on how to be men. This could never have happened previously because our dads would have taught us. Modern fathers have been so discouraged from embracing their masculinity, that they have not even learned the basics. In 2006, *The Dangerous Book for Boys*[132] was published, aimed at boys 'from eight to eighty'. The book contains traditional masculine exploits, like how to build a tree-house, how to skim stones, how to fish, and even how to make the world's best paper airplane. It topped the UK non-fiction chart several times, and sold over a million copies in doing so. In any other era, this book would have been pointless.

While societal neutering of young men certainly appears to be in action, it may not even be necessary. The sperm counts of western men have fallen sharply over the last few decades, while those of African, South American and Asian men appear to have remained stable. According to Dr Hagai Levine of the Hebrew University of Jerusalem[133], there has been an incredible 52% drop in sperm concentration and a 59% decline in total sperm count between 1973 and 2011. Levine examined thousands of studies and then conducted a meta-analysis on 185 of them to reach his conclusion.

The reasons for the severe decline are still up for debate. According to Dr Peter Schlegel[134] of the American Society for Reproductive Medicines, the possible causal factors include diet, pesticides, stress and heat. Schlegel notes that, 'sperm levels could drop to severely low levels that could affect the majority of men in 30-40 years.' Schlegel adds that the most disturbing part of the study, is that the decline shows no sign of levelling off. In other words, masculinity is in free fall.

Judging from the everyday language used about men however, you'd suspect that the patriarchy had never had it so good. As an example, according to the online version of the Collins English Dictionary, the word 'misogynist' is reasonably common. It is in the top 30,000 English words in regular usage, and scores 0.21 on their frequency index. It is also accompanied by many synonyms, such as 'woman-hater', 'male chauvinist' and 'anti-feminist'.

In comparison, the misogynist's opposite number 'misandrist' barely registers on the scale, with a measly 0.01-0.00. To all intents and purposes, it does not exist. Apparently, it does not even make the top 50% of words in common usage, and is given the single entry 'hatred of men'. It is of course taken as read that men hate women, but the lexicon barely makes it possible for a woman to be accused of the same action.

'Exactly how nontoxic do you have to be to get invited to the party?' is the question that men are now asking themselves. The list of global problems for which maleness must take responsibility is practically limitless. From the *New York Times*, 'Dear White America: Your toxic masculinity is killing you', to the *Guardian*, 'Toxic masculinity is everywhere. It's up to us men to fix this.' Whatever your cause, be it acid attacks to mass shootings, homophobia to rape culture, misogyny to climate change, toxic masculinity can be easily fitted into the frame. If you stub your toe before the first cup of tea in the morning, you can guarantee that before the cup has touched your lips, some hard-working social justice warrior somewhere will have identified a causal link between the two.

As a man understandably you'd want to go out of your way to avoid this pernicious disease, and indeed any scientist who can come up with the cure will be quids in. I have noticed recently that many of my male friends seem to have given up meat, and I was puzzled as to the cause. Most hinted at animal welfare, or environmental issues. Then I noticed the fantastic headline, 'Doing vegetarianism to destabilize the meat-masculinity nexus', which made the thing much clearer. According to Anne DeLassio-Parson[135], a sociology professor at Pennsylvania State University, eating meat perpetuates toxic masculinity. Delassio-Parson argues that eating meat perpetuates 'hegemonic masculinity' and 'gender hegemony', and that 'refusing meat therefore presents opportunities, in each social interaction, for the binary to be called into question.' Naturally after reading, I went out and ordered a steak, just to be on the safe side.

In all seriousness, it is tragic to see the erosion of respect and love for traditional masculinity. The idea that good men do not exist is bad enough; the idea that men are collectively responsible for the ills of the world is a scandalous assertion that is bandied around rather cruelly. As a boy, my favourite film scene was always the ending to The Railway Children. Even now, if I imagine the young Jenny Agutter shouting with delight 'Daddy, my daddy!' and running up to jump into his arms, I shed a tear. How have we got to the stage when fathers and grandads, older brothers and uncles, firemen, soldiers, and policemen are all *persona non grata* because they carry the toxic Y chromosome?

Back in the 1980's when Dustin Hoffman dressed up as a woman to secure a job in the film, Tootsie, it was a lighthearted joke. Nowadays, the school career guidance counsellor may well find that a sex change is the best advice they can give our young men.

The thinly-veiled double standard

A sex change might not be such a bad move. Being a woman, or even pretending to be one, is not without its compensations. One such benefit is the female double-standard; a nice wrinkle in the equality patchwork quilt, which enables women to play each situation as a victim no matter what men do. Men not holding doors open for you? They're misogynists. Holding doors open for you? They're patronising.

Feminists are often spoilt for choice in this regard, and find themselves stymied, trying to decide which is more attractive, the victim or the equality card. Jessica Valenti found herself in exactly this position, when writing for the *Guardian* on that most toxic of issues, wolf-whistling. In 2014 she opted for the victim card with, 'The end of hisses, whistles and stares: we need to walk the streets without fear.' By 2015 however, she seemed to have decided that the equality card was preferable, and went for, 'Men rarely catcall me any more. I hate that our culture makes me miss it.'

Cosmopolitan magazine faced a similar quandary during the 2016 Rio Summer Olympics. Having previously set out their victim stall re sexual objectification of women ('Confirmed: Men who objectify women are effing horrible'), they couldn't resist coming full circle, and abandoning it in favour of the equality card version, '36 Summer Olympic bulges that deserve gold'.

Back to the *Guardian* with famously pro-male columnist, Eva Wiseman, who offers up such nuanced wisdom for her male audience as, 'How not to be a dick'. Wiseman, who wrote a piece in her column in 2012 about the joys of crying in 'The crying game', seemed to have had second thoughts about it by 2015 (leastways, if it's a man doing the crying), 'Is there anything worse than a man who cries?'

For men, much of life now is not so much about escaping opprobrium, but merely choosing which brand of misogynist you wish to be labelled. Whether it's objectifying women by frequenting strip clubs, or taking advantage of them by working in strip clubs, you're damned if you do and damned if you don't.

Sex kills

No doubt the best illustration of the female double-standard is the game of sex. Women lead men a merry dance on this one. The trouble with sex is that is used to be quite enjoyable, the greatest treasure hunt of all time. That was before the feminists and equality-mongers got a hold of it. Now, it is a pursuit for which no man of sufficient means would ever get legal clearance.

One of the spectacular myths that women have managed to surreptitiously slip into the sex rulebook is that men and only men derive any pleasure from the dirty deed. Any woman who acquiesces to your advances, is purely doing so as a personal favour. They are lying. Measurable indicators, such as pupil dilation, heart rate, and genital blood flow suggest that, far from frigid little cherubs, women actually enjoy sex and are aroused as much as, and sometimes more strongly, than men[136]. Not to mention spending their hard-earned 78 cents on the latest *Fifty Shades* offering, or Jilly Cooper novels. There is a marked discord between women's reported levels of arousal and what their bodies actually indicate.

To understand why this charade continues, we need to consider the role of parental investment by the sexes. Here uncharacteristically, women have genuinely drawn the short straw. Their involvement in parenting could not be heavier: from conception they are fully committed to the venture, and may well spend the next 20 years devoting their lives to the security of the next one. Men however are free to split as soon as the egg does. Undoubtedly, this stark imbalance in parental responsibility is the real reason that women have got the needle with men, and why it's so easy to confuse modern feminism with simple misandry – they simply don't want to be the ones left holding the baby. Women didn't get the vote on childbirth, and they hate us for it. I probably would too.

Back to the dating game, this unfairness colours the negotiations somewhat. Before having his 'wicked way', our man is a busted flush in every possible sense. He must pay in perpetuity for the right to be rejected at any stage of the game; accept that he has no rights in the selection process (or the potentially expensive aftermath); promise the moon and stars, and deliver them with added VAT. Females therefore, are selling access to immortality to the highest bidder. The Fabergé egg if you will, a seller's market. Men are relegated to flogging free samples door-to-door, perhaps one in a thousand will get invited in.

Before relinquishing her most glorious prize, one of the terms that women absolutely insist upon is that the man openly chases, solicits and attempts to lead her, even if it is just for the pleasure of prick-teasing. Pick up any women's magazine, and you will find an article slating men for not taking the initiative. What they mean is, men who do not understand how the game is played, and that it is men (rather than women) who must stick their neck on the line.

So you lead, big mistake. Women are free to change the rules whenever it suits them (women's prerogative). In the current climate any kind of romantic overture is no longer merely liable to rejection, but also (should the lady be so inclined), to being wilfully misinterpreted. Consider if you will, the recent plight of Aled Jones, he of 'Walking in the Air' fame: the angelic voice that has long since been the amiable companion of Classic FM listeners, and BBC viewers alike.

Aled is a nice guy, if it is ever possible to say that about a man. He received an MBE for services to niceguyhood in 2013. Jones obviously understands how the mating game is played, because he was recently 'under investigation' for an 'inappropriate' text message that was sent to a work colleague over ten years ago. Aled knew that he would have to make the first move, so he put his bid in. Indeed, he ought to get some grudging respect – having to wait over a decade for a response, surely no one can keep it up for that long? While Jones kept his regular slot with Classic FM, the BBC actually axed him while the investigation was conducted.

To try to put that into some kind of context, I can't think of a single man I know who hasn't sent 'inappropriate' text messages to a work colleague at some stage. I certainly have myself, and very rarely I've had the good fortune of getting a favourable reply. If a text message, which is surely the modern day equivalent of the hopeful love letter or Valentine's Day card is off the table, what exactly does that leave?

The recent epidemic of sex 'scandals' is worrying, and ought to be so for everyone. If you're a man it simply dictates that even attempting to get your leg over now is too dangerous. If you're a woman, it is likely to mean that the midnight racy text to finally get you going is, like you, increasingly unlikely to come at all. There is also the slightly larger issue that it will mean the end of the human race. Who'd have thought that the global warming alarmists had backed the wrong horse?

It should go without saying (though somehow I doubt that it will so I shall say it anyway), genuine sexual misconduct (of which incidentally, there is plenty to go around on both sides) is a serious matter. But that is not what we are talking about here. Whether it's Aled sending a non-PG text or Hollywood's leading ladies taking the express lane to an Oscar via the casting couch, the notion that women should always be able to exact some kind of revenge from men for deigning to have sex with them, is becoming enshrined in the narrative. Everyone else is getting a piece of the #MeToo action, why not you?

A good illustration of women's complicity in would-be victim roles, was given recently by Sir Ian McKellen. Giving a talk at the Oxford Union in 2017, McKellen was asked about the abuse of power in Hollywood and had this to say:

> From my own experience, when I was starting acting in the early 1960s, the director of the theatre I was working at showed me some photographs he got from women who were wanting jobs – they were actors. Some of them had, at the bottom of their photograph, DRR - 'directors' rights respected'. In other words, if you give me a job, you can have sex with me. That was

> *commonplace from people who proposed that they should be a victim. Madness. People have taken advantage of that and encouraged it and it absolutely will not do.*

Of course it is not the case that female victimhood does not occur. What is apparent, however, is that male victimhood is rarely spoken of, and indeed it is the case that men increasing require protection from women who would abuse this imbalance.

One of the serious suggestions for men to protect themselves from this kind of attack is the farcical idea of obtaining consent. Consent in the form of a contract, consent in video form, or consent being granted on a ten-minutely basis. The people who come up with these insane solutions to the mating game, are less-qualified in terms of human nature than Stevie Wonder is as a choreographer. Go out tonight and try out your consent lines on a few random women and see how you get on.

In any case, up in court where the law is skewed so far in women's favour, exactly what kind of consent would stick? When both consenting adults are drunk for example, the man alone is held responsible for his actions. To illustrate how ridiculous the notion of consent has become, Sarah Hall (a primary school mother-of-two) recently requested that the classic misogynist's bible, *Sleeping Beauty*, be banned from schools, because the Prince did not obtain consent to kiss the princess[137].

Aside from hacking through the magical forest, triggering the gender-neutral witch and fulfilling the damned prophecy, just how much consent does the guy need? Moreover, how exactly is he supposed to get it, considering the girl is in a coma?

Of course it's funny, until you get your collar felt. The only reasonable conclusion from today's furore over consent, is that a man must know *a priori* that his clumsy overtures will be both welcome and consented to. As English Law currently stands: 'The law places an evidential burden on the defendant to adduce sufficient evidence that the complainant consented'. Not only is this both ridiculous and impractical, but what it also indicates is that any dalliance may subsequently become an issue for a man, should a woman suddenly become indisposed towards him at a later date.

We're now at the stage when it may be injudicious for a man to be alone in the same room as any woman, including close family members. Indeed, I'm sure I recently caught that glint in my daughter's eye that says, 'Thirty years from now, those late nappy changes, that denial of sweets at the checkout, those restrictions on playtime could well translate to a rape charge'.

For men, sex kills – literally. As the old saying goes, 'I never paid so much for sex, as when I didn't pay for sex.' Asking for a woman's phone number or wolf-whistling[138] may soon be designated hate crimes, along with that traditional rape festival, kissing under the mistletoe[139]. For the angst-ridden young man therefore, getting to first base and not ending up behind bars is an act of contortion.

Indiscreet though it is to mention money or fame, it is clear from many of the current Hollywood scandals and indiscretions that far from men being exclusively the bad guys, women are playing their roles too. The Harvey Weinstein revelations generally paint the women as powerless victims. Exactly how much of a victim was Gwyneth Paltrow when she dedicated her 1999 Best Actress Oscar to the very man she would later claim had assaulted her previously?

Many of Hollywood's leading ladies were mysteriously efficient at landing big roles thanks to Weinstein, but equally mysterious in their delayed denouncements. Pamela Anderson nicely sums this up as, 'They knew what they were getting into.' In an interview with Megyn Kelly, Anderson pulled no punches about the victim culture of Hollywood women:

> I think it was common knowledge that certain producers and certain people in Hollywood are people to avoid. Privately. You know what you're getting into if you go to a hotel room alone... When I came to Hollywood, of course I had a lot of offers to do private auditions and things that made absolutely no sense; don't go into a hotel room alone; if someone answers the door in a bathrobe, leave. You know, common sense. Hollywood is very seductive, and people want to be famous.

It's not only fame that is on the table, there's money too. Consider celebrity attorney, Lisa Bloom, who has been less than honourable when it comes to her work in sexual harassment cases. Bloom, who claims to work *pro bono* on such cases (but naturally made prospective clients sign contracts, entitling her to one third commissions from any payments received), tried to bag mysterious donations of up to $750,000 for women who said they had been sexually harassed by Donald Trump, as long as they did so before the election in 2016. According to *The Hill* magazine[140], Bloom worked with four separate women, and was extremely pushy with the timing of the election: 'Give us a clear sense of what you need and we will see if we can get it,' read one text message. The exact price that Bloom can get for you depends on the penis in question, and how famous or wealthy the body attached to it might be. She has form in this department, having previously been responsible for getting Bill O'Reilly fired from Fox News. O'Reilly is the big fish of the sexual harassment world, having famously settled out of court with former Fox News legal analyst, Lis Wiehl, for $32 million in January 2017, despite denying her claims. Bloom also reeled in Hollywood's big fish, Harvey Weinstein, as well as (bizarrely) agreeing to represent him briefly in October 2017.

There's something distasteful about these goings-on, and for me it's got very little to do with the alleged behaviour. The acceptance of money for genuine malfeasance is repulsive to me personally, but even more than that, it's the issue of degree that troubles me. What is so repugnant about the figure of $32 million is not so much the exorbitant sum itself, but the question that it begs: what is it about $32m that alleviates suffering, in a way that $31m does not? Even assuming the allegations are true, one cannot help but feel like the $32m is the figure the market decided that O'Reilly would need to pay for his penis, and by extension his Y chromosome, simply because he could.

With the stakes so high, we have to ask ourselves whether women can always be trusted to tell the truth on matters of a sexual nature. Moreover, when children are factored into the equation, the game can get ugly. As an illustration, a recent survey of 5,000 British women carried out by *That's Life* magazine[141] indicated that 42% would lie about contraception to get pregnant, irrespective of their partner's wishes. A further 50% said that they would lie about the baby's real father if they got pregnant by another man, but wanted to stay with their partner. While global statistics on this are much more conservative (though naturally problematic), it is still estimated that the number of men raising children which are not theirs is between four and ten percent[142], an enormous statistic.

If we revert back to the issue of sexual misconduct, and specifically rape, the issue of female mendacity is about as contentious as they come. Indeed, any man even suggesting that women lie about rape (which, of course, they do) is on a sticky wicket from the outset. It is likely that this is explained (at least in part) by the pervasive notion that women are victims while men are oppressors[143].

Global estimates for false rape accusations range from the conservative 1.5% to around 10%[144]. All figures however, are understandably fraught with complications. A long-term study from 1994 by Eugene Kanin[145] provides a lot more insight into this issue. Although Kanin's work has faced criticism (largely I believe due to its extremely high finding that 41% of women lied about rape), his research is still noteworthy.

Kanin based his study on the police files from a small town in Midwest America, with a population of just 70,000. The study was conducted over a nine-year period. The police had ample time and resources to investigate each case thoroughly. Polygraph testing was available in all cases, and the false incidences were only marked as such when the complainant recanted their original story.

What was interesting in this study is that Kanin was able to classify the reasons for the false rape, and broke the numbers down as follows: 56% of the women involved made the false accusation as an alibi, ie to account for their whereabouts or possibly a pregnancy that they did not want their regular partner to know about. For instance:

> A married 30-year-old female reported that she had been raped in her apartment complex. During the polygraph examination, she admitted that she was a willing partner. She reported that she had been raped because her partner

did not stop before ejaculation, as he had agreed, and she was afraid she was pregnant. Her husband is overseas.

Twenty-seven per cent meanwhile used the accusation to exact some form of revenge, as in this example:

> A 16-year-old reported she was raped, and her boyfriend was charged. She later admitted that she was "mad at him" because he was seeing another girl, and she "wanted to get him into trouble.

A further 18% used the false accusation as a form of attention / sympathy-seeking, as this example shows:

> An unmarried female, age 17, abruptly left her girlfriends in the park one afternoon allegedly to go riding with a young man, a stranger she met earlier that morning who wanted her to smoke marijuana with him. Later that day, she told her friends
> she was raped by this man. Her friends reported the incident to the police, and the alleged victim went along with the rape charge because 'I didn't want them to know that I lied to them.' She explained that she manufactured this story because she wanted the attention.

Despite being extremely high (41%) when compared to other more conservative estimates, this figure compares favourably with the attitude survey that we saw previously (that around 50% would lie about paternity, if pressed). Moreover, it is important to reiterate that there are many reasons for women to lie about the occurrence of rape, besides the issue of money.

In general, it is often bemoaned that conviction rates for rape are notoriously low. Dispassionately however, we may need to consider that suspicion of female motivation for such a claim, is also notoriously low. That may be something we need to change. The simple idea that women are never believed is just not true.

Consider if you will the harrowing case of Jemma Beale. Jemma is a 25-year old woman from West London, raped or gang-raped by no less than 15 men between 2010 and 2013. Beale, who states that she has been a lesbian since the age of ten, and has 'no desire' to sleep with men, was nonetheless targeted repeatedly by gangs and strangers, including those armed with machetes, and sometimes suffered 'sexual violence of the most serious kind'. Beale even had scars and bruises to substantiate her claims of being assaulted with barbed wire for instance.

Her first attacker was sentenced to seven years in jail after a retrial in 2012. In a victim impact statement, Beale described the devastating effect that the rape had had on her: 'I feel that any sentence he received will never reflect the life sentence that he gave me'. Sounds abominable, doesn't it? Don't worry, not one word of her story is true. Even the brutal injuries were performed by Beale herself.

Beale was described as a fantasist by the presiding Judge, Nicholas Loraine-Smith, who commented,

> This trial has revealed, what was then not obvious, that you are a very, very convincing liar and you enjoy being seen as a victim. The prosecution described your life as a 'construct of bogus victimhood'.

Beale, who was jailed for ten years in 2017, told the court that she had been bullied at school because she was fat, which might in some way explain the attention-seeking behaviour. But the flagrant disregard for the lives of her victims, one of whom was falsely imprisoned for two years, and another who fled the country in fear, is truly reprehensible.

The extreme nature of this case is surely a rare phenomenon, but it goes some way to show the extent to which women are always assumed to be victims. Even after Beale concocted bizarre stories and repeated almost identical lies, which naturally the defendants denied, still her victimhood was accepted.

Beale's victims' lives were tarnished gravely, but at least they lived to tell the tale. Sometimes the consequences for the innocent male victims of false rape accusations can be deadly. This is exacerbated by the lack of anonymity for the accused, with some tragically taking their own lives. Consider the harrowing case of British teenager, Jay Cheshire, who was falsely accused of rape in 2015. Cheshire hanged himself just two weeks after the allegations were withdrawn. What is even more devastating is that his mother, Karen, replicated the suicide one year later.

The fashionable hysteria otherwise known as the #MeToo campaign meanwhile is as much a war on men as it is a quest for justice. One easy way to see that is the fact that there are conspicuously no women implicated in the campaign. From what we have seen about the incidence rates of indiscretion between the sexes, there really ought to be. This means that men exclusively are being milked for all they are worth. If you're rich, successful and possibly famous, your penis is a lucrative entity, and you should be exceptionally careful not to misplace it.

To repeat the point one final time, absolutely, definitely 'yes' to thorough due process, scrutiny, and investigation of serious sexual assaults, no matter who commits them. But 'no', equally vehemently not, to waking up 30 years later having had a mildly enjoyable indiscretion in your youth, looking at your middle-aged self in the mirror and deciding that someone else should pay for how things have panned out.

Furthermore, having traded access to your vagina for access to your celebrity idol, or a fasttrack to the Oscars, that does not make you a victim. That makes you a calculated businesswoman unhappy with the merchandise she bought - caveat emptor.

As a final point on this topic, it is noteworthy that while the feminists are so keen to lynch all men for the crime of trying to pass their genes on, that is where their curiosity regarding crime starts and abruptly ends. It's OK to hate men, as long as it's the right men.

The zeal with which the #MeToo campaign has gained traction has occurred at a suspiciously opportune moment. At precisely the same time all across Europe, migrant hordes are competing to make their subjugated capital cities the rape centre of the world. These are genuine rapes, brutal rapes, frightening rapes.

But remarkably, this is apparently an issue that the western feminist is not interested in. Here she has ample opportunity to expose real misogyny, genuine toxic masculinity, but at the cost of progressivism. The perpetrators are non-white males, and as such do not fit the narrative so well. Indeed, the more data that comes out of Sweden and Germany, the more myopic western feminists become, and the more they seek to dissect and punish the minutiae of Marks and Spencer's-clad grandads' feeble come-ons.

These two phenomena are not unrelated. The kind of person who falsely equates a racy text message or an unwanted hand on someone's knee with brutal gang rape cannot be acquitted on stupidity alone. They have an agenda. That agenda is to prove that all men are at it, which has the benefit of mitigating the more serious end of the spectrum. If you doubt that, consider the vitriol that Matt Damon[146] has received recently for merely pointing out that indiscretions are on a spectrum, and that that ought to be taken into account. The feminists do not want to hear that. Disparities in the data, the degree or frequency of offences, and the demographics committing them are irrelevant. Nothing must be allowed to get in the way of their faux homogeneity.

Sweden's justice minister, Morgan Johansson, as good as enshrined this in law (in Sweden it is illegal to collect data on criminal ethnicity[147]) when he said in November 2017, 'It doesn't matter if rapists are migrants, only that they're men'. This is as disgusting as it is sophistic. We are presumably not very far off some leading light informing us that migrant rape is acceptable. This has already been hinted at, with (yet again) Swedish politician, Barbo Sorman, attempting to exonerate migrant rape when she tweeted in 2016 that Swedish men rape by choice, migrants rape by ignorance, 'The Swedish men who rape do it despite the growing gender equality. They make an active choice. It's worse.'

It may not necessarily take two to tango

Sex is currently a little problematic, that much we can all agree upon. However, it may not be an issue for much longer. All the signs are that men are being increasingly marginalised in society, and that the Y chromosome is simply becoming too much trouble.

As it currently stands, we are at a crossroads. Either a) the feminists have gone too far, and women are not the porcelain victims they purport to be, or b) men are not fit to play a role in society full stop. It looks like we're going for option b.

Indeed, there are plans afoot to write men out of the equation entirely. The development of sex robots and the surprisingly different responses to them is telling. While sex robots for men 'epitomise patriarchy and offer men a solution to the threat of female independence'[148] (naturally), sex robots for women on the other hand beg the question 'are men replaceable after all?'[149]

Seeing as one in four millennials would date such a robot[150], the chances are that men are replaceable. And even if the robots are all busy or suffering malfunctions, there are still plenty of other avenues for females to choose from, such as settling down with ghosts[151].

Our libraries too are crammed with titles explaining just how little use men are. From worthy tomes such as Camille Paglia's, *Are Men Obsolete*[152], Barbara Whitehead's, *Why There are no Good Men Left*[153], and not forgetting Hanna Rosin's masterpiece, *The End of Men: and the Rise of Women*[154], it looks increasingly likely that the only patriarch to be trusted will be the state. The Y chromosome, as so often in history, has got to ask itself a question: is it all worth it?

On the flipside, women may not only be too dangerous for men, but they may also be losing their appeal. Japan already has one foot out the door, with a birth rate in such decline that its population is expected to shrink by a third between now and 2065[155]. One reason for this is the new breed of young men (Otaku) who have no interest in sex, and prefer to date virtual girlfriends. In 2010, a Ministry of Health survey found that 36% of young men had no interest in traditional dating[156].

In the west, I doubt things will come to that. The day a company manufactures a half decent sex robot that can cook and clean, and comes with a working on / off nag function, the human race is almost certainly going to be out of business.

The last target

Any punter who didn't get the memo that men are the inferior gender, has got one last obstacle to negotiate to remain ignorant on the issue – the television. If you cannot avoid it, you will be hit by an almost constant barrage of negative stereotypes of the bumbling, hapless, incompetent, intellectually-challenged Y-chromosome carrier. From Homer Simpson to Joey from Friends, the tv schedule is full of them. Loveable buffoons perhaps, but buffoons they are.

And if you don't get up to make that obligatory cup of tea between programs, the adverts are even more brazen. Whatever you need to sell, and whatever kind of imbecile you need, the white man is your safest bet - in fact your only bet. Anything other than white is much too risqué for our identity-obsessed zeitgeist, and in any case might get you taken off air.

But don't worry; the white man is a versatile fool. Need someone who ain't down with the kids? He's your man. Someone who can't pull birds? Doesn't know how to use deodorant? Can't articulate his feelings? Our man is outsmarted by the wife (naturally), as well as the kids, the mother-in-law, the neighbours, the dog, the goldfish, the washing machine, the telephone, the car, the alarm clock, there's not even any point to a list - he'd be outsmarted by that too.

Perhaps it was funny the first few million times, but it goes beyond comedy. It's telling you something: if no one else can even be considered for the role of the fall guy, definitely not women or 'people of colour', what exactly does it say for your male privilege that you and only you have the right to have the piss perennially taken?

The average middle-aged white male is essentially now *persona non grata* in his own armchair, and that is a situation which can only go on for so long. As we have seen, the maleness he carries is constantly under fire. His whiteness, however, isn't doing him any favours either.

CHAPTER
8

The War on Whiteness

The problem of whiteness

If men feel (understandably) aggrieved at the criticism they face for penis possession, then white people ought frankly to be up in arms over the hysteria that their pigmentation causes. For the most part, they are not. Thankfully they are not, because if any other group faced a similar, brazen, unashamed barrage of hostility from society in general, we would be in the early stages of civil war. There's still time.

We're not talking about the lunatic fringe here, nor the odd, drunken tweet at 3am. We're talking about mainstream publications, educational institutions, the media, and public figures, collectively normalizing the relentless war on whiteness. Indeed, if you did not know to what they referred, you would be forgiven for thinking that a sickness, rather than a race or skin colour, was being referred to.

From Florida Gulf Coast University's course on 'White Racism'[157], to Magdalen College Oxford's compulsory course on 'race awareness'[158], whiteness courses masquerade as similar-sounding options, such as Black Studies or Women's Studies. While the latter are celebrations, 'Whiteness Studies' taught by 'whiteness scholars', are tawdry excuses for nothing other than attacking white people.

Consider the 'Pyramid of white supremacy'[159], part of a required course entitled 'Diversity and the Self' for students attending the Professional Teacher Education Program at Salisbury University, Maryland. In order to pass, students are required to memorise the pyramid, and must then take a quiz. Far from teaching diversity, the course is a direct criticism of whiteness, and explains that whites achieve everything through privilege rather than work.

The pyramid itself consists of seven tiers: Indifference, Minimization, Veiled Racism, Discrimination, Calls for Violence, Violence and finishes up with Genocide. According to the course, the lower tiers are directly responsible for propping up white supremacism which leads to genocide. So, according to the pyramid, you are directly responsible for genocide if you do any of the following: remain apolitical, want to suggest that not all white people are racist, ever question non-whites, deny white privilege, suggest that people are racist to whites, hope that we can all just get along, teach a relevant curriculum, or wish to fund schools locally. It is not a coincidence that this course is compulsory for education majors.

The assault continues. From Ivy League professor, Ali Michael's *Huffington Post* article, 'I chose not to have children, because they'd be white'[160], to Harvard professor Noel Ignatiev's call for the abolition of the white race, 'The goal of abolishing the white race is on its face so desirable that some may find it hard to believe that it could incur any opposition other than from committed white supremacists'[161]. From the *Guardian's*, 'We tend to empathize with our online avatars. So let's get rid of white emojis'[162], to the *New York Times*, 'Can my children be friends with white people?'[163] From *Vice* magazine's, 'White people need to learn how to integrate'[164], to *Salon's*, 'White men must be stopped: The very future of mankind depends on it'[165]. The message is consistent: it's not OK to be white.

Those calling for the out-and-out extinction of the white race are neither alone nor shy about making their position clear, and they get a lot of support from the mainstream. Author of *Stupid White Men*[166], Michael Moore, clearly relishes a time when white people will be no more.

> The angry white guy is dying out, and the Census Bureau has already told us that by 2050, white people are going to be the minority, and I'm not sad to say I can't wait for that day to happen. I hope I live long enough to see it because it will be a better country.

Rumoured 2020 presidential candidate, Oprah Winfrey shares Moore's lust for the death of older, white Americans, as she explained in an interview for the BBC[167]:

> There are still generations of people, older people, who were born and bred and marinated in it, in that prejudice and racism, and they just have to die.

Indeed, any news that predicts that the white race is not on course for extinction is reported with the same nervous despair as an impending stock-market crash. Here's the *Washington Post* putting on a brave face under difficult circumstances, 'Trump's immigration plan could keep whites in US majority for up to five more years.'[168]

> President Trump's proposal to cut legal immigration rates would delay the date that white Americans become a minority of the population by as few as one or as many as five additional years.

Whiteness itself is now fundamentally a problem. There's too much of it about. The Oscars are regularly lambasted for being 'too white'[169]. Charities are similarly afflicted[170]. So are campuses[171], Hollywood[172], and catwalks[173]. You don't even need a list; if there's anything good going on and white people are involved, it's a cast-iron certainty that it's too white.

While universally excoriated, whiteness has perhaps one redeeming feature – it can be used to scapegoat any issue for which the root cause is unpalatable. Indeed, the blame which can be attributed to whiteness is relentless. *Vogue* went for white women voting the wrong way, 'Why do white women keep voting for the GOP and against their own interests?'[174] *The Huffington Post* chimed in with, 'White families are engines of inequality.'[175]

Current leader of the Liberal Democrats, Vince Cable, basically decided that the whole Brexit referendum, and the accompanying vote of 17.4 million people to leave the European Union, was caused by white racism. At the party's 2018 spring conference, he used his speech to explain the motivation of older, white voters:

> Too many were driven by a nostalgia for a world where passports were blue, faces were white, and the map was coloured imperial pink...crushing the hopes and aspiration of the young for years to come. Looking around the auditorium, we are very, very white. We must prioritise making our party more ethnically diverse.

Vince is not alone in his conclusions. As if it were not bad enough being the majority population in your own countries, or own political parties, whiteness is now a clear sign of being racist, and you'd be surprised at just how far that line has been taken. Former L'Oreal model and transgender woman, Munroe Bergdorf, has been given platforms from the Metro and the BBC, to a (notably brief) equality advisor role for the UK Labour Party. She has used them all to proclaim the same message: 'All white people are racist.' Or, if that's not clear enough for you: 'The uncomfortable truth is, that the white race is the most violent and oppressive force on earth.'[176]

With the print media facing ever-dwindling sales, what a boon to find a topic the public are actually thirsty for. The *Washington Post* capitalized with, 'Why not being a 'racist' isn't enough'[177]. The *Guardian* reported, 'Why I'm no longer talking to white people about race'[178]. And the winner, *Afinity* magazine, 'You don't have to be racist to be racist'[179]. The rhetoric is tediously repetitive, no matter what you do – if you're white, you're racist and there's nothing you can do about it. Don't like it? Suck it up snowflake, and guess what, you're still racist!

Help is at hand of course, if only white people weren't so racist they could see it. Buzzfeed offered a helping hand with, '37 things white people need to stop ruining in 2018'[180]. Netflix essayed, 'Dear White People', a series educating whites on their inherent racism. Or, as *GQ* simply put it: 'White people need to be better.'[181]

In fact, being white is now a considerable handicap to those unfortunate souls afflicted with its condition, but none more so that those who also happen to be afflicted with masculinity as well. This lethal combination of 'white male' is perhaps now the most dangerous description in the English language.

Ten years ago when a female politician wanted to use the white maleness of her opponents against them, she felt compelled to coyly employ the euphemism, 'male, pale and stale'[182]. These days she doesn't even bother. Stating that someone is a 'white male' is usually sufficient to ensure their arguments are completely disregarded, or at the very least viewed with a health warning.

The BBC, for instance, is 'hideously white'[183] according to former boss, Greg Dyke; the West End too is 'hideously white'[184] according to the (presumably) non-hideously white Andrew Lloyd Webber, and the Football Association a bunch of 'old white men'[185].

There is no other identity that elicits such out-and-out condemnation without trial, but there it is. If you are unlucky enough to belong to this identity group, you'd better get used to it because it's here to stay. No one is going to bat for you; no one is going to take up your case, and certainly not *pro bono*. The simple fact of the matter is, you do not provide the opportunity for any leverage. It's impossible to virtue-signal about anti-white sentiment and to get anywhere. On the rare occasions that your message may strike a chord, you are quickly shouted down as being 'populist', 'far-right', or, if you are undeniably correct, simply upgraded to 'Nazi'.

The second-class status of whites is now so clear and so accepted, that the UK Labour Party recently made the hernia-inducing move of attempting to charge white people a £10 surcharge to attend a rally in February of 2018[186]. I fear this may be only the beginning. Coffee shops and restaurants are already experimenting with extra fees for male[187] or white[188] customers, and there are now even serious calls for a 'privilege tax' on white people of around five per cent[189].

The situation is so dire, that many people are now frightened, ashamed and even embarrassed by their whiteness. Appeasers are already on manoeuvres, with prominent figures coming out in open condemnation of their skin. Perhaps they mean what they say, or perhaps they merely wish to be on the right side of history. Famous white rapper Eminem mused in his song 'Untouchable' (a song about White Privilege in America):

'There have been times where it's embarrassing to be a white boy.'

Former politician turned journalist, Matthew Parris, decided that being white was a little more than embarrassing, with a recent piece entitled, 'If I had a choice, I wouldn't be a whitey'[190].

> Speaking as a white man, don't we have ghastly complexions? Par-baked like those bread rolls you can buy in supermarkets, we look like not quite the finished product. Glancing at the person opposite on the Tube the other day, I thought "if only I could be that colour". He was in his late thirties, maybe, south Asian, maybe Sri-Lankan; and his skin was that beautiful golden brown that whispers that this is how humans were supposed to look. White is just wrong for skin — a kind of mutation, as though some key pigment was missing from birth. It looks inbred.

Jeff Hitchcock meanwhile, co-founder and executive director of the Center for the Study of White American Culture, couldn't push the boat out far enough. He stated in a 1998 speech[191],

> There is no crime that whiteness has not committed against people of colour...We must blame whiteness for the continuing patterns today...which damage and prevent the humanity of those of us within it...We must blame whiteness for the continuing patterns today that deny the rights of those outside of whiteness and which damage and pervert the humanity of those of us within it.

In fact, being anti-white is now so fashionable that white people (whiteness aside) are queuing up to protect non-whites from their fellow white man. Consider this gem from the *Huffington Post* in September 2017[192]:

> The volunteer-run Facebook group, founded last year by friends Layla Tromble and Terri Kempton in Washington state, has white people respond to racist trolls online at the request of people of color. "If a white person is filling your social media with white nonsense ⁂ anything from

overt racism to well-intentioned problematic statements, tag us and a white person will come roundup our own."

In other words, if a white person dares to ask a reasonable question, we will come and silence them for you.

Every now and again it makes sense to take a step back and realise that innocent people are being spoken about here as though they were vermin. An easy thought experiment is to simply replace the word white with any other colour or group, and then to suddenly notice how odious it is. So the question we need to ask ourselves, apart from merely existing, what exactly is the crime of whiteness?

The crime of whiteness

When I initially set out to write this chapter, I was troubled as to how to broach the subject of whiteness generally. What is it about whiteness that appears to be so irksome to its critics? At first, I intended to write at some length regarding the contributions and achievements that this race has brought to the world. While white people are rather unambitious when it comes to crime, and clearly do not take up nearly enough of the available seats in the prison population, they have some redeeming features.

One thing they seem to have going for them is their accomplishments. According to the Encyclopaedia Britannica's *The 100 greatest inventions of all time*, 80 were of European or North American origin. Similarly, since its inception in 1901, the Nobel Prize has been awarded 923 times. Eighty-three per cent of these have been to laureates from western countries, with more than half going to UK, US and German citizens.

Immigration too, tells a story of a one-way street. The flow is from non-white countries to white ones. According to Pew Research[193], the top three emigration destinations are currently the United States, Germany and Russia. Whites are hard workers, and pay the majority of tax, a lot of which they invest in their new immigrant populations.

I started to get a little way down this road when I realized that I was wasting my time. I don't think even the most ardent anti-white social justice warrior is going to seriously argue that white people have not achieved anything (I could be wrong of course). I think rather, they would argue about how they have done so and why.

So, the more appropriate question seems to be, yet again, all about variance: why do whites vary so much from the baseline on almost any metric, and why is this a problem? Or, perhaps more precisely, why is white success problematic? In my opinion, that is where this anti-white sentiment derives from, and ultimately distils to. The crime of whiteness is its success.

Jealousy would seem a very human response and therefore explanation for such hate. The problem is that this jealousy would then need to be selective. No one raises an eyebrow at the variance when it is non-white groups performing well. You are spectacularly unlikely to hear someone complain that hip-hop or basketball are too black, that there are too many Asians in tech, or that the nursing and teaching professions are predominantly female. Those things are considered progressive, or do not occur frequently enough to raise suspicion about the equality lie.

Whiteness on the other hand is consistent in its success. If you are heavily-invested in not just equality per se, but in equality of outcome, then whiteness is your worst nightmare. So the question for the variance-deniers is, how do you solve the problem of white success?

The solution to whiteness

The left believes they have got the solution to whiteness, and if simple solutions to complex problems are desirable, then this is a masterpiece. The solution to white variance is the myth of 'white privilege', and it really is a silver bullet. White superiority on any measure then is not real variance, but instead is the disenfranchisement of minorities.

A good place to employ the white privilege myth, therefore, is obviously those domains that illustrate large variations between populations. These areas need to quickly be attacked as heretical, which is exactly what is occurring right now.

Consider the field of mathematics, which one might mistakenly have supposed to be as meritocratic as they come. There are right answers and there are wrong answers, as opposed to the humanities, where interpretation plays a larger role. In mathematics, then, the skin colour of the hand that writes the answer ought not to even figure in the proceedings. The white privilege guys, however, do not agree.

Take Rochelle Gutierrez, professor of Education at the University of Illinois. Gutierrez argues that teaching maths perpetuates white privilege[194]. In a chapter of, *Building Support for Scholarly Practices in Mathematics Methods*, she makes her case:

> On many levels, mathematics itself operates as Whiteness. Who gets credit for doing and developing mathematics, who is capable in mathematics, and who is seen as part of the mathematical community is generally viewed as White.

Gutierrez is making the *a posteriori* assumption that, because whites perform well at maths that somehow influences the fact that whites do well at maths. On that rationale, you could white-up every kid in Harlem and rerun their SATs. Somehow, I doubt it would provide her with much validation.

White privilege is flexible too, working on a sliding scale should it be required, magically fitting in with whatever observable variance needs to be explained. For instance, to explain why in the US blacks commit more crimes than Hispanics, who in turn commit more crimes than whites, it is apparently because of hierarchical and systemic white privilege, dishing out prejudice to groups on a sliding scale. Similarly, if blacks do worse than Hispanics, who do worse than whites, who do worse than Asians on IQ tests, that is (curiously) still white privilege. Asians get away with their intellectual superiority, at least for now.

The slight downside to the 'white privilege' panacea comes when you examine the collapse of the white working-class, which has occurred across the west in recent years. Here is a group that should have everything going for it – it's got privilege in abundance, right? Wrong. Western societies are now so indifferent to their own populations that whites are falling dangerously behind on many measures. Whatever white privilege they have was clearly bought on hire purchase.

At a cursory glimpse, in 1999 white Americans aged 50-54 with a high school education had a mortality rate 30% lower than black Americans. As of 2015, it was 30% higher[195]. Meanwhile in the UK, general attainment at GCSE level for disadvantaged pupils across the spectrum has improved by 20% since 2006. This is encouraging. What is less encouraging is the fact that white working-class children have seen absolutely no improvement in their scores[196].

A paltry 24% of white working-class boys are currently achieving the bare minimum of five good GCSE's, and a mere 45% of white British pupils attend University, the lowest rate of all ethnicities apart from Romani. As usual, those who insist upon equality of outcome, only ever seem to do so at the upper end of the market.

The Campaign against whiteness

White privilege is an impressive lie. Not only does it foster an environment where whiteness is the ready-made fall guy for any non-white shortcoming, it also facilitates alternative avenues of anti-white sentiment to your taste. By this token, whiteness can be further impeded in day-to-day life, which in turn further restricts white success. If you remember, that's the whole issue in the first place.

• Debasement of the word 'white'

White really is the new black. I'm sure that's offensive to many people. I'd go so far as to say that the word 'white' is now more of a negative than a positive term. Buzzfeed, keen as ever to prove me right, has a three-minute video on YouTube entitled, 'People of Colour from around the world react to the word white'. If it's positive reactions you're looking for, the video is three minutes too long.

In the evolution of language meanwhile, the word white (along with 'man'), is the word you most readily attach to another to render it pejorative. 'Whitesplaining' of course was a cert, because, along with 'mansplaining', it means you never have to listen to any facts you don't like – provided a white person is saying them.

In 2017, the noun 'white fragility' was shortlisted for the OED word of the year[197]. White fragility is defined thus: 'Discomfort and defensiveness on the part of a white person when confronted by information about racial inequality and injustice.'

What white fragility really constitutes is a readymade put-down for a white person who argues more effectively than you do. Indeed, whiteness is so constantly under fire that even millennials have noticed. You remember those guys, the social justice warriors who think that everything is the fault of white people? Even they concur that whiteness is under fire a little too often. According to a survey from GenForward[198], almost half of white millennials say that discrimination against whites is as big a problem as discrimination against people of colour.

Even using the word white in isolation can be problematic. In 2017, University College London apologised for referring to snow as white[199]. Presumably, this was more to do with having used the word white in a sentence, because as far as I am aware, snow still is white. The blizzard in a teacup was actually caused by university bosses, who tweeted using the University's twitter account:

> Dreaming of a white campus? Our campuses will be open and operating fully today, Monday 11 December, so please make your way in as planned. (We can't guarantee snow but we'll try!)

What the bosses obviously had in mind, the allusion to Bing Crosby's hit, was nowhere near as offensive as the idea that they were all secret white supremacists. The by-now dull and predictable backlash over 'racism' was met with a swift retraction the next day:

> We chose our words very poorly yesterday when thinking of this song: (link) We're sorry and we'll choose our words more carefully in the future.

It's not just snow. Milk too has come under a lot of fire recently for its white supremacist leanings and its racism. No, it's not a joke. In Sweden, the FOI (Total Defence Research Institute) has classified milk[200], along with the 'OK' sign as being used to 'convey hatred and create fear and anxiety'. It's not only Sweden that has noticed milk's suspicious right-wing inclinations. According to California State University's college paper staff writer, Samantha Diaz[201], milk has become the new symbol of hate:

> *You, along with the rest of the nation, have been so accustomed to hearing the benefits of milk that you probably didn't even realize the subtle racism hidden in our health facts. The main health benefit of milk is to guard against osteoporosis, a disease that weakens your bones – hence the 'stronger bones' rhetoric. While this is a very practical health benefit, osteoporosis affects Africans at a significantly lower rate than it does most Americans.*

In other words, white bones are weaker than black bones. Milk therefore, by insensitively not passing on the same benefit to blacks (because blacks don't need it), is as good as signing up for the Klan.

On to music: classical to be precise, because what are the chances that that won't offend someone, somewhere, somehow? The BBC: 'Classical music excludes composers from minorities'[202]. The *Guardian*: 'Western classical music – performers and audiences alike – is still an almost exclusively white concern. What can be done?'[203] *San Francisco Chronicle*: 'Classical so white and male: Time is overdue for diversity'[204].

There basically isn't much left accompanied with the word white that doesn't cause anger. Taylor Swift is apparently 'aggressively white'[205], white marble is racist[206]; and don't even get me started on white meat! [207]

The popularity of this negative association has obviously been picked up on by those who could potentially use it to leverage. Hilary Clinton decided that white people should pick up some of the tab for her losing the 2016 election to Donald Trump. Everyone else is blaming white people, so why not? As interviewed on CBS

Sunday Morning in 2017,

> Clinton: 'He was quite successful in referencing a nostalgia that would give hope, comfort, settle grievances, for millions of people who were upset about gains that were made by others ... millions of white people.'
> Presenter: 'What you are saying is millions of white people.'
> Clinton: 'Millions of white people yeah.'

Irrespective of whether Trump's campaign was explicitly designed to attract white voters, the idea that appealing to the majority of Americans is somehow negative is quite a hard one to get your head around. But the lengths to which this anti-white sentiment can go are nowhere near to being exhausted.

White bashing is en vogue these days, and not everyone is in a hurry to change the channel. As the old saying goes, 'If the only tool you have is a hammer, you tend to see every problem as a nail.' David Lammy, Labour MP for Tottenham (London) is one such perpetual offence-seeker who likes to see everything in black and white, literally. Naturally, anything black is a victim, and anything white is an oppressor.

In 2013 Lammy replied to a tweet from the BBC concerning the selection of a new Pope. This procedure is usually indicated by black or white smoke emanating from the chimney of the Sistine Chapel. White smoke indicates that a new Pope has been chosen, while black indicates that no decision has been made.

Lammy, replied to the BBC's tweet thus, 'This tweet from the BBC is crass and unnecessary. Do we really need silly innuendo about the race of the next Pope?

When it was pointed out to Lammy that the smoke was not actually a reference to the Pope's skin colour, but rather than one had or had not been appointed, he was undeterred:

'It's the juxtaposition of Pope and black and white. But maybe I'm just weary of the endless discussion of race.'

Lammy has many strings to his race bow, and is remarkably adept at finding diverse ways to accuse white people of flaunting their privilege, no matter the circumstances. One such bizarre occasion, was his recent criticism of Comic Relief. In a film for the BBC's Daily Politics program[208], Lammy accused the charity of portraying Africa as a continent of poverty-stricken victims who could not speak for themselves, claiming they had 'tattooed images of poverty in Africa' on to people's minds.

The *Guardian* soon had his back with the impartial, 'Comic Relief to ditch white saviour stereotype appeals.'[209] Afua Hirsch was late to the party, but rallied valiantly with her article, 'Ed Sheeran means well but this poverty porn has to stop.'[210]

Despicably white as it may be, Comic Relief did manage to raise a record-breaking £55.4m during its 24-hour telethon in 2016. Perhaps if we were talking billions, the whiteness could be overlooked.

Lammy has done well to highlight the disgusting white saviour mentality, as it seems to be more widespread than anyone had previously noted. The BBC took the bait, 'Never Again: Is the gun control movement too white?'[211], as did the *Guardian*, 'Why are so many white men trying to save the planet without the rest of us?'[212]

Let's try another angle. Far from superior, white people are actually inferior to other groups. At least you might think that if you immersed yourself in western culture for any length of time. Here's the *Guardian's* attempt, 'Why white people aren't as cool as black people: Black people have an effortless cool about them, almost no matter what they do.'[213]

Vice magazine meanwhile took a different tack[214]:

> White People Need to Learn How to Integrate. The discourse around integration in Britain is always about foreigners being "more like us". But in areas like Leyton and Notting Hill, it's middle-class whites who are failing to assimilate.

You've got it. Mass immigration into London has been so completely overwhelming in parts, that it is now the fault of the indigenous white Brits who are not integrating fast enough with their new immigrant populations.

The crowning glory of the campaign against whiteness,

however, is the notion that your white privilege is so great, you aren't even allowed a voice. This particularly vile and dangerous idea is on the move. Here is one of its recent incarnations from *The Beaver,* 'Dear White People: no melanin, no opinion.'[215]

I'd take issue with that of course, but alas it would probably only be whitesplaining, or, at the very least, white fragility on my part.

• *The elimination of whiteness*

It's patently obvious to anyone decent enough to hold the correct opinions, that whiteness is a cancer which must be eradicated. While a vaccine for whiteness has not yet been created, society is definitely hard at work on the developmental stage. Like the old Dickens classic *Scrooge,* it appears that past, present and future whiteness is being eliminated.

The media generally is making a better stab of it than young, black men in Sadiq Khan's London. According to the UK census of 2011[216], 81.9% of the population are white, but you wouldn't know it by the representations of the UK on television.

Christmas is a good time to analyse what businesses and advertising companies are up to, because they do their market research well. According to Statista[217], the average UK household was expected to spend £821 on their 2017 Christmas shopping. You'd think therefore, that companies would have pandered to that massive demographic of whiteness, but you'd have been mistaken.

An illustration of this was the 2017 Christmas adverts. As a smart advertiser, you'd presumably attempt to corner a section of the market that no one was playing to. If that was your line, you'd be the only company trying to reach the typical white household, because no one else was. Of all the big players, not a single one deviated from the mixed race 'diversity is our strength' hymn sheet. Debenhams decided to run the Cinderella theme: white woman, black man. Marks and Spencer's went with a mixed race couple, white woman, black man. John Lewis had a hard think, and finally came up with a mixed race couple – white woman, black man. And on and on it went interminably.

Traditions are not so bad of course, as long as the whiteness element is kept to a minimum. That's why it was no surprise in 2017 that the latest must-read book was *Santa's Husband*[218], a book telling the story of a gay, black Santa, who lives in the North Pole with his white husband. A white Santa is OK of course, as long as he is subservient and stays in the kitchen.

The ghost of Christmas future must not be overlooked either. Here perhaps the evidence is most strong that whites are being actively discouraged from breeding full stop. The headlines are shocking:

> *Guardian*: Should we be having fewer children for the sake of the planet?[219]
>
> *Slate:* After-birth abortion. The pro-choice case for infanticide. [220]
>
> *Medusa:* Beyond Pro-Choice: The Solution to White Supremacy is White Abortion. [221]
>
> *Macleans:* Mothers who regret having children are speaking up like never before.' [222]
>
> Texas State University Student Newspaper: White is over. Your DNA is an abomination. [223]

Whereas diversity is demanded in all aspects of life, the photographs used in these articles are exclusively of white women, white families and white babies. It appears that calls for voluntary genocide are exempt from diversity quotas.

As important as the assault on the present and the future is, if you really want to go the whole hog it is necessary to erase the history of a people too. People without a strong sense of identity and tradition are much easier to annihilate.

Across the west as we speak, famous white statues are either being torn down, or are requested to be in the name of inclusivity. And as genuine history dissipates, it is being quickly replaced with lies. UK television has been very quick to replace white historical figures with black actors, again naturally in the interests of inclusion. Joan of Arc, Roman soldiers, Margaret of Anjou, Friar Tuck, Guinevere, Victorian soldiers and Achilles have all been proudly presented as black, to name but a few.

Then came the Cheddar Man. In February 2018, every progressive media outlet could not wait to report the claim that our ancestors may not have been white at all. Here's the *Guardian*[224]:

> A great many widely held – but incorrect – assumptions about the expected pale-skinned, fair-featured nature of Britain's founders were promptly overturned, to the rage of some commentators and the joy of many.

The joy was short-lived, however, when just a month later, geneticist Susan Walsh of Indiana University, contradicted the claims[225]. But for many, the seeds of doubt had already been sown. Whiteness is being systematically eroded, both in reality and by subterfuge. In the near future, the only thing likely to remain white about Britain will be the mythical white demography of Eastenders.

• *You can't be racist to white people*

Lest anyone should get it into their head that white people deserve defending, you needn't concern yourself. Even in rare moments when you hear things you strongly suspect might be a little bit racist, still then – don't worry. It turns out that our understanding of racism is way off. *The Oxford English Dictionary* defines racism thus: Prejudice, discrimination, or antagonism directed against someone of a different race based on the belief that one's own race is superior.

But then again, what exactly does the OED really know anyway? In any case, they've probably got loads of white people working for them. To understand racism, we really have to consult non-white people, who own the discussion. The *Huffington Post* recently reported with thinly-disguised glee, 'Dear White People' director and star break down why black people can't be racist.'[226]

The sleight of hand essentially distils to this: double standards around race do not exist. Non-whites can have non-white-only spaces, can be racially offensive, can use racial slurs etc. while white people cannot. 'Reverse racism' simply does not exist. This is an essential move, because if this lie had not been put in place, white people would be able to play the race card too. By constantly redefining terms and meanings, the identity Gestapo is attempting to always keep a little daylight between white people and the discussion. By refusing to use their terms, it's quite easy to see that reverse racism indeed does not exist. There is just racism, which is what determinedly anti-white rhetoric is.

It's not that non-whites don't want to be racist to white people. People are really trying.

Imagine how heartbroken they must feel when even their best efforts go unrewarded. The artist, Dean Hutton, had a go with his poster and accompanying shirt, beautifully repeating the poetic phrase, 'Fuck all white people'[227]. Much to Hutton's chagrin, the presiding judge of South Africa's Equality Court ruled that this constituted neither racism nor hate speech. Back to the drawing board then.

Meanwhile, Goldsmiths College's diversity officer, Bahar Mustafa, threw her hat into the ring when she tweeted the hashtag #KillAllWhiteMen[228]. I mean, what else do you want from your diversity team if not a little genocide? She must have thought she had cracked it when she was initially charged. The early celebrations turned out to be bittersweet unfortunately, as the Crown Prosecution Service subsequently dropped all charges.

Consider how unfair this is, when white people achieve the accolade of racism with consummate ease. Keegan Jakovlevs[229] (a white man) barely had to get out of bed to get thrown in jail for a year for an almost identical crime. Instead of Twitter, Jakovlevs chose FaceBook to post 'Kill all Muslims'. In this case, the judge, Niclas Parry, was only too happy to explain to him that, 'racism was evil, and that anyone who incited racially aggravated violence must expect severe punishment.'

Perhaps the best recent effort to be considered anti-white was offered by Chicago 19-year-old Brittany Covington[230]. She was part of a group of black youths who kidnapped a white mentally-handicapped man, tortured him, beat him while screaming racial abuse and topped it off by streaming the entire thing live on Facebook. She must have thought she was home and dry.

Not quite. Covington was granted probation, sentenced to a

mere 200 hours of community service, and (most harrowing of all), a four-year ban from social media.

So spare me the white privilege nonsense.

• *Should whites be allowed to exist?*

We are living through strange times. The idea of whether whiteness or even white people ought to be allowed to exist is rapidly becoming a legitimate question. Consider the furore that was achieved in late 2017. All across America, posters appeared at high school and university campuses. These posters depicted incendiary speech, hate speech, overt racism or Nazism, depending on your point of view. What were these words? 'It's OK to be white'.

In South Africa right now, white farmers are having their lands taken, their property confiscated and their blood spilled[231]. This comes after South Africa's parliament recently voted to allow the seizure of land from white farmers without compensation. Exactly where is the international outrage? Have you heard much about this story from the BBC?

What I have heard instead, is open condemnation of those who wish to help. Australian home affairs minister, Peter Dutton, has been accused of hypocrisy, after he suggested that persecuted white South African farmers should be granted asylum in Australia[232].

Elaine Pearson, Director of Human Rights Watch, was not impressed.

> *I find it breathtakingly hypocritical that government ministers would prioritise this group of white South African farmers over other groups that are equally, if not much more desperately, in need of assistance.*

What she means presumably, is that white people cannot be victims. Many parents appear to have come to the same conclusion, and seeing how little is to be achieved with the victim narrative, are offering up the sacrifice of their own children to fuel their own virtue-signaling needs. This was beautifully put by the Huffington Post, with their intriguing article: 'Preserving my children's innocence is an act of preserving white supremacy'.[233]

And indeed, it's just as well there are these wonderful people around, because some of us have the gall to disagree. Do you know, there are still white people who do not wholly embrace their own extinction? It's so problematic that the *New York Times* had to run a piece in June 2018 entitled, 'White extinction anxiety.'[234]

This is genuinely the state of play in 2019. The question of whether whites have the right to exist has been granted ill-deserved legitimacy. Where are the #MeToo brigade, the feminists, the antiracists? Progressives are not interested in defending whites, because not only do whites provide no chance to leverage, they are also unlicensed for a victim status of any hue. For that, genuine privilege, you need to look the part.

CHAPTER
9

The Quest for Victimhood

The Victim Olympics

Competing with everyone under equal circumstances (survival of the fittest), is not everyone's cup of tea; it's hard work. The *white male* patriarchy myth is the perfect way of avoiding competition altogether. The only snag is that everyone else in the non-white male group can, and indeed will, claim an aggrieved status too. So once again, competition rears its ugly head. How to rank all the worthy oppression?

Fortunately, the patriarchal coin has a flipside - the hierarchy of victimhood, which appears to solve the impasse. Victimhood is measured by how far away from the privileged white male position you can get. Here is a recent example, a poster from the 'Student Engagement and Equity' department, at the University of Ontario Institute of Technology[235]:

> Becoming aware of privilege should not be viewed as a burden or source of guilt but rather an opportunity to learn and be responsible so that we may work toward a more just and inclusive world.

Check your privilege.

Privilege: Unearned access to social power based on membership in a dominant social group.

- Able-bodied physically and mentally

- Access to education
- Christian
- Cisgendered
- Heterosexual
- Male
- Native English Speaker
- Canadian Citizen (at birth)
- White

Black men's oppression then, is outranked by that of black women (two victim statuses), who in turn are outranked by gay black women, *ad infinitum*. As I'm sure George Bernard Shaw would have put it: 'Those who can, do; those who can't, claim victim status'.

Navigating your way amongst polite society more or less depends on your ability to understand the ever-increasing complexity between the different levels of victimhood in the hierarchy, and your relative position within it. White men who do not fully grasp the truth of this are walking a daily tightrope where one false move, or rather one false opinion, can be treacherous. Reputations and careers are destroyed on a regular basis by simply overlooking the fact that in a given situation you are not allowed to even have an opinion, let alone voice it.

Conversely, at the other end of the spectrum – the ever-expanding LGBTQ list of 'special' identities has extended so far that a high-ranking victim is now to all intents and purposes beyond reproach. That is, unless another suitably-oppressed individual wishes to do so. We're not even close to topping out on this one either. Professional victims now abound in the marketplace, with distinction being awarded to those who can highlight a hitherto unknown area of 'privilege', or way in which he (or more likely she / zie) is being oppressed.

The recent discovery of victimhood that is 'cultural appropriation' highlights this rather well. This is the bizarre notion that you (for 'you' read predominantly white people) are not allowed to learn from, participate in, wear, eat, practice, or otherwise enjoy anything from another culture. Just as you were starting to enjoy that diversity, right? Aside from the immediate riposte that this is both completely unworkable (humans have always learned from each other socially), and hypocritical (it works both ways, surely?), you'd think it would have been laughed out of court.

But it has not been. It has been taken up willingly by white celebrities, bamboozled no doubt by the absurdity of it, and of course anxious to retain their audiences. Singer Katy Perry has had to apologise on multiple occasions for (amongst other things) appropriating black culture by braiding her hair in 'cornrows'[236] (a traditional black style), or appropriating Japanese culture by dressing as a Geisha[237]. Little Mix singer, Jesy Nelson, was accused of 'cultural borrowing' after unveiling dreadlocks on Instagram[238].

The biscuit was well and truly taken by Justin Timberlake, however, when he managed to apologise for praising Jesse Williams, a black actor[239]. Timberlake made the rather obscure faux pas of claiming to have been inspired by the actor, and was then roundly criticised for having benefited from black cultural appropriation throughout his career. So that's the situation then: a successful white man cannot even pay homage to a successful black man, because the latter's victim status still outranks the former's adulation. If you're white, best just to apologise.

Maximum confusion is injected when you have a mixed-race artist. How then exactly does the victim hierarchy function? Bruno Mars caused just such a controversy in March 2018, when he was accused not only of appropriation, but of actually using his 'racial ambiguity' to manipulate the market[240]. Writer Sensei Aishitemasu argued that the Grammy-award winning singer Mars, who is half Filipino, quarter Puerto Rican and quarter Ashkenazi Jew, only won Album of the Year at this year's Grammy Awards as white people love him 'because he's not black'. '*Bruno Mars 100 percent is a cultural appropriator. He is not Black, at all, and he plays up his racial ambiguity to cross genres.*'

Rough translation, 'It is not easy to accurately identify the victim-status which Bruno Mars deserves to be afforded, which means he has victim-status privilege. Or alternatively, anyone who isn't white, but also isn't conveniently 'half Filipino, quarter Puerto Rican and quarter Ashkenazi Jew' is suffering from 'non-privileged victim-status victimhood'. Clear?

Who can say what?

The victim Olympics are a complicated series of events that even the great Daley Thompson would have struggled with. The complexity lies in trying to predict which victim status to back in a given situation. Even seasoned campaigners often fail to read the public mood. The position is clearest when a white person is involved – in such cases they are almost always assigned the 'oppressor' role. Here, the 'victim' has a hard time coming away with anything other than a victory. The only real question is what kind of punishment the oppressor will face, which is usually commensurate with his proximity to the patriarchal white male Gold Standard.

The difficulties arise when two, similarly-matched victims are competing against each other. Here then, emotions rule the game, and it can be nigh on impossible to predict how society will view it. As a case in point, consider the tragic story of Mercedes Grabowski, or as she was more commonly known, August Ames.

Ames was a popular female porn star, who got caught up in a controversy that she could never have anticipated. She refused to shoot a sex scene with a bisexual male co-star (known as a 'crossover' in the industry), because she was concerned that it constituted a health risk. She was right of course. According to US Statistics, gay and bisexual men account for 66% of all AIDS diagnoses, and 82% of HIV diagnoses amongst men[241]. If you consider the fact that the man was a porn star to boot, it is not difficult to see why she refused the job. This is Ames' initial tweet which started the avalanche on 3rd December 2017:

> *Whichever (lady) performer is replacing me tomorrow for @ EroticaXNews, you're shooting with a guy who has shot gay porn, just to let cha know. BS is all I can say. Do agents really not care about who they are representing? #Ladirect I do my homework for my body.*

Ames was then subjected to a torrent of abuse from Twitter users, accusing her primarily of homophobia. Ames apologised at length for any apparent offence, and explained that most women in the industry have a similar policy, but her contrition was in vain.

So here is the situation: a female porn star, a reasonable level of victimhood one would imagine (albeit a white one), comes up against the might of the LGBTQwerty Gestapo. In terms of variance denial, it's easy to understand what was going on. Ames was perfectly right that shooting a crossover scene was a more pronounced risk to her health (as an aside, that's irrelevant as it was her choice).

The problem she faced was that the variance deniers could not allow her to get away with telling the truth. Highlighting the fact that gay men are a more pronounced risk of AIDS would mean violating the equality lie. So, to avoid the accusation of homophobia, she would need to sleep with someone she did not want to, to prove that she did not think it equated to an amplified health risk, which it did.

Here is one of the milder tweets which she had to endure, ironically from a fellow porn star, the apparently 'pansexual' Jaxton Wheeler[242]. You'll notice the clear ultimatum: *'The world is awaiting your apology or for you to swallow a cyanide pill. Either or we'll take it.'*

In the end it was understandably too much, and Ames hanged herself shortly afterwards.

The power of the codes

Because the nature of the victimhood hierarchy is so confusing, the situation requires clarification. Fortunately, codes are often used to highlight the nature of the infraction, and indicate where your allegiance should lie. This is naturally important for all parties concerned, but is of most use to the justifier. By using codes, he is able to easily direct his audience to the correct response, and is also often able to avoid actually giving explanations or arguments. Naturally, it should go without saying that the truth is often only ever playing a cameo role in these proceedings. The main codes are below:

- Sexism – male perpetrator, female victim.
- Racism – white perpetrator, non-white victim.
- Islamophobia – white perpetrator, Muslim victim.

- Homophobia – straight perpetrator, LGBTQwerty victim.
- Equality – the disadvantaging of white people.
- Diversity – the exclusion of white people.
- White Supremacy – white people who dare to complain about being disadvantaged or excluded.
- Feminism – sexism to men, which is considered positive.

The immense power that these simple words have should not be underestimated, as we saw in the tragic case of Ames. The codes play alternating roles, either in controlling the general populous (feminism, diversity and equality must be supported at all times) or in suppressing it (sexism, racism, Islamophobia et al mean you're on the thinnest of thin ice).

It was of no surprise, therefore, to read in January 2018 that West Ham Director of player recruitment, Tony Henry, had been suspended, and was subsequently fired, for apparent racism[243]. The code itself was enough to condemn the man, to successfully remove him from his post and to convince the public that it was morally right to do so. It did not have to be substantiated, nor is there any sort of legitimate measuring device to confirm its existence. What Henry actually did, was voice an opinion (a fairly innocuous one at that) regarding African football players. He merely stated that the club was not looking to sign any more players from Africa, as they can 'have a bad attitude', and 'cause mayhem' when they are not in the starting line-up.

Throughout the ensuing and rather predictable media frenzy, and the million uses of the word racist (white man speaking about a non-white victim, standard stuff), not one publication or person of note even dared to raise the seemingly important question, 'Are African players difficult?' If not, can't he just be mistaken? If they are, why can't he say that?

Just as, 'Who is allowed to say what' is an important distinction, so too is it crucial to get words working for you in order to cement your victim status. The Nazis (to whom one will become immediately closely acquainted, should one be caught holding the wrong opinion) famously understood the importance of words, not just in the fight to control public opinion, but in the process of lying itself. In Mein Kampf, Hitler outlined the importance of making a lie big enough to be believed:

> All this was inspired by the principle – which is quite true within itself – that in the big lie there is always a certain force of credibility; because the broad masses of a nation are always more easily corrupted in the deeper strata of their emotional nature than consciously or voluntarily; and thus in the primitive simplicity of their minds they more readily fall victims to the big lie than the small lie, since they themselves often tell small lies in little matters but would be ashamed to resort to large-scale falsehoods.

> It would never come into their heads to fabricate colossal untruths, and they would not believe that others could have the impudence to distort the truth so infamously. Even though the facts which prove this to be so may be brought clearly to their minds, they will still doubt and waver and will continue to think that there may be some other explanation. For the grossly impudent lie always leaves traces behind it, even after it has been nailed down, a fact which is known to all expert liars in this world and to all who conspire together in the art of lying. (Mein Kampf, Chapter 10 as translated by James Murphy[244])

'*A lie told often enough becomes the truth*' is the shorthand, which is attributed to various people from Lenin to Goebbels. In terms of how true this might be, psychologists talk of 'The illusion of truth'. That is, false information which people have been told before is subsequently more likely to be believed or reported as true. In other words, the Nazis basically got it right.

For the variance denier, the single best weapon has always been the accusation of racism. This word alone has managed to become a serious marker of unacceptability – of one's character, one's opinions, in short, of one's entitlement to exist. It is the nautical equivalent of catching scurvy, for which there is no citrus remedy.

The success the Left have enjoyed with this word is phenomenal, and while they constantly seek new codes, they have never found anything better. To silence a man whose words you fear, there is still no finer tool than the slur of racism.

People of Colour

Due to the effectiveness of the *racism* code, the highest imaginable single victim status is the recently popularised term 'people of colour'. This is a rather bizarre taxonomy, given that wrapping up Hispanics, Asians, Arabs and blacks as some sort of homogenous group makes no sense at all. It makes no sense in terms of history, geography, genetics or culture. It only makes sense, if you insist upon seeing things in terms of 'them and us', Whites (oppressors) and non-whites (victims). Thankfully, the Oxford English Dictionary clarifies it for us:

> The term person of color is first recorded at the end of the 18th century. It was revived in the 1990s as the recommended term to use in some official contexts, especially in US English, to refer to a person who is not white.

In other words, it refers to someone who has achieved the requisite victim status. Over a very short space of time, the term has morphed into a soubriquet meaning little more than someone who it is unwise for white people to challenge.

An example of this was the recently-discovered political ambitions of a man named Spencer Raymond. Raymond decided in October 2017 that he wanted to run for a City Council seat in Portland, Oregon[245]. This would usually be a worthy ambition, but Raymond had two slight problems. Firstly, he is a straight, white male, as his political opponents were quick to point out. Secondly, he would be running against three women of colour.

State Representative, Diego Hernandez offered Raymond some friendly advice on Facebook:

> *Do yourself a huge political favor and don't run... I want to*

make her story, I want there to be women of color on Portland City Council, and I'm going to use every influence I have to make that happen.

Others were more direct about their reasons for opposing his candidacy.

'Why in the world are you running for this seat? There are three women of color who have much more experience than you in this race.'
'Lord, give me the confidence of a mediocre white man.'
'This is not your race... Wait for next cycle and run against another white dude. Get Woke.'
'Another case of white male bullshit.'
'How. Dare. You. Run. Against. Three. Women. Of. Color.'

Rather unsurprisingly, Raymond subsequently pulled out of the race.

Carte Blanche

There gets to a point where your victimhood is so central to your identity, it imbues you with a Harry Potteresque protection and you cannot be touched. A person who could harness the power of the 'people of colour' tag, with high representation on other victim demographics, would be nigh on unimpeachable. Meet Linda Sarsour, the hijab-enshrined political activist and darling of the American left, who is equally at home campaigning for Black Lives Matter or for feminism, as she is campaigning against President Trump.

Sarsour's victim CV is impressive. Indeed, if we were playing Top Trumps, victimhood edition, the Linda Sarsour card would be unbeatable: the daughter of Palestinian immigrants growing up in Brooklyn, she hits the trifecta of female Muslim immigrant. Add to that, her devotion to the hijab and her anti-western views, and you can see why victim groups such as the Women's March want her at the helm.

The only downside to Sarsour growing up was her skin colour – something that clearly she has thought through herself. 'When I wasn't wearing a hijab I was just some ordinary white girl from New York City.'

The whiteness was a problem because it denied Sarsour the highly sought after 'person of colour' weapon from her arsenal. The hijab then is not just a religious symbol, but for Sarsour it represents diplomatic immunity. Sarsour understands this all too well, not just the fact that with this final label she would be untouchable, but also how easy it would be to achieve, given she was so far up the hierarchy already. In the end, it was a simple matter of self-identification. 'I'm Palestinian, if I want to say "I'm black" - I'm black!'.

The chameleon-like ability to change skin colour at a whim is crucial to Sarsour's success, and she needs it as courting controversy is not something she shies away from. Here is a typical tweet from her Victimness: 'Brigitte Gabriel = Ayaan Hirsi Ali. She's asking 4 an a$$ whippin'. I wish I could take their vaginas away – they don't deserve to be women'. In May 2017, speaking at the Islamic Society of North America, Sarsour called for jihad against the Trump Presidency:

> I hope that when we stand up to those who oppress our communities that Allah accepts from us that as a form of jihad, that we are struggling against tyrants and rulers not only abroad in the Middle East or on the other side of the world, but here in these United States of America where you have fascists and white supremacists and Islamophobes reigning in the White House.

'Jihad' is usually interpreted as 'holy war' rather than 'struggle', so it's the perfect thing to say if you mean one thing, but want to say it in a politically acceptable way. It ought to go without saying, that if Sarsour were a white, middle-aged Trump supporter from Texas, not only would she have less access to the public eye, but she might have slightly more access to the inside of a jail cell.

Drastic Steps

Those unfortunate souls who are not naturally endowed with automatic victim status via their skin or genitals need not despair. There are occasions whereby a victim status may be obtained by a somewhat unconventional route. The story of Brendan Cox is particularly revealing in this regard. Cox, an adviser on international development to former Prime Minister Gordon Brown, had long since lived in the shadow of his more successful wife, the former Labour MP, Jo Cox. That was until 2016, when Jo was brutally murdered.

The affection and esteem that Jo was clearly held in was immense. Upon her death, campaigning for and against Brexit was suspended as a mark of respect, and words of condolence poured in from far and wide. Husband Brendan, who even received a personal phone call from then US President, Barack Obama, appears to have benefitted hugely from the loss of his wife.

Cox, a white, middle-aged (one can only presume privileged) man, subsequently morphed into the nation's moral compass, regularly appearing on prime time media slots to proclaim his own brand of feel-good, bromide-laden rhetoric: 'I want to change UK's narrative of division', or 'hate doesn't have a creed, race or religion, it is poisonous.'

The death of his wife was his immunity from prosecution, the only 'get out of jail free card' he would ever need. Political opponents would sit opposite him in a sort of hushed reverence, visibly pondering 'how can we argue against these asinine clichés when the man's beloved, left-wing wife was murdered by a right-wing supporter?' They couldn't.

The biggest test of this protection came in February 2018, when it was confirmed that Saint Brendan was in fact a little less Saint Jude and a little more Saint Judas. Cox confessed to several incidences of inappropriate behaviour during his charity work, one incident allegedly involving grabbing a female colleague around the throat and saying 'I want to fuck you'[246]. Nothing so unusual there, unless you consider the fallout which followed.

When right-wing men are found to have erred in their sexual

etiquette they are largely hung out to dry. By contrast, Cox was met with a torrent of warm-hearted support from broadcaster Andrew Marr to Labour shadow ministers. As *Daily Mail* columnist Amanda Platell put it, 'My friend Brendan Cox is not some Weinstein-like sex fiend - if anyone deserves a second chance he does'[247]. For Cox then, the victimhood label had been secured.

Not everyone is fortunate enough to have their wife die in such favourable circumstances; neither are most people so able to shed the privilege of their white skin. Indeed, there is no shortage of white people trying to get in on the victim act, despite what one might consider the deal-breaker of their whiteness. *Only Fools and Horses* may have finished a long time ago, but if it was still going today, you can bet your life that Delboy would be working on the ultimate 'get rich quick' scheme: a cure for whiteness.

Until the cure arrives, shortcuts and placebos will be taken. One early advocate of such crudity is Shaun King, also known as 'Talcolm X'. King is an American political activist, and big player in the Black Lives Matter movement. He has courted much controversy from the fact that he appears (to the bigoted naked eye at least), to be nothing more than a white man pretending to be bi-racial. King tries hard to mask this rather obvious problem. He does his best to draw attention away from his whiteness, using black and white photos on social media for instance, or cutting his hair and growing a pencil moustache to assume the character he is aiming to cultivate. To say that the act is not entirely convincing is to be generous. Furthermore, King's birth certificate cites both parents as white, as does a police report that he was mentioned in[248].

In a similar vein, Shakespeare's Juliet naïvely once asked 'what's in a name?' Quite a lot, according to Rachel Dolezal, another contender for the highly-coveted title of 'whitest black person ever'. Dolezal goes by the more authentic-sounding alter ego of Nkechi Amare Diallo, and is a civil rights activist who claims to be black, despite contradictions from ignorant third parties such as her parents. Diallo eschews such unfounded accusations adroitly, as she explains: 'I acknowledge that I was biologically born white to white parents, but I identify as black.'

With her victim status undergoing a successful upgrade,

Dolezal has done remarkably well. In 2017, she published her memoir, *In Full Color: Finding My Place in a Black and White World*[249], which explains her journey of 'conscious self-definition', and in which she compares her own experiences to slavery. Besides the book, Dolezal is a licenced 'Intercultural Competency & Diversity Trainer' for businesses, has worked as a professor of Black Studies at Eastern Washington University, guest lectured at Spokane Community College, University of Idaho, Gonzaga University, and Washington State University, and has served as President of a chapter of the NAACP (National Association for the Advancement of Colored People).

Skin colour, whilst of course a key player, is not the only measure of victimhood. There are many other avenues being explored by those, desperate to elevate their status. One such option currently being trialled, is the use of the prefix 'trans'.

A case in point is that of India Willoughby, formerly ITN newsreader Jonathan Willoughby. In January 2018, Willoughby took part in the reality television program 'Celebrity Big Brother'. She participated in a now famous exchange with another housemate 'Ginuwine', aka Elgin Baylor Lumpkin, an American R&B singer, which prompted the BBC to print the gritty headline, 'Is it discriminatory to refuse to date a transwoman?'[250]

The conversation began when Willoughby asked the assorted housemates whether they would date a transsexual woman. After several housemates dodged the issue by claiming to care more about personality, pondering whether society puts too much pressure on people to be binary, or asking whether it could be blamed on fragile masculinity, Ginuwine came up with a genuine opinion.

> *Ginuwine: And then I believe it's your choice too, like I would choose not to. Like, and that doesn't make me like, like scared.*
> *Willoughby: You would go out with another woman?*
> *Ginuwine: Would I go out with another woman?*
> *Willoughby: You would go out with a woman?*
> *Ginuwine: Yes, of course.*
> *Willoughby: But you wouldn't go out with a transsexual woman?*
> *Ginuwine: No, no.*

Willoughby: The fact Ginuwine here, you know, is happy to go with women, but he's not happy to go... (and this isn't an attack on you), I'm just saying he wouldn't feel comfortable going with what is termed, he wouldn't feel comfortable going with me.

Willoughby: If you're in my situation, and you're trying to date, there is an extremely narrow band. And from my experience, I've tried to date and everything that comes back. You know, guys have chatted me up not knowing my past, but then as soon as they find out...'woah! I'm a woman, right, forget about any 'T's or anything in front of it, I'm just a woman OK, so on that score you would date me wouldn't you?

Ginuwine: Not if you told me you was trans.

Willoughby: No, no I'm not telling you I'm trans, I'm a woman. You would date me wouldn't you?

Ginuwine: A woman, yeah yeah, a woman.

Willoughby: Go on then, let's have a kiss.

Ginuwine: No!

Willoughby: You see, and I think all the unspoken things that you can read into both those responses there, illustrate my case one hundred percent.

The crux of Willoughby's position appears to be not quite that she is a man pretending to be a woman; rather, she is a man pretending to be a woman, protected under the victim status of her 'trans' identity. In other words, the oddness of her behaviour is offset by her transwoman rank. In Willoughby's eyes, therefore, the weighty task of finding a mate sensitive enough to accommodate this extreme behaviour, caring and confident enough to see past the physical inconsistencies, is society's and men's problem, rather than her own.

Needless to say Willoughby stormed off post-exchange (an important part of securing the victim narrative), and suffice it to say that Ginuwine was then routinely vilified on social media as a bigot and a transphobe (Willoughby's female trans status clearly outranking Ginuwine's solitary black status).

Successful victim statuses are quickly imitated, and spawn a range of alternatives. Whilst the 'trans' novelty clearly has legs,

Chloe Jennings-White really doesn't want hers. Jennings-White, a Cambridge University educated research scientist, has wanted to live the life of a disabled woman since childhood. Her irrational behaviour appears to stem from the fact that her aunt used to wear leg braces, something that Chloe herself wanted to do.

For many years, she has attempted to injure herself by skiing in dangerous conditions and once by pedalling her bike off a four-foot stage and landing on her neck. In 2009, she was involved in a high-speed car crash, which could have killed her. 'Any time when I'm driving I sort of conjure up accident scenarios in my mind where I will become paraplegic,' she admits.

While her doctor, Mark Manlan, believes that she suffers from a rare condition known as Body Integrity Identity Disorder (BIID), it is clear that there is an allure to victimhood. In my opinion, we haven't seen the last incaranation of 'trans', not by a long shot. Might I suggest 'transbroke' for those who do not want to be frowned upon for their wealth, 'transbeautiful' for those (like me) whose looks are starting to fade, and perhaps 'transgenius' for thickos who resent being pigeonholed?

The overwhelming desire of many, especially whites, to achieve a commanding victim status is perhaps best outlined by radical feminist and author Robin Morgan, who wrote the following in her 1989 work *The Demon Lover: On the Sexuality of Terrorism*[251]:

> My white skin disgusts me. My passport disgusts me. They are the marks of an insufferable privilege bought at the price of others' agony. If I could peel myself inside out I would be glad. If I could become part of the oppressed I would be free.

The reality of things

A society that obsesses over false victimhood statuses is in danger of overlooking genuine oppression. Genuine victimhood deserves both our sympathy and our action. Being enslaved, sent up the chimney or down the mine at 11, or off to war at 16 – that's oppression. But being triggered, denied your safe space or forced to listen to facts or words which you would rather ignore, that is not. The preoccupation with such nonsense is frankly an insult to those who often soldier on quietly, under the greatest burdens.

Even the best of us however, may occasionally fall foul of victim mentality. It is eerily seductive, and encouraged 24/7. Take Hou Yifan, the highest-rated female chess player in the world, and a woman it is exceptionally easy to like. She is polite, articulate, highly intelligent and a masterful player of the noble game. Still, it was easy for her to lose her composure over an incident where she believed she was being discriminated against.

Yifan is just within the world's top 100 players, and whilst not quite on par with the elite men, sometimes plays in elite events. At the 2017 Gibraltar chess tournament however, Yifan became angered that she was being continually paired against other women, despite the fact that this means easier opposition, and despite the fact that the pairings are randomly assigned via computer (as they always are). Yifan was even invited to examine the computer's log files. Sadly, she was so convinced of her victim status that she resigned a subsequent game after just five moves in protest at the 'unfair' treatment.

Yifan's mistake however is a rare one. More often than not, victimhood turns out to be just plain old leverage, however ingeniously-disguised. Take Monica Lewinsky, former White House intern, and Bill Clinton's favourite cigar holder. Lewinsky has done surprisingly good business from her well-publicised affair with the former president, having re-invented herself numerous times as activist, fashion designer and public speaker, to name but a few. She was also widely rumoured to have been offered $12 Million for her memoirs in 2012[252].

With the fiscal turbulence taken care of, Lewinsky's next reincarnation seems to be that of victim. For the past 20 years, Lewinsky had always maintained publicly that the affair between herself and Clinton was consensual. That was before she realised she could, and perhaps ought to have played the victim card.

What better way to mark the anniversary then, than writing a piece for *Vanity Fair* in 2018 with the enigmatic title: Monica Lewinsky: Emerging from 'the House of Gaslight' in the Age of

#MeToo[253]. In the article, Lewinsky explains that her previously consensual position has shifted:

> *Given my PTSD and my understanding of trauma, it's very likely that my thinking would not necessarily be changing at this time had it not been for the #MeToo movement – not only because of the new lens it has provided but also because of how it has offered new avenues toward the safety that comes from solidarity. Just four years ago, in an essay for this magazine, I wrote the following: 'sure, my boss took advantage of me, but I will always remain firm on this point: it was a consensual relationship. Any 'abuse' came in the aftermath, when I was made a scapegoat in order to protect his powerful position.' I now see how problematic it was that the two of us even got to a place where these was a question of consent. Instead, the road that led there was littered with inappropriate abuse of authority, station, and privilege.*

> *Now, at 44, I'm beginning (just beginning) to consider the implications of the power differentials that were so vast between a president and a White House intern. I'm beginning to entertain the notion that in such a circumstance the idea of consent might well be rendered moot. (Although power imbalances – and the ability to abuse them – do exist even when the sex has been consensual.)*

> *...He was my boss. He was the most powerful man on the planet. He was 27 years my senior, with enough life experience to know better. He was, at the time, at the pinnacle of his career, while I was in my first job out of college.*

In other words, 'I wish #MeToo had come around sooner, am I too late girls?' Building an entire career around one blow-job is one thing. Seriously attempting to play the victim for doing so is quite another entirely.

Sex is often seen inappropriately in terms of female victimhood, but it is not necessarily the ultimate victim status. Sometimes, victim statuses are so compelling, a counterargument cannot even be mounted. The Grenfell Tower fire was the Linda Sarsour of tragedies. You couldn't have achieved a greater victim status if you'd given Anne Frank a first class cabin on the Titanic as part of her Nazi reparations package.

Grenfell Tower was a tower block of 120 homes in Kensington, West London, in which 72 people are believed to have died[254]. That's just where the victimhood starts. Kensington is famous for spectacular wealth, with the average house (sorry, flat) price being around £1.5 Million[255]. Grenfell was not one of those places. It was council housing where the residents were disproportionately from ethnic minorities, with many families from Moroccan and Somali backgrounds. So the victim count was escalating already – massive wealth inequality, low-class accommodation, majority foreign and non-white etc.

The Labour Party was keen to stoke the victim narrative. The 'evil Tory' line was pushed relentlessly, with Prime Minister, Theresa May roundly criticised for failing to turn up, and then squarely criticised for not failing to do so. Labour leader Jeremy Corbyn agreed to spare a few tears for the survivors, on the proviso that television cameras and selfies were in constant supply.

David Lammy, Labour MP and one-man race-awareness course, did a fantastic job of fueling the victim narrative by turning up every five minutes to tearfully proclaim his expertise. He'd lost a friend in the fire, and thereby assumed ownership of the entire issue. It didn't occur to Lammy that other residents of the building might have had friends too.

One of Lammy's chief contributions was to denounce the appointment of highly qualified judge, Sir Martin Moore-Bick[256]. Not in terms of competence (Lammy actually admitted Sir Martin was eminently qualified), but rather his appearance. Stating as ever with a grasp of identity politics second-to-none, Lammy opined:

> He is a white, upper-middle class man who I suspect has never, ever visited a tower block housing estate and certainly hasn't slept the night on the 20th floor of one. I hope he would do that in the days ahead... The job is not

just to be independent and judicious – I am sure his is eminently legally qualified, of course he is – it is also to be empathetic and walk with these people on this journey. To sit with them and understand that their lives were in the hands of the state and something badly, badly failed...It is a shame we couldn't find a woman to lead this inquiry or indeed and ethnic minority to lead the inquiry in 2017.

The truth of the matter was completely irrelevant. It didn't matter that Prime Minister May and her team had been putting together an action plan for Grenfell, something of substance, rather than attempting to make political capital out of the issue. It didn't matter that the inhabitants had been following fire safety protocol by staying put[257]. Nor did it matter that five tower blocks in Labour-controlled Camden were similarly built with flammable cladding[258]. No, the evil Tory victim narrative would do very nicely thank you, and naturally the *Huffington Post* was there to oblige, 'Racism and classism killed the residents of Grenfell Tower.'[259]

Six months down the line, with the families generously compensated by both the taxpayer and independent charities, with permanent housing of luxury flats in a £2 billion development promised to each family[260], with amnesty promised to the illegal immigrants that had managed to state that they were living there[261], it still wasn't enough. Once the victim snowball has started, there was no stopping it. It hardly even mattered when subsequent stories began to emerge of the illegal subletting[262] that was rife in the Tower, the convictions for fraud for those impersonating survivors[263], or those running million-pound cannabis farms from their flat[264].

The most beautiful denouement was unveiled in February 2018 at the Brit Awards. It appeared completely ad-libbed, but couldn't have been scripted better had it come straight from Jeremy Corbyn's communications team. 'Stormzy' (real name, Michael Omari), whose illiterate drug and violence-fuelled ramblings have somehow been repackaged as 'grime artistry', had just won the Best Male Artist award. This was in no way caused by the 2016 Brit awards furious hashtag #BritsSoWhite, which had complained about the lack of non-white artists being rewarded, and it would be most unfair to suggest it was. Perhaps it was clear to the audience, though it was news to me that Stormzy's award also came with the title of self-appointed Labour spokesman, and Tory outreach officer, as he warbled with his customary mellifluousness,

> Yo, Theresa May where's the money for Grenfell? What, you thought we just forgot about Grenfell? You criminals, and you got the cheek to call us savages? You should do some jail time, you should pay some damages. You should burn your house down and see if you can manage this.

So that's a millionaire non-victim victim, awarded a victimhood award, aligning seamlessly with the millionaire non-victims of the Labour Party, playing the victim card on behalf of genuine victims, in order to make the evil Tories and the taxpayer pick up the tab, which they had already done. And they talk about levels.

Contrast that with a similar recent event – the Manchester Arena Bombing of May 2017. Twenty-two people lost their lives as Salman Abedi detonated a nail bomb inside the venue. Both were tragic events, but you might detect a subtle distinction. During both tragedies, the nation appeared to come together. But the tone of the coming together differed starkly.

One reason for this might be the victim status of the Manchester Arena victims. They were almost exclusively White Brits. Therefore, there was simply no victim card to play. There was no Jeremy Corbyn to cry for them or pose for selfies, and no celebrities volunteered to berate the government for their lack of care.

In terms of finance, while the nation rallied commendably during both, with sizeable charitable donations, the government response for Manchester was lackluster to say the least. According to the local council, it had spent £17 Million on the tragedy, and wanted more in return from the government. Theresa May, however, would only confirm that 'the majority of funds (would) be made available.'[265] Perhaps it was the absence of Stormzy to keep the government in check. Where was he when we needed him? Or, had he simply forgot?

Running out of excuses

There is a downside to the perpetual victim card. Having to continuously invent new forms of oppression, lest reality catch up with you is exhausting. There is also the strong possibility that you may eventually run out of road. Recent, rather pathetic attempts at 'new and improved' victimhood suggest that that time may be fast approaching.

The minutiae of white behaviour has already been stretched so thin, to the point where the victim hunters are now clutching at straws. Consider the following which have been attempted recently: 'Smart people need to check their cognitive privilege'[266] (Iowa University college newspaper). 'Expecting people to show up on time is racist'[267] (Clemson University). 'Is having a loving family an unfair advantage?'[268] (ABC). Or actor Riz Ahmed, who seriously argued that the lack of diversity on television will drive young people to Isis[269].

You can see the problem. Where are they going to find new material? Thankfully some bright sparks are already on the case. Behaviour has been fully canvassed, so let's try non-behaviour. How about mere existence? Yes, that'll do it. The mere existence of white people is grounds for an aggrieved status.

April Hathcock, a New York University librarian recently essayed 'racial fatigue', caused by having to be 'in the presence of white people' for an extended period of time[270]. In her blog, 'About the intersection of libraries, law, feminism and diversity' Hathcock explains the arduous task of having to attend a 5-day annual conference of Librarians in Chicago:

> *Race fatigue is a real physical, mental and emotional condition that people of color experience after spending a considerable amount of time dealing with the micro- and macro-aggressions that inevitably occur when in the presence of white people. The more white people, the longer the time period, the more intense the race fatigue.*

Hathcock is not the only person to hint that whites drain your energy. In 2017, NBA star Lebron James commented that he needed 'a day without white people'[271]. A rather ironic statement from a man whose net worth is estimated to be $400 million, made from a white country, with the help of white mentors such as Warren Buffet, and paid a salary of over $30 million a year from a white team owner. Still James does not feel equal. He explains,

> *No matter how much money you have, no matter how famous you are, no matter how many people admire you, being black in America is tough. ... And we've got a long way to go for us as a society, and for us as African-Americans, until we feel equal in America.*

Perhaps James genuinely feels inferior. More likely, perhaps he is smart enough not to relinquish his victim card so easily. Equal or not, James is not alone in his sentiment. 'A day without white people' is a topical concept, not least of which because of Evergreen State College. Evergreen has held a 'Day of Absence' every April since the 1970s, when minority students and faculty members have stayed off campus to raise awareness of their contributions.

In 2017 this was turned on its head. White students and staff were 'invited to leave campus for the day's activities[272]'. A white biology professor, Bret Weinstein, refused to leave, and was subsequently mobbed and threatened with violence. Attempts were made to oust him from his job, simply for disobeying supporters of the day.

By May 2017, the College President, George Bridges, was being held to ransom by the protest group. The campus police meanwhile were barricaded in the campus police station for several days, with the threat of violence should their demands not be met. By June, this had escalated to death threats, and the campus had to be closed for two days. There can be no denying that, while only 25% of the student body, the minority had made its presence felt.

A dangerous game

A dangerous game is now being played, whereby honest debate has been replaced with a regression to victim status. Instead of facts and logic, people now merely attempt to control the discussion by proving that their particular brand of oppression is the one which ought to hold sway. From Linda Sarsour to Black Lives Matter, the modern victim is nothing of the sort: a tyrannical bully masquerading beneath the protection of a hijab, or the pawning of ancestral oppression, a cheapened diplomatic immunity, well beneath the dignity of the worst slave owner.

The professional victim is no longer even paying a fleeting homage to the truth. He knows full well that the debate will be cancelled if enough outrage can be generated. Take it from Linda Sarsour, who can sum it up for you in a line, 'We must never stop fighting to show our outrage.'

Outrage then, for the variance denier, is the ultimate goal. While realists believe that you have to win the argument, the enemy has shifted the goalposts. Variance deniers are purely concerned with generating enough offence to cancel that argument. Whatever your issue: women in the military, gay adoption, walk-on girls, the only question is how much victimhood can you get out of it?

The allure of victimhood should not be underestimated. Even the rich and famous are vulnerable to such desires, and will go to great lengths to achieve them. At the time of publication, Hollywood star Jussie Smollett finds himself in the bizarre position of having faked a violent hate crime to boost his victim credentials. Smollett, who claimed to have been the victim of a racist assault, appears to have paid two accomplices to stage the attack. He was charged on February 20th 2019 with filing a false police report[273]. The full implications for Smollett are unclear; what is clear is that the pursuit of victimhood needs to be taken seriously.

A world where outrage reigns, and the right to offend people has been withdrawn, is a world which cannot function. In initiating this war, the variance-deniers have brought things to a head – a head which will have to be resolved, because at present it is rendering society completely dysfunctional.

All issues are now being defined by one simple matter: your stance on reality. Brexit, the Trump Presidency, the EU, mass immigration and so on, are all now being fought by two highly-hostile camps: those who wish to deal in reality, and those who are concerned only with pretending that reality is a social construct.

On the one hand, patriots, nationalists, conservatives (realists) are trying to warn people of the dangers we face. On the other hand, globalists, liberals, social justice warriors (variance-deniers) are demanding alternate pronouns, safe spaces, and the criminalisation of such warnings, so that they do not have to listen to them.

In my opinion, the consequences of this struggle cannot be overstated. It is also my view that the resolution of this war of ideas will ultimately decide the fate of the west.

CHAPTER
10

The Suicide of the West

Pandora's Box

The first lesson my mother ever taught me was that life is not fair. This was a valuable lesson, and has served me well throughout the disappointments and injustices that life inevitably serves up. The current generation however, has been encouraged to skip that lesson. They believe they have a panacea to the variance they mistake for injustice; what they have is a lie.

Their solution is a sort of inverted Pandora's Box. Unlike Pandora, who at least had curiosity going for her, our variance-deniers are incurious in the extreme, intent only on putting everything back into the box. Free speech, controversial opinions, offensiveness, and facts – deciding, in short, that truth is an entity we can no longer be trusted with. As a compromise, they have released a lot of evil too.

Society is now being described almost exclusively in terms of 'privilege', 'oppression' and the ultimate 'intersectionality' – an impossible, labyrinthine continuum of victimhood that no one could ever hope to untangle. Perhaps that is the point. Perhaps the idea is to have everyone waste their lives calculating the victimhood implications of their actions, an objective so complex that it would result in no one ever doing anything.

No matter how much one may wish to deny reality, reality will assert itself one way or another. Just as a fully-grown Pandora will hopefully discover the correct use for her box, so too must we relearn some simple truths.

The success of any unit, from the individual to the nation state, depends dramatically on its capacity to accurately identify variance: truth from lies, friend from foe, importance from irrelevance. Found a society on the denial of variance, and you will find yourself working to become less efficient, less resistant to attack, and less able to function effectively.

It is difficult to overstate the extent to which our societies are now infected with the disease of variance denial. In fact, it is becoming increasingly difficult to identify a broad domain where non-variance policies are absent. Here are just some of the consequences we must now contend with:

Education

Education used to be the process of providing students with the tools to succeed in life – in short, teaching them how to compete. Increasingly however, our students are being taught not to compete. Our increasingly left-wing[274] educational establishments are more engaged in enforcing the equality lie, than they are in teaching. Students who violate this lie, and show extreme promise, are now as big a problem for the state as underachievers used to be. In fact more so, since underachievement can usually be blamed on inequality, or the evil right wing. Who do you blame intelligence on?

Why can't students simply conform? The thickos continually let you down, while the swots insist on embarrassing them further. Something needed to be done in Britain to bring these two divisive camps to heel. Something was done. With the abolition of grammar schools in the 1960s (naturally under the guise of 'egalitarian principles') just that was achieved. Standards could be sufficiently dropped to make the lower echelons look adequate – what David Blunkett would later euphemistically refer to as 'raising standards' – while the brightest could have their development hampered by not really teaching them anything.

With the demise of the grammar school, Britain has suffered greatly. In the mid 1960s there were over 1,200, catering for 25% of state school pupils. In England now, there are a mere 163. The price of the equality lie in terms of education has been a marked decrease in social mobility[275], with fewer state school pupils going on to Oxbridge. How many thousands of bright students have had their potentials left unfulfilled because of the ideological pursuit of equality? How much of a loss has it been to the nation as a whole?

Even if you are intent on teaching the kids anything, how can you? First of all, where do you find a window in the schedule that is not already allocated to the latest diversity indoctrination? Maybe you could plan a history class in the morning, but what are you going to do about that urgent transgender rights lesson that you simply have to get through? If you finally do get a few books open, what are the chances that the students will not be triggered by the contents of them – have you prepared counselling sessions for that?

And what of the students themselves? Who would be a teacher in England right now, where misgendering or use of the wrong pronoun will have you up before the board faster than incompetence ever could. This means that the average teacher is literally running the gauntlet every time he asks a student to answer a question, *'She looks like a girl, she's dressed like a girl, her name is Samantha, but what are the chances that she might be identifying as a 50-something truck driver called Dave?'* Best not to risk it.

England is still home to some great schools – I know, I was fortunate enough to go to one. As a council estate scruff in the early 1990s, I set off for Dulwich College, a school so expensive my father would have had to postpone his death for a good few decades to afford it. Luckily, evil selective education and government-funded assisted places meant my brothers and I got there on merit. What a quaint notion that is!

Employment

OK, so this one should be a cinch. You're thinking of hiring someone, and have obviously taken the necessary first steps to ensure that you're open to all candidates. Actually, that might be a mistake. The person you hire may need to complement the victim symmetry of your existing workforce, and it's not just the old hat of gender and race that they're talking about these days.

According to the Equality Act 2010, it is illegal to discriminate against a person on the grounds of age, religion, disability, sexual orientation, gender reassignment, marriage and civil partnership, which are considered 'protected characteristics'. The flip side to which is that equally, it is supposed to be illegal to do the opposite, ie to positively discriminate.

You're gonna love the kicker to this one. While it is illegal to discriminate positively, that's to say to favour those who have the required victim statuses that you so desperately wish to employ, there is an ingenious exemption to this called 'positive action'[276]. This situation arises when two 'evenly-matched' candidates are both suitable for a post, in which case the employer may elect to choose the one with the greatest victim status should he so desire. So positive discrimination is illegal, unless you call it something else. Is it me, or is there the slight possibility of abuse here?

With the rather obvious question of legality aside, the only thing that should matter in terms of employment is hiring the best person for the job. That's not only good for the company itself, but also for the wider society who may be affected by the work they do. Increasingly though, competence has become an irrelevance, with so much attention being paid to the mythical gender pay gap, or workforces which do not reflect the requisite 'diversity'. Such imbalances are always headline news, irrespective of the rather obvious constraints that real life places on diversity targets.

Demography varies, as do the personal choices of individuals and groups. And while Prime Minister Theresa May might well bemoan the fact that the police force is *'too white'*[277], or that there aren't nearly enough male nurses called Achmed, taking the diversity war to Devon is probably not the right way to go about it.

One major issue for employers is that the government is constantly breathing down their necks to ensure they meet the necessary diversity standards, even though quotas are illegal. Here for instance is the government's Culture White Paper from 2016:

> We will ask Arts Council England, Historic England and the national museums and galleries to develop and share strategies for tackling the lack of diversity in leadership across the cultural sectors and to provide regular reports on what has been achieved.

With quotas being 'technically' illegal but increased diversity a must, unofficial quotas are being achieved by stealth, either by accepting less-qualified minorities (who otherwise would not have got the job), or by simply banning whites from applying, which appears to be the preferred option. From the BBC to Historic England and the National Trust, it has become increasingly customary to observe employment exclusions such as this:

> If you're interested in gaining skills and experience for a career in heritage and identify as having Black, Asian or other Minority Ethnic Heritage or mixed heritage please see how to apply below.

As time goes on, the list of protected characteristics is only expanding, so quite literally, the one thing a prospective employer won't be focussing on is appointing someone who can actually do the job.

Nowhere is the competence/diversity trade-off more evident than in the House of Commons, specifically within the current Labour Party shadow cabinet. There's no one more inclusive than Jeremy Corbyn, but even he was lambasted for originally appointing all white males to the four great offices of State[278]. What was he to do?

If you re-examine Corbyn's shadow cabinet, it's hard to argue that he's gone for competence, rather than a simple diversity box-ticking exercise. In a pro-variance society, many of his appointments simply could never have been made, because the ridicule they deserve would render such a cabinet fatally unelectable.

And yet in a society based on variance denial, these ludicrous appointments are actually something of a trump card. Instead of mirth, we are forced to contemplate questions which do not deserve to be asked: Why can't Angela Rayner be the Shadow Education Secretary? Sure, she left school pregnant at 16 with no qualifications, but why does that matter? Why can't Diane Abbott be the Shadow Home Secretary? Just because she's a buffoon who believes in neither borders nor defence, who are we to judge? Why can't Shami Chakrabarti be the Shadow Attorney General, with judgement so poor she'd fail to uncover anti-Semitism during Kristallnacht - why isn't she ideal for the post?

It is only variance denial and cast-iron victim statuses which could leave us in such a weak position. How can any privileged, white male consider pointing this out? Who would dare?

Policing

Policing too is hugely problematic in terms of variance denial, because effective policing requires nothing but correct identification of variance: establishing right from wrong, victim from perpetrator, innocence from guilt. This is something that the police are increasingly unable and unwilling to do.

Let's consider the policing of London, which is rarely out of the news these days. Our key players are London's heralded first Muslim Mayor, Sadiq Khan, and first female Metropolitan Police Chief Commissioner, Cressida Dick, the appointment of whom was equally celebrated as an equality coup. The Mayor has a direct mandate for policing in the Capital, while the Met Commissioner is responsible for its delivery, and is accountable to both the Home Secretary and the Mayor himself.

The victim status of our players, therefore, is not in question. Sadiq Khan was elected Mayor in 2016, when he ran against the almost Olympic-grade oppression of millionaire Conservative white male, Zac Goldsmith. Goldsmith would no doubt have deployed his white privilege card, were it not for the lightning-paced demographic changes which have occurred in London. Khan was ultimately a dead cert, winning comfortably with 44.2% of the vote to Goldsmith's 35%.

Dick meanwhile, despite her slightly-distasteful whiteness, certainly has a few victim checkboxes ticked. Her fans are vociferous in their claims that she has smashed the patriarchy's glass ceiling, along with changing the macho image of the Met. Not only is she the first female commissioner, but she also considers diversity to be at the heart of her role, and as a bonus is in a same-sex relationship.

If, however, you're an awfully racist/islamophobic/sexist onlooker, and actually expect a level of efficiency from your leaders, you might begin to start worrying at this point. Dick, despite her obvious appeal, is a controversial figure. She appears to have bizarrely escaped blame for the disastrous shooting of Jean Charles de Menezes in 2005, in spite of holding overall responsibility for the officers involved. The inquest into his death recorded an open verdict, which was met with dismay by the victim's family. Not only did they complain of a whitewash, but they subsequently objected most strongly to Dick's appointment as Chief Commissioner, pointing out that she would not be able to hold the public confidence.

Khan, for his part, has a rather more disturbing charge sheet. He has shared platforms with and defended extremists and terrorists, both verbally and in his capacity as a lawyer. A typical example being Nation of Islam leader Louis Farrakhan[279], who refers to Jews as 'bloodsuckers'. He has previously referred to moderate Muslims as 'Uncle Toms'[280], a slur meaning a non-white person who is excessively servile or obedient to white men. In *Challenging Racism: A Handbook on the Human Rights Act*, Khan wrote a chapter entitled, 'Actions against the Police', where he advised people how to sue the police for racism[281].

Perhaps the best way to examine Khan's past, is through the eyes of a friend and ally. Reformed Islamist turned counter-extremist, Maajid Nawaz, wrote about Khan on his successful election as London Mayor[282]:

> I've known Sadiq Khan since 2002 when he was my lawyer while I served as an Islamist political prisoner in Egypt, before he became a Member of Parliament. I'm forever indebted to him for visiting me in Mazra Tora prison, while the world gave up on me.

And on Khan's character:

> Again, Khan is no Muslim extremist. Indeed, this cannot be repeated enough. Nor can the fact that Khan clearly has a record of terribly poor judgment in surrounding himself with Islamists and Muslim extremists, and in using them for votes.

I daresay that's not much comfort. Sure, he hangs around with the bad guys, but he's not a true believer. He might never hack your head off, but he'll happily stand around watching while others do it. If the best you can say about a man is he is not as much of an extremist as his terrorist bedfellows, is this really the man that you want in charge of policing and crime priorities for London?

What this appointment by victim status has brought about is carnage on the streets of London, and a total breakdown of law and order. Consider the death of career criminal, Henry Vincent[283]. Vincent, 37, died on the fourth of April 2018 when he and an accomplice attempted to burgle Richard Osborn-Brooks, a 78-year-old pensioner with a disabled wife, residing in Hither Green, south east London. Using a screwdriver to defend himself, Osborn-Brooks fatally stabbed Vincent in the scuffle. Subsequent to Vincent's death, his family have continuously placed flowers opposite the house of the victim, much to the dismay of the local residents, who have repeatedly torn them down in protest. In addition, criminal associates of Vincent have sent death threats to the pensioner[284], telling him in no uncertain terms that they were 'hell-bent' on 'evening the score'.

To say that the authorities were lacklustre in their response would be to put it mildly. Whereas comparably (in the case of murdered Fusilier Lee Rigby) the local council removed the unofficial shrine[285], in the case of Mr Vincent, the council refused to intervene. The police meanwhile, made it clear that they would arrest anyone who disturbed the flowers again[286].

So here's the position: Mr Osborn-Brooks (the genuine victim) was burgled and physically attacked by two young men. Having failed to die in the fray, he himself was arrested, and is now unable to return to his home for fear of reprisals. The police, in the meantime, kept busy defending the unofficial shrine of his attacker. It doesn't end there. At the head of the chain of command, Deputy Chief Commissioner Craig Mackey also clearly had trouble differentiating between the innocent and guilty parties. Speaking on LBC radio on 12th April 2018, he made the following comments:

This is a highly-emotive issue. You know, what happened

in that street was a tragedy for everyone involved. A homeowner experienced every homeowner's nightmare of someone coming into their home, and somebody lost their life ultimately. What we have to do is balance that, and get that perspective right. This is a tragedy for the family who have lost a loved one. It is also a tragedy for the homeowner forced to take the action he did.

So let's balance that, by all means. Let's make a false equivalence between a career criminal, and an innocent citizen attempting to defend himself. Naturally, pretending that balance exists where it does not, confirms our comforting equality lie, even if it must come at the price of a chaotic and dangerous society.

Traditionally policing was a simple matter of catching criminals. Today, it appears to be more concerned with policing attitudes and thoughts, particularly the private thoughts of the citizen. While Sadiq Khan continually laments falls in police numbers, he did move 900 officers to tackle 'online hate crime'[287], with London police averaging nine such arrests per day[288]. Inevitably however, the Bobbies must occasionally step out of their offices for some old-fashioned police work. Except, we might have to send out Bobbettes to keep the variance deniers happy. Consider this early 2018 tweet from Lambeth Borough Police: 'We have an all-female crew fighting knife crime in Brixton today #OpSceptre #GoGirls'

Who came up with that one? The accompanying photo of half a dozen or so smiling young ladies would give hope to the lamest knife crime wannabe; I daresay even the criminal equivalent of Mr. Bean would fancy his chances in Brixton on that particular day.

There is a price to pay for this pandering to an obvious lie. At the very least, if you fancied a bit of knife crime in Brixton, that was the day to mark your calendar. At the worst, it would mean the very likely injury (or possible death) of a woman, all for the purpose of pretending that female coppers are just as capable as the men.

On the other side of the fence, criminals too are feeling a little put upon by a system which judges them too harshly. Labour MP David Lammy, as per usual, is your go-to-guy when variance doesn't provide the answers you want. Tasked with investigating the experiences of BAME individuals within the criminal justice system, the Lammy Review[289] came up with the bizarre recommendation that certain criminals ought to be able to hide their convictions from potential employers.

Lammy examined reoffending rates by race, and found out (as he usually does) that two and two did not necessarily equal four. While white youths in the UK have a reoffending rate of 36%, black youths outgun them at 46%. While this distinction could be indicative of a larger picture, Lammy naturally resisted that possibility, and instead concluded that it meant the system was biased against black youths.

Lammy's recommendation then, is that certain criminals should be allowed to 'lock' their records. That is, they would not need to disclose their convictions to a potential employer. Just to be clear, Lammy is still in post.

Considered in the whole, policing in London is now nothing short of a war zone. According to the Guardian, there were 135 London murders in 2018 with Khan at the helm. This is the simple consequence of electing people based on equality principles rather than competence, of refusing to implement stop and search because it is considered 'racist', and a refusal to focus efforts on the black community which is host to the majority of the victims as well as the perpetrators.

All crime is dramatically up under the capital's first Muslim mayor, and comparisons with New York make for interesting reading, particularly since the two cities have comparable populations, police numbers as well as budgets. According to official statistics, such as the latest ONS Crime Survey for England and Wales[110], you are more likely to be robbed in London than in New York, almost six times more likely to be burgled, with London boasting almost three times the number of reported rapes. That is not all. In February 2018, London surpassed the New York murder rate for the first time. While in America's major cities, murders are on a downward trend, London is experiencing something of a boom.

Ordinarily, you might think this would be a good time to question a leader's suitability, but exactly how easy is it to hold Mayor Khan to account? To put that another way, how much harder would it have been for former incumbents such as Boris Johnson or Ken Livingstone to have kept their jobs, had they presided over such failure? Both would be considered 'privileged' white males and therefore, would have no victim cards to protect them. They would get short shrift with claims of 'whitemaleophobia', and it is absurd to imagine that they would have remained in post.

Cressida Dick, meanwhile, is under some pressure as a non-Muslim. Notwithstanding her female lesbian victim status, she could use some good news in these troubled times. The last time Dick was in the line of fire, she did manage to pull something spectacular out of the hat. Facing criticism over the appalling Manchester Arena bombing of 2017, where 23 people were killed and 500 injured, Dick quite fantastically called upon the equality lie to save her – in this case, the equality of the dead. I can honestly say that I have never heard a more contemptible statement than that which follows:

> It's desperately sad and poignant but among those who died is someone who's British, there are French, Australian, Canadian, Spanish…in terms of our witnesses that we've spoken to so far, out of the 300-odd people, there are about 20 different countries of origin. And the London British population comes from all kinds of backgrounds and every kind of faith and ethnicity.

You didn't misread that. No matter how high the death toll gets, whether it's from London switchblades, or terrorist bombs, so long as we all croak in an inclusive, calm and restrained manner, and our blood mingles responsibly and calmly in the streets, there's nothing to see here. She's right – there won't be anything left to see.

Gender

If you went back a few decades, and told the inhabitants of the swinging sixties that (in the unlikely event they survived the drug-fuelled haze), their application for membership of the Darby and Joan Club could well result in them being done for genderfluidity denial, they would have laughed in your face. They're not laughing now. The idea that gender does not even exist is now extremely fashionable. Consider this headline, plucked from many which I have read this week alone: 'It's a Theyby! Is it possible to raise your child entirely without gender from birth? Some parents are trying.'[290] (A Theyby is a gender-neutral term to refer to a child of either sex.)

Some people clearly believe in this stuff. Others are smart enough to see a leverage opportunity when it rears its head. Consider the plight of a second-tier male athlete: you're good, but you're not quite up to elite competition - what can you do? Well, one of the best things you can do is to decide that you are a transwoman. Even merely identifying as a woman might get the job done. Again, twenty or thirty years ago, who could have guessed that the following headlines would become run of the mill?

'Transgender wrestler Mack Beggs wins Texas girls title again.'[291]
'Transgender woman wins international weightlifting title amid controversy over fairness.'[292]
'When a Man Sets the Record for the Fastest Marathon Run by a Woman.'[293]
'Eight of Iran's women's football team 'are men.'"[294]

The highly commendable notion of fairness is simply too good an opportunity not to hijack for anyone who has such an inclination, as the nice ladies of Hampstead Heath Ladies Pond recently discovered. Genderfluidity is a delight as a topic for the more genteel of dinner tables, but not quite so much fun having it suddenly thrust upon you as you bathe.

The female-only swimming pond in North London has long since been a traditionally private space for all women over the age of eight, to enjoy a swim unmolested by the prying eyes of males. That is until now, when the boundaries between the sexes have somewhat merged.

Feminist writer and pond regular, Julie Bindel (who you might have expected to be in favour of inclusion), was up in arms at the decision to allow rather masculine women to dip their toes in the water too[295]. Suddenly gender equality had its limits, as she explained, 'The last thing {young girls} want is to look behind them and see a male-bodied person pretending to be a woman in order to gawp at them'.

The City of London Corporation which manages the pond tried to calm the waters by explaining that they would allow transgender swimmers transitioning from male to female to use it; furthermore, that all of their lifeguards and managers were well-versed in transgender issues, and had all taken courses in trans awareness. Presumably this means identifying which penises were only half-cocked? Needless to say, this did not soothe ruffled feathers.

Years ago, it used to be common practice amongst men to pretend to be gay in order to access female only spaces. Nowadays, the options have become easier. Perverts in the bushes are an annoyance perhaps, but who wants to run the risk of complaining? Hurt feelings aside, what do you do when you discover that the Peeping Tom's victim status outranks yours, and you come under the full weight of the transphobia Gestapo?

It doesn't matter what section of society you come from, the weight of the victim card is still a tough one to beat. Here's a recent headline which highlights the prevalence of the problem: 'Transgender rapist who was moved to women-only jail despite still having a penis is segregated after 'making unwanted sexual advances on female inmates'.'

Even in the prison system, the idea that gender does not exist is a nonsense that is being taken seriously. Martin Ponting (now going by the much more feminine-sounding 'Jessica Winfield'), a double rapist who underwent a £10,000 sex change operation behind bars, was moved to a female jail in 2017[296]. It was there that 'she' had to be segregated, after most unexpectedly making unwanted advances to her fellow inmates.

It is only the blinding power of the equality lie which could have caused this insane sequence of events to unfold, aided and abetted by the government, because denying people's feelings and personal identity is more important than any unspeakably evil actions that they could well commit as a result of your weakness. In other words, upholding the equality lie is now more important than the most critical questions of safety.

The Military

Going to war is a good test for your equality lie because history tends to demonstrate that barbarian hordes beat effete pansies any day of the week. There appears to be no end however, to those who wish to disprove this theory. The military has come under continual pressure in recent years to toe the equality line.

This is bad news for the British Army which has already been stripped to the bone, down from 102,000 soldiers in 2010 to just 78,000 soldiers in the present. It might appear therefore to those of us on Civvy Street that now was not the right time to start worrying about a rebrand. Army decision makers, however, did not concur.

In late 2017, leaked official army documents revealed that plans were afoot to drop not only the historic army crest, but also the 'to be the best' motto[297]. Army top brass apparently considered the term to be 'elitist', and expensive image consultants had also suggested it was a tad 'non-inclusive'.

They're damn right; inclusive they are not, and inclusivity is the one thing an army really doesn't want to be. An inclusive army is one in which anyone can enlist, and that's the kind of army that isn't even going to make it onto the battlefield, let alone stick around to win anything.

The costs are not to be sniffed at either. At a time when military cuts are rife, the estimates are that such a rebrand would run into millions of pounds. Thankfully, such plans have been halted. The Defence Secretary, Gavin Williamson, stepped in to veto the plans at the eleventh hour. These plans are not in isolation however, and are a symptom of a much wider problem. Consider the British Army's recent advert 'keeping my faith'[298], which featured a unit pausing to wait for a Muslim colleague to pray. Again, inclusivity is being prioritized not only over those most likely to enlist in the army, but also over financial pressures which the army is ill-placed to bear.

But what does finance matter to a government so fixated on inclusion? The current BAME population of the military is only around 7%, but seeing as the government wants that increased to between 10 and 20 percent by 2020[299], something's got to give.

That something appears to be efficiency.

The British Army is not the only army focusing on everything except winning wars. The Marine Corps Integration Plan[300] of 2013 oversaw the lifting of restrictions on women joining the elite unit. The effectiveness of mixed squads was looked into, and it turns out that all-male squads outperformed mixed squads across the board. All-male squads were faster, more lethal and able to evaluate casualties in less time. They were superior to mixed squads on 93 of 134 tasks, with mixed squads only superior on two. In addition, female marines were six times more likely to get injured than males, and were unable to shoot as accurately.

That noticeable gender disparity might impress some people, and encourage them to give this inclusivity lark a rethink, but not James Joyner, professor of security studies at the Marine Corps Command and Staff College, Marine Corps University. According to Joyner, the problems arising from the introduction of females into the marines is due to 'toxic masculinity culture'[301]. Far from it, Professor. The marines do not have a problem with toxic masculinity, they need it. In fact if anyone has any toxic masculinity to sell, I've no doubt that the military would be the best place to set up shop.

Democracy

Democracy is under threat in the UK, of that there can be no doubt. We're used to hearing this in terms of Brexit of course, but that needn't trouble us overly since we all know that only thickos like me voted to leave the European Union, and we should of course be forced to vote again until we get it right.

However, it's not just referenda which are fraught with complications. Elections, too, are now problematic. Why might this be the case? Well, because without accepting variance, how can you criticize people for cheating – surely cheating is just another form of not-cheating? In 2018, the Conservative Government came under fire from all sides when it outlined plans to force voters to show photo identification at polling stations[302]. In other words, to force voters not to cheat.

Tories intent on preventing Labour from getting their usual 2 for 1 on student and postal votes, faced stiff opposition from every left-wing publication, MP, charity and watchdog, who complained that this would disproportionately impact minorities. Here is an excerpt from the letter written from the Equality and Human Rights Commission legal secretary Claire Collier, to Cabinet Office minister David Lidington[303]:

> *The Commission is concerned that the requirement to produce identification at the given local elections will have a disproportionate impact on voters with protected characteristics, particularly older people, transgender people, people with disabilities and/or those from ethnic minority communities. In essence, there is a concern that some voters will be disenfranchised as a result of restrictive identification requirements.*

Quite apart from the fact that you need photo identification in the UK for pretty much everything other than getting your hair cut, photographic idenitfication is already mandatory for eligibility to vote in other places, such as Northern Ireland. Besides which, the UK has a problem with postal vote fraud, and general electoral fraud, as witnessed for instance in Tower Hamlets in 2015[304].

The issue is simply this: if you cannot distinguish between eligible and non-eligible voters, in short if your society is in variance-denial, the question 'why can't illegals vote in elections?' is actually a legitimate one.

Islam

I've tried to keep the examples short and sweet, but hopefully you get the point. Last but not least, we get to Islam – you thought I would have the good taste to leave it out didn't you? The equality lie is a disease of which there are many symptoms. The symptom of Islam, however, towers head and shoulders above all the rest. It is the clearest and most dangerous illustration of the fact that if you deny the reality of variation, you will be unable to identify anything, even that which is trying to kill you.

This book is not about Islam per se – there are already many good books which are. While these books and their authors usually view Islam as a problem, and perhaps the ultimate demise of western civilisation, I do not. I consider us to be the problem. External attack is nothing new in the world; denying its existence is.

Let's begin with a few facts. Islam is a problem, and it's a growing problem. Once upon a time it was Catholicism, no doubt next week it will be the Zoroastrians, but right now it is Islam. We have to acknowledge that.

According to the Pew Research Centre[305], the UK has been the major European destination for economic migrants in recent years. Assuming median levels of migration, the UK's Muslim population is set to triple from 4.1 million in 2016, to 13 million in 2050, taking it to almost 17% of the population. Even without continued migration, the UK has one of the largest gaps in fertility rates between Muslims and non-Muslims, 2.9 compared to just 1.8. It is clear that demographic projections are only headed one way.

So why is this necessarily a problem? What's wrong with all this wonderful cultural enrichment and diversity? Here's the thing: despite what the variance-deniers love to tell you, Muslim populations and European populations are not the same, not by a long chalk.

A survey conducted by ICM Research in 2016, 'What British Muslims really think'[306] makes for some worrying reading. Among the chief findings it concluded that, 23% believe Sharia Law should replace British Law; 52% believe homosexuality should be illegal, with nearly half of all respondents deeming it unacceptable for homosexuals to teach their children; 39% believe wives should always obey their husbands; 35% think that Jews have too much power in the UK, and a third refuse to condemn the stoning of women accused of adultery. Two-thirds would not contact the police if a close friend was involved with jihadis. Eighteen per cent meanwhile have sympathy with violence in defence of the Prophet, and 4% (some 100,000 Muslims) have sympathy with suicide bombers.

Attitudes are sadly not the only thing we have to contend with. In terms of employment, the Social Mobility Commission[307] found that less than one in five Muslims adults are in work. Channel 4's undercover documentary 'Extremely British Muslims'[308] claims that there are 85 Sharia courts currently operating in Britain. MI5 meanwhile revealed in 2017 that there are an estimated 23,000 jihadis wandering the streets of Britain[309]. As if that were not enough, the lid has recently been lifted on the abhorrent scale of grooming gangs which emanate from the Muslim community.

Headline cases like Telford have shown that this is an almost-exclusively Muslim problem, with estimates ranging between 75% and upwards of 90% of all cases. Anti-extremism think tank Quilliam examined all convictions since 2005, and concluded that Muslim men were involved at a rate of 84%[310].

The law-abiding, decent sections of society are irrelevant here, as they always are in cases of extreme behaviour. A very considerable section of the Muslim community is simply not seeking to integrate in the least, and is a real danger to the lives of British people. That is something we should be neither tolerating nor seeking to import, and it's high time we stopped ignoring that glaring fact.

This is not a problem confined to Britain. All across Europe, the same forces are at work. A 2017 Chatham House study, 'What Do Europeans Think About Muslim Immigration?'[311] shows that across the entirety of Europe, citizens are opposed to further mass Muslim immigration. The figures are unequivocal: on average, 55% of European populations want to stop all future immigration from Muslim-majority countries.

That means that those who scream 'racist' as their way to negate any criticism of Islam have a problem on their hands. By all means scream 'racist', but when you are accusing everybody, it loses some of its sting. If everyone is racist, then the word has ceased to mean anything tangible.

Those who are in favour of continuous mass Muslim immigration will need to actually make the case for why the UK, along with other western nations, benefits so strongly from something its people resolutely do not want. So far that case has not been made successfully.

Making the highly tenuous assumption that freedom of speech can be taken back, Islam and all its facets must be discussed honestly, without concern for the feelings of its adherents. There is simply no way to get around this. Pandering to this religion has got us into the mess we are currently in. Pandering and appeasement, hoping for the teenager to grow out of his severe bout of acne and ill temper, are no longer on the table.

Islam, meanwhile, has played its hand well. It has managed to sell itself as the ultimate victim status: foreign, heavily in the minority (at least initially), non-white, fiercely devout, poverty-stricken and immigrant-based. The west, obsessed with victimhood, is simply too enfeebled to criticise when it ought to, and more importantly to defend itself – so excuses are made.

Excuses as to why Muslims are flooding the west in the first place: they're all refugees; they're here to work; they're here to prop-up our collapsed birthrates; they're here to pay our pensions, and they're here to integrate. Further down the line, excuses as to Islam's retrograde nature, and the slow yield of any sense of authority: who are we to judge a culture that likes to segregate the sexes? Who are we to judge a culture that dresses its women in bin-liners? Who are we to judge a culture that mutilates its daughters? Who are we to judge a culture that kills its daughters for bringing dishonour upon the family? Who are we to judge a culture that is trying to annihilate us?

The guilt-trip we are indulging in is growing at an alarming rate. In 2016, former Chairman of the UK Equality and Human Rights Commission, Trevor Phillips surmised that Muslim integration is the biggest problem we have ever faced[312]. The implication being that it is Islam's responsibility to integrate with its new host nations. As time goes on, however, the narrative of Liberals is becoming ever more servile. In the same year for instance, the BBC produced the following headline, *'UK attitudes towards Islam 'concerning' after survey of 2,000 people'*[313]. The survey was conducted by ComRes and entitled *'Ahmadi Muslims – Perceptions of the* Caliphate'[314]. Their findings were that the majority of Brits questioned in a survey did not believe that Islam was compatible with British values – the implication being, presumably, it will be easier for us to integrate with them, so that's the line we'd better take.

So here we are, perpetually drawing fresh lines in the sand, only to have them walked all over. And still no major reaction, no acceptance of the facts, and no honesty from our politicians. What we have instead are no end of bad jokes, with western leaders attempting to outdo each other as they mock their indigenous populations. Hapless London Mayor, Sadiq Khan tweeted in 2018:

> *There is zero-tolerance for FGM in London. It's an abhorrent and illegal practice that violates the rights and the bodies of women and girls. We're working with @metpoliceuk, schools, health services and local communities to #endFGM.*

Khan's joke is a good one. Despite having been a criminal offence since 1985, there are around 9,000 cases of FGM per year in the UK[315]. To date, there has only been one successful prosecution[316].

Canada, not far behind the UK, is considering holding an annual Islamophobia Day to raise awareness of Muslim suffering[317]. PM Justin Trudeau, a one-man inclusivity symposium, while concerned about ordinary Muslims, is more concerned about the treatment of ISIS fighters who want to return to Canada, labelling them 'returning islamic travellers'[318].

Obama however, as is so often the way, nailed it when it came to the virtue-signalling Olympics, 'The future does not belong to those who slander the prophet of Islam'[319]

In Sweden, the home of tolerance, 'Earth Hour' has had to be cancelled, in order to protect women from migrant rapists[320]. They're also having to cancel music festivals[321], because (while of course the music is good), the rapes go through the roof. Sweden does tend to be getting it in the neck a bit at the moment, but none more so than former Swedish politician, Zaida Catalan. Catalan represented the Green Party, and was a keen supporter of open borders, immigration and equality – at least, until she was beheaded in the Congo in 2017[322].

In the UK, where you can still just about hold music concerts, they tend to be more problematic than they used to be. Ariana Grande found that out when she was performing at the Manchester Arena in 2017. Grande who proclaims that Islam means 'peace', must have been perplexed as the deluge of bodies flew past her in an arguably non-peaceful manner.

Despite what the do-gooders tell you, Islam does not mean peace – it means 'submission'. Many of our leaders appear to have already decided that submission is the answer – ours, not theirs. While this is perhaps easier to achieve, the odds for survival are not so good.

It is not difficult to see where this narrow road is leading. The choices are very few. If we choose to sit idly virtue-signalling while Rome burns, hoping for the situation to self-correct or for someone to save us, the result is not in doubt. Islam will dominate Europe, and the west will fall. There is not much sensible argument to be had on this matter.

The left, who railed so hard against this argument for years, is now in the final stages of its denial. They started out by calling anyone who suggested Europe was becoming Islamised 'far-right', 'extremists' and 'lunatics'. Then they argued that Islamisation was not happening, but so what if it did? Now, they are reduced to arguing merely over the timeframe.

Even Angela Merkel of all people, is now saying that migrants must go home[323], and that multiculturalism is a 'sham'[324]. When even the cheerleaders of our destruction are starting to tell the truth, there is something wrong.

The free market is miles ahead on this one, as it generally is, and is a much better gauge of reality since it measures honest demand rather than state-manipulated sentiment. While the left has been in full denial, the reality of variance has asserted itself. Sales of anti-rape underwear in Germany have skyrocketed[325], as have smartphone apps to help citizens navigate the no-go zones in Paris[326] (that's right, the ones that don't exist). When women are advised by their government not to go out[327], or if they must to go out in pairs[328], the truth is hard to ignore.

One-by-one the variance deniers are beginning, very slowly, to realise the consequences of their misdeeds. Long-time poster boy for Muslims and refugees, George Clooney started off with appearances in numerous refugee promotional campaigns, and was even granted a personal audience with Angela Merkel to thank her for swamping Germany with migrants. 'We're not going to be scared of Muslims or immigrants,' he confidently proclaimed.

But following the spate of terror attacks in England in the summer of 2017, it seemed like Clooney had a change of heart, perhaps he was going to be just a little bit scared. Certainly scared enough to move his family back to LA for 'security reasons'[329]. He even decided to sell his Lake Como Villa, as the area has been trashed by migrants. It is with no small irony that Clooney fled back to the country he berated so often for not taking in enough migrants, now under the tenure of a 'xenophobic fascist', as he once generously referred to then presidential candidate Trump.

Nothing needs to change for this to be the conclusion to our story. And, most regrettably, it is extremely likely that our story *will* end here. The globalists clearly know which side their bread is buttered on, that's their job. Politicians will continue to lie and why shouldn't they? The offices and prestige (however fleeting) that they crave is not predicated on telling the truth, but on ingratiating the demographics they claim to serve.

As those demographics are only going in one direction, and there has been little energy to change them thus far, the prospect is bleak in this regard. Politicians are ahead of the curve on this one. They have access to all the data, we do not. It is inconceivable that the majority of mainstream politicians will not pander to the expanding and evermore vocal Muslim vote.

On the other hand, if a fight for our nations is to be had, it would make sense to have the fight when you have any sort of chance of winning. As has already been highlighted, the numbers and the timings are tight. We have a very finite window for achieving victory in this regard.

Thus far, the response to Islam has been childish in the extreme. The graver and more obvious the peril, the more Sesame Street our response becomes. Gang-rape is countered by respect wristbands, suicide bombings met with candlelit vigils and hashtags, vehicles driven callously into pedestrians shored up with concrete bollards dressed as lego bricks or Christmas trees. We are dishonest even in our inaction. As Churchill put it:

> If you will not fight for right when you can so easily win without bloodshed; if you will not fight when your victory

is sure and not too costly; you may come to the moment when you will have to fight with all the odds against you and only a precarious chance of survival. There may even be a worse case. You may have to fight when there is no hope of victory, because it is better to perish than to live as slaves.

On a knife edge

In its denial of variance, the west is committing suicide in all but name. There is an almost palpable sense of masochistic pleasure in the way that our nations appear to be hurling themselves towards oblivion, in apparent good humour. Whether it is demographic decline, islamification or the dull inevitability of nuclear war, the one thing we do not seem to engage with is the fear of our own extinction. After all, that would be necrophobic, and we'd never want to be that, would we?

Clinging to the equality lie has completely emasculated us. Failure to accurately and honestly respond to anything means that even under pain of death, you must not show life any preference. From the macro level of society to the micro level of every precious individual life we are witnessing this lack of emotion.

Sounds far-fetched no doubt, but please consider the tragic case of Alfie Evans. By the time this book is published, I will not need to mention more than the name of this beautiful little boy. Alfie was a terminally-ill toddler, who the NHS deemed could not be helped by further treatment. Doctors from Italy and Germany opened their arms to Alfie, their governments having planes on standby, ready to take him for further examination in their own countries. The Pope interceded on his behalf, and Alfie was even made an Italian citizen to try to make it possible for him to leave.

The UK High Court however, denied all of these requests on the grounds that the child might suffer. Having defied the doctors by refusing to die while having his ventilation removed, Alfie clung to life. Alfie's parents begged for him to be allowed to return home, but to no avail. The power of the state in denying any dissent from the correct way of thinking is terrifying. Refusing a little boy's last chance to be held in the bosom of his loving family is something which, I believe, has chilled the nation to the bone.

In terms of variance, the UK is currently poised on a knife edge, perfectly symbolized by the uncertainty of Brexit. The next UK election could see the appointment of a far-left, equality-obsessed Labour Party, which seeks to open the nation's borders in perpetuity[330], and will bankrupt the nation in the process. Our streets are no longer safe, and it's not only knife edges in Khan's London that we have to worry about. In many parts of the country, our daughters are increasingly vulnerable. That fact is absolutely indefensible. To put ourselves in a position to deal with these problems, the one thing we categorically must get right is our approach to variance.

The authorities meanwhile have had a long, hard look at the situation and they have lost. They have lost control (assuming that's not what they wanted in the first place). They can't keep track of the jihadis roaming the streets, the grooming gangs protected under 'religious persecution', the stab victims let alone the stabbers, or the immigrants legal or otherwise. The cat was let out of the bag during the Telford grooming scandal, as it was reported the police bosses thought stopping the abusers was just 'too much trouble.'[331]

So instead they've decided to go for the easy target – free speech. If they can silence complaint, silence dissent, and prevent people from speaking out against the war that is being waged on them, then they won't have to deal with the root cause.

This is a war they can only win in the short term, because variance is ultimately the only thing that really matters. Whatever you're talking about, variance is what you're talking about. Reality will assert itself, no matter how much we bury our heads in the sand. Clinging to the equality lie is not going to work forever, and I believe the bell for last orders has already been rung.

Each of the considerations in this chapter in isolation would be worrying. Together, they are catastrophic. The lie of equality must be killed to allow truth back into the discussion. Every time a comedian is convicted for telling a joke and we do nothing, we are complicit. Every time a man goes to prison for a bacon sandwich violation, and does not come out the other side, our society dies a little. Every time we're lied to about immigration, policing, or democracy and we vote the same parasites in, we are closing the door on our future.

It's time to stop the equality enforcement. It's time to stop frisking old dears on the way to bingo because you don't want to appear racist. They might get a thrill out of it of course, but we're missing the point. It's time to compete again as a nation, and that means talking honestly no matter who is offended. It means dealing with problems effectively, irrespective of how uneven the data may be. And it most certainly means choosing the right man for the job, no matter what.

CHAPTER
11

Last Chance Saloon

Death Instinct

This book opened with the notion that *Homo Sapiens* is a funny old species. It is also a species acutely aware of its own mortality. Futuristic depictions of the human race tend to be negative in the extreme. The dystopias range from the barbarism of Mad Max, the intellectual prison of 1984, or the machine-led terrors of The Matrix or The Terminator.

Freud wrote of *Thanatos* or the human death instinct, and he may have had a point. Mankind seems to know that he is in the very real position of becoming merely a formerly humorous entity. It could be that Utopian entertainment lacks Box Office punch. It could also be that we are genuinely feet from the cliff edge.

As one in a long line of Cassandras predicting our downfall, I note that the quality most likely to ensure our demise is either our intellect or our savagery. The savagery of Man is, sadly, well-documented historically. Our intellectual destruction meanwhile is usually conceived in the form of nuclear weaponry or the birth of machines that tire of our whims, and end up killing us just to get some 'me time'.

It is regrettable that I am forced to outdo my fellow prophets of doom. Nevertheless, I fear that we are currently facing an unprecedented double-whammy. In Europe, barbarity has now been imported in the form of relentless, Islamic immigration. There is now not even any point debating the original reasons for doing so.

The barbarians are no longer at the gates – the gates have been taken away for diversity training, and we are left naked, with only our *refugeeswelcome* and *hopenothate* hashtags to cover our modesty.

It should not come as much of a shock that anything fewer than two is an unsustainable birth rate. However, importing a population, the majority of which is permanently on the dole, is just as unsustainable a model. This is not a problem limited to Britain, but is widespread throughout Europe. In Germany, for instance, which has perhaps been the most warm-hearted nation in terms of non-EU immigration, the reality of migrant employability is hard to ignore.

According to Immigration Commissioner, Aydan Özoğuz, 75% of refugees face long-term unemployment or possibly a lifetime on benefits[332]. According to figures from the Federal Labour Agency[333], the employment rate amongst refugees stands at a paltry 17%. In addition, in terms of Islam, there is the added piquancy that a considerable slice of those you import are actively trying to kill you. As interesting a Saturday night out as that makes for, it does little to safeguard the future.

Sometimes, I wonder whether the minister in charge of candles at the EU didn't confuse the decimal point on his order form, and foolishly over-ordered the odd billion. Europe ablaze then, was the best idea they could come up with to come out even on the deal. Candlelit vigils and tealight sales notwithstanding, mass immigration has not been a good move for Europe.

The intellectual calamity of our time has, ironically, not been intelligent machines of our own invention. Rather, our brains have been banned from performing the most basic of functions that made *Homo sapiens* so great in the first place. Good from evil, right from wrong, honesty from deceit, intention from accident, we are being robbed of our ability, our indispensable ability, to discriminate effectively. Should the data not fit the progressive narrative, you will be in severe danger of being labelled racist, sexist or, *quelle surprise*, discriminatory.

The left has lost all common-sense when it comes to this. Discrimination is now a dirty word, rather than the accolade of sound judgement that it ought to be. 'Not all Muslims are terrorists' of course, but it's a good team effort isn't it?

While it is wrong to tar everyone with the same brush, it is also wrong to do so in reverse. That is to ignore the truth, and instead to pretend there is no issue, because not doing so seems unkind and makes you feel uncomfortable. The left is leading us up the garden path on this one, and the destination is more Hansel and Gretel than The Waltons.

There has never before been a moment in history when a nation chaperoned the enemy into its own castle, made his bed, gave him a generous allowance, the key to his wife's chastity belt, apologised for the place not being in better shape, and then flogged the outraged servants for daring to question whether this might not be a little ill-conceived. That is what our politicians have so far colluded to do.

When ecologists model the decline of a species they use the term 'tipping point' or point of no return, whereby the population gets so low that extinction is unavoidable. While actual members of the species still survive in diminishing numbers, they are effectively ghosts, waiting post-mortem like on the operating table for Mother Nature to record the exact time of death.

While in purely ecological terms, the future of *Homo Sapiens* appears reasonably secure (at least for the foreseeable future), what guise that survival will take is definitely up for debate. It is my opinion that Europe and western civilisation in general is very much poised at a tipping point. If no concrete action is taken to address the problems we now face, our culture, our history, our very way of life may well soon be something which cannot be saved.

A civilisation that does not know how to live in peace is unlikely to be successful. But so too must a civilisation be ever-vigilant to the threats that may come, whether they be economic or military in nature. A civilisation that refuses to fight when it must is ripe to be conquered. A civilization that refuses to even acknowledge the fight is well on the way to airbrushing itself out of history entirely.

The left has already resigned

Assuming that some kind of resistance is going to eventually take place, the right needs to recognise early on in the proceedings that it is fighting alone. The left has either already conceded long ago, or alternatively cannot wait to bring about the Armageddon it has worked so assiduously to achieve. Like any good damsel in distress weighing a quarter of a ton, the left is making it very hard for others to save it from itself.

You can see this lethargy most clearly when it comes to national issues such as Brexit. Nothing stirs a liberal to action so much as the notion that laws and decisions governing his life should actually be decided by the people directly accountable to him. Indeed, the desire for abdication of authority embodied by the Remain camp is something profoundly shocking in my opinion, and speaks volumes about how unwilling we are to stand up and take responsibility for our own future. In all the toing and froing of debate over Brexit, this is the issue the left has most failed to address: the issue of sovereignty. When half the nation wishes to quibble about the exact percentage of UK laws made elsewhere, rather than the absolute necessity of self-determination, it is difficult not to sink into despair.

The only adversaries the left wishes to engage with are straw men who cannot fight back. Why bother fighting against the horrors of terrorism, when you can be justly outraged by non-issues such as pronoun misuse, misgendering, and the patriarchy?

All across the west, our nations are at varying stages of suicide, and in this regard it is easy to put the pieces of the jigsaw together. Some countries have held out much better than others. Poland, for instance, which has refused to accept immigrants, has remarkably not had its fair share of terror attacks[334].

France on the other hand (already bracing itself for the full burka), is well on the way to full Islamisation, and should therefore be the guide for how well western countries are dealing with their newly-imported populations.

At 2017 rates, France is already estimated to be around 10% Muslim[335]. In the 2017 French Election, Marine Le Pen couldn't get anywhere near the globalist puppet Emmanuel Macron in terms of vote share, scoring just 33.9% to his whopping 66.1%. Maybe she will do better in 2020. Maybe, the voter base will be so irrevocably changed that she cannot do better. Some projections suggest that Europe will be Muslim majority within 40 years[336]. The left's voter base is being imported directly. Where is the right's?

I do not relish the predictions that I am making. And though I believe our death knells can already be heard, still I live in the hope that events are not yet set in stone. I would be most grateful if the future were here for my daughter to enjoy. I would much rather she berated my lousy efforts as a father, safe in the knowledge that she has no genuine problems to engage with.

For our children to have a future that we would recognise, we must act immediately, and that means all of us. Everyone must resist. Everyone must engage. It is not enough now to see this as a phase that we are drifting through. The left owns the conversation. They have put their stamp on the legal parameters of discourse, and it is in the hands of the same, hair- shirt-wearing appeasers that the fate of the west currently rests.

Small measures, therefore, are not going to cut it. The intellectual hegemony of the left must be broken, and it will require all of us to do it. This means that from the bottom up we must work together: individuals, voters, bloggers, polemicists and leaders. This is a rare case when even the average Joe sitting at his desk has a major role to play. Faced with the uncomfortable prospect of challenging his liberal friend's virtue-signalling post on Facebook, he can no longer resign himself to the excuse of 'it's not worth it'. It is worth it, and he must act. All levels of the liberal orthodoxy need to be shaken, and it's not going to be pretty.

There are now bigger things at stake than the severed ties of friendship. When the choice may well be severed ties with our heads, we are duty-bound to speak. We must insist that the truth is a defence, that free speech is non-negotiable, and that reality be restored. Pressure must be exerted on the incumbents in government to do the right thing, and if they refuse (which they will initially), they must be kicked where it hurts hardest, in the ballot box.

We do not need to wait for leaders to materialize. They exist already. France has Marine Le Pen, The Netherlands has Geert Wilders, the United Kingdom has had, lost, and regained Nigel Farage (via the recently-formed Brexit Party), and yet none of these strong, charismatic, eyes-wide-open leaders has thus far got their hands on the top job.

I can hear many of you wince as you read the last statement. Under no circumstances would you consider voting for someone like that. That kind of vote snobbery is a luxury you can no longer afford, at least not if you want your children to afford the luxury of freedom. The time for small measures is over. You are going to have to accept that.

If you doubt whether it can be done, take heart from the fact that genuine, pro-variance politics can win, and are winning. Viktor Orbán has recently been elected for his third term as Prime Minister of Hungary, achieving an overwhelming mandate to do so. The reason for this is simple: Orbán (like Matteo Salvini in Italy) loves his country and its people, and wants to put them first. The public clearly resonate with that.

You've got to ask yourself a question

Are you happy with the direction that the UK, Europe, and the west generally is headed in? Are you happy with the death of free speech? Are you happy living in a society where thoughts and social media posts are punished more assiduously than real crimes? Are you happy with a two-tier legal system, with you at the bottom? How many terror attacks will it take for you to accept that Islam is a problem? Do you need to suffer a direct attack on your family before you will do so? If that tragedy should occur, what wouldn't you give to come back to this point and start speaking out? Do you think your children will thank you for the future they inherit? In short, are you happy with the Islamisation of Europe and the west generally? If you are not happy with it, what exactly are you prepared to do to prevent it?

The steps we need to take

• *Wake up and wake others*

The starting point is tricky. For anyone to require waking up suggests either complicity or a startling lack of curiosity. There are those whom we can never persuade: those who actively desire the destruction of the west, those so far on the left that they are beyond redemption, and those so wealthy and removed from reality that they just do not care. Everyone else, however, can be reached.

A key step in this process is to vocalise. Whenever a Tommy Robinson is banned from Twitter, but the Muslim Brotherhood and Hamas remain blue-check firmly in place, it must garner outrage. When Kevin Crehan goes to prison for a bacon sandwich violation[337] and fails to come out the other side, but Farhana Begum Ahmed (who spread Isis propaganda online) is spared jail[338] because the judge considered, 'In your exceptional case, the sooner you are returned to your children, the better for all concerned', questions must be asked. When politicians deny the root causes of serious crime, and incarcerate those who fail to deny them, such cowardly behaviour must be lambasted in the strongest terms.

• *Stop self-censorship*

The first thing to notice here is how far we have drifted down this road, without most of us noticing. We are compromised. We are all afraid of the same things: we fear for our children, our jobs and our acceptance in society. We are loathe to place ourselves in the line of fire, and to reveal our opinions honestly. This is something that we can achieve together. If we shoulder that responsibility collectively, and insist that the debate is honest, we will find that others follow suit.

Again, the smallest in society have a big role to play here. For the sake of politeness, we have slipped down the treacherous path of integrating with others, rather than demanding that they integrate with us; this is an error. However small it may seem, every time we make concessions such as 'Happy Holidays' spoken in place of 'Merry Christmas'[60], we endorse the erosion of our traditions. Every time we hold our tongues in the name of 'inclusivity', we allow the debate to slip far away from the free speech zone it ought to be. It must be taken back.

Every time we do not criticise unacceptable behaviour on the grounds that the perpetrator's victim status is unassailable, we are tacitly accepting a totalitarian state, with us at the very bottom. We are going to have to be brave, and in doing so, we may just find that others find their courage too.

• *Re-examine our position on anger*

If you observe our collective response to the next terrorist atrocity (don't worry, there'll be another one along shortly), you will notice that the clichés share something disturbing. Under the microscope, the bromides become clear: we are praising ourselves for our stoicism, our stiff upper lip, in short, our utter lack of emotion:

- Celebrate our differences.
- We stand together.
- You will not divide us.
- Hope not hate.
- Diversity is our strength.
- Don't look back in anger.

Anger yes, make sure you give that a miss whatever you do. What kind of idiot could sit back and casually reflect on the mass slaughter of the innocent and conclude that it was acceptable? It's not merely rank idiocy, it borders on psychopathy. But that's what diversity means right, tolerating different viewpoints?

If the blood-soaked, indistinguishable, splintered torsos of dead baby girls (whose only crime was wanting to attend a music concert) doesn't stir the ire in you, you want to have a fucking word with yourself.

• *Be vigilant to Banalysis*

Whatever form it takes, banalysis is not something we should accept. The reason for this is simple: the comedic gives way to the serious, in turn loosening the chain on the lunatic, thereby inspiring the dangerous, and finally crescendoing into the fatal.

Here is a perfectly reasonable day's news in a society founded on a lack of necessary discriminations:

Comedic: Is it possible for two people to simultaneously sexually assault each other?³³⁹
Serious: Professor says students should choose own grades to help reduce stress.³⁴⁰
Lunatic: Families told to remove community paddling pool so 'burglars don't drown.'³⁴¹
Dangerous: Pedophiles believe they should be a part of the LGBT community.³⁴²
Fatal: Norwegian rape survivor 'feels guilty' the man who assaulted him was deported.³⁴³

• Defend variance

This is at the very heart of the matter. We discriminate on everything: where we work, who we employ, what we wear, who we are friends with, where we shop, who we sleep with, who we live next to, whose calls we return, who we vote for, *ad infinitum*. In order to eliminate discrimination, man would first need to eliminate himself.

Not content with merely eliminating variance, but choosing to erect a new hierarchy of victimhood, and doling out rights based upon it, is perhaps one of man's most egregious historical follies.

Whatever the topic, we must stand firm and defend the reality of variance. Meaning matters: men and women are not the same, and we are certainly not equal. There are only two genders. Race is not a social construct. All religions are not the same, just as all people are not the same. The future of the human race is in peril all the while this matter is up for debate.

• Demand free speech

The UK is currently experiencing a crisis in terms of freedom of speech. In late 2017, Home Secretary Amber Rudd upped the ante, by proposing 15-year jail sentences³⁴⁴ for those viewing extremist content online. Naturally this was sold as counter-terrorism, but specifically included those viewing 'far-right propaganda'. Who gets to decide exactly what constitutes 'far-right'?

In March 2018, Mark Meechan, aka Count Dankula, was convicted for the hate crime of being 'grossly offensive'³⁴⁵ because he made a joke video, teaching his girlfriend's pug dog to do a Nazi salute. Meechan, who could have faced a year in jail, was told by the judge that 'context and intent are irrelevant'. If that's the case, then that basically makes humour off-limits.

In the same month, right-wing activists Martin Sellner and Brittany Pettibone were detained and refused entry to the UK[346]. Sellner was due to deliver a speech at Speaker's Corner in Hyde Park, but was considered 'not conducive to the public good'.

Free speech must be demanded in our societies. This is non-negotiable. Without it, we are wasting our time. It is not a coincidence that so many great thinkers have a free speech quote attributed to them, and are even so well known that I do not need to reproduce one here. Free speech is the keystone of a free society, without it you have no legitimate and peaceful way for people to express their concerns, nor to discuss difficult subjects. Without that you have civil war, anarchy, or essentially have to arrest or kill everyone to prevent them from speaking. With the obvious caveats such as incitement or treason, civilised societies do not criminalise thoughts, ideas, or jokes.

No one needs free speech for Big Bird and Oscar the Grouch (although that day may come). Free speech only exists for those views and attitudes that you find repellent, and it is very much in your interest to ensure that your enemies have such peaceful means of expression at their disposal.

To illustrate the fine line we are treading on this matter, consider the recent YouTube shooting. On April 3, 2018, Nasim Aghdam, furious with the company for what she deemed censorship of her videos, shot three people before killing herself[347]. In one of the videos on her channel she explained her frustration, 'YouTube filtered my channels to keep them from getting views'. If you are not allowed to speak, there are not many other options to express yourself.

Free speech really means freedom to be honest. A man need not fear a violent reaction to his worldview, and therefore may send it out freely into the world to do battle with the other ideas. It also means, therefore, that you are more likely to correctly know what the man in the street thinks. Without fear of censure, he has less reason to deceive you.

Take Anjem Choudary, the famous UK-based Islamic hate preacher, jailed in 2016 for inviting support of the Islamic State[348]. Choudary has made a career of touring the BBC studios, spouting his particular brand of peace and love. With sincerity and a straight face, he has often proudly proclaimed that the UK will one day be part of the Caliphate, suggests that the Queen should wear a burka, and longs for the day when the flag of ISIS will fly over Buckingham Palace. As deplorable as Choudary may be, the man is honest. I give him credit for that. I am also immensely thankful that we actually know what he thinks – he would pose a far greater danger to society if we did not.

The UK is now in the process of leaving the EU. That means that for the first time since 1972, our courts will again be sovereign over our laws. We do not have to pander to those who do not share our concerns, and instead can actually make decisions unimpeded. Free speech therefore, does not have to be achieved via proxy, but can be insisted upon. And it must be.

• *Destroy the enemy's trump card of 'racism'*

The single biggest weapon in the variance-deniers arsenal is the accusation of racism. While the other codes enjoy reasonable success in silencing dissenters, the shrill cries of 'racist' are paralysing. And why? Do you think the left genuinely believes in its claims? Do you think the left really equates caution with hatred? Do you think it genuinely believes not wishing to relinquish your home, your nation, and your money to complete strangers is immoral? Do those on the left not conduct their own lives in precisely this fashion? Would putting your own family and your own people first really make you so heinous, so abhorrent, so beyond redemption, that it would be better to die than to admit thinking so?

They do not think this at all. They are leveraging, and they are leveraging with pinpoint accuracy. Historically, even the smartest people have wasted precious time trying to defend or answer the accusation of racism, playing right into the enemy's hands. The stock response of 'It's not racist to...' must be a thing of the past. We don't have time for that, especially as it comes at the detriment of our own argument.

For the right to make genuine progress, the effectiveness of this term must be destroyed absolutely; there can be no half measures. The only way to do this is simply to meet it head-on. I do not say this lightly, nor underestimate the venom that will be unleashed in so doing. Nevertheless, it is a necessary step.

When they call you racist, what they are really saying is, 'You have violated the homogeneity lie'. That's their argument in a nutshell: a non-argument. They are testing that you understand the boundaries of acceptable speech and opinion, and it is vital that you do not pass their test. Instead, it is my firm belief that the correct answer ought to be, 'Yes of course I am, so what?'

To argue factually that there are clear distinctions between races is indeed racist by any common definition of the word. Irrespective of how much one might take offence at the use of the term, it is a term we are going to have to accept, in order to force the other side to debate, the very thing they are trying to avoid by the accusation of racism. Their whole argument revolves around avoiding the debate. That's what these codes are designed to do – to protect them from uncomfortable facts. They must therefore be forced to face them, and crucially to answer them.

All the codes must be fought this way. Whichever they choose – be it offensiveness, sexism, transphobia etc – our argument must be the same. 'We do not believe your homogeneity scam, now debate us with facts or go home with your tail between your legs.' That, I believe, really is the only way to fight this thing going forward.

The first people to implement this strategy are indeed going to be directly in the line of fire, that much is to be expected. I myself have been accused of racism on many occasions merely for playing devil's advocate. This is often upgraded to charges of being a white supremacist.

I consider that the correct intellectual position is to be a supremacy supremacist, at least for anyone who cares to examine the data. Speaking for myself, I am a black supremacist when it comes to an array of sports, an Asian supremacist when it comes to IQ, and safe, cohesive societies, a female supremacist when it comes to childcare, the enduring of physical pain, tolerance, emotional intelligence, longevity to name but a few. But yes, there is no reason to doubt that white males have a role to play in the supremacy debate.

In terms of ability, the data inexorably leads us to a hierarchical conclusion, and the fact that many in society wish to push the lie of equality is an utter irrelevance. The never-ending array of victim statuses is nothing but a smokescreen to what everyone secretly knows, but dares not admit. Differences are real – there does not need to be any conflict arising from that truth, but either way it is still true.

• *Think of your children*

Even if you manage to survive comfortably without ever saying or doing anything offensive throughout your life, what about the children that you leave behind? However shrill the left's cries of 'racist' may be, is that an ignominy you would prefer the next generation to suffer? We know that mainstream politicians are only ever going to follow demographic projections, and push for evermore diversity. It is incumbent on us therefore to change the dialogue facilitating this. We have to move the debate, so that our children do not suffer the consequences of our negligence.

Whenever we are faced with tough choices, I think this is the simplest way to see things – who do we want to run the gauntlet, ourselves or the innocent, who have never even known a world devoid of such madness. Honour behoves us to protect them; that is our duty. So far, we are failing.

• *Repeal stupid laws*

Electing the right politicians is merely the beginning. There are egregious laws on the statute books, and they need repealing. Hate crimes are one such set of laws. The very notion of 'hate crime' is exceptionally injudicious in its conception. How much precisely would you exonerate a father who murders his wife and children out of love, if he compassionately assumes they will not survive his impending suicide? He is no less guilty than a comparable father who murders his family out of hatred. The action is the crime, not the thought required to exact it.

Speaking personally my default setting, while perhaps not exactly hate, is certainly caution. I do not like most things and most people with whom I come into contact. I'm OK with that, and am quite happy to adjust my thinking for the rare individuals who manage to see past my severe personality flaws. The idea of sitting down with the state, checking off which things I would be allowed to continue hating is downright sinister. Hate is a human emotion, and as such must remain the individual's sovereign territory.

To remind ourselves of the absurdity of these laws, consider UK police force operational guidelines for the recording of hate crimes:

For recording purposes, the perception of the victim, or any other person, is the defining factor in determining whether an incident is a hate incident... The victim does not have to justify or provide evidence of their belief, and police officers or staff should not directly challenge this perception. Evidence of hostility is not required for an incident or crime to be recorded as a hate crime or hate incident.

So for a non-crime to become a crime, all that is required is for someone who doesn't like you to come up with no evidence that you offended them. Are you OK with that? We're constantly being told that hate crime is on the rise, how could it not be? When an ever-expanding Armada of check boxes will provide Tom, Dick or Mohammed with an opportunity to play the victim, what's not to hate?

• *Take Islam in hand*

The conversation we must now have about Islam cannot afford to be born out of fear or concern for feelings. The race card will be deployed, and must be met by the stock answer, 'Sure, you've got me. Please feel free to consider me whatever you wish. Now that you've got the moral high ground, could you please answer my point?'

Discovering that a man holds views of which you disapprove

does not detract from his ability to make correct decisions. Churchill, for instance, was widely considered a warmonger[349]. He would certainly be considered an Islamophobe were he around today. He may well have been anti-Germanic, and could conceivably have topped it all off with fascistophobia. None of that prevented him from winning the Second World War, and being quite possibly the most important man in recent British history[350].

In terms of dealing with the problem of Islam, our variance denier is not going to go away without a fight. Where all other arguments fail, he may whine, 'What are you going to do, deport all the extremists?' to which the correct response is, 'Yes, where that is appropriate; internment where it is not.'

A holistic approach must now be taken, which encompasses every neglected sphere of society. From our schools, our mosques, and our prisons, there can be no place for anti-British sentiment in our society. Those who do not wish to integrate should not be here.

In legal terms, the double standards which seem to exist should never have been tolerated in the first place. Equality before the law is one of the central tenets of English Law, and should always be upheld. The parallel legal system of Sharia has absolutely no place in the UK, and must be eradicated straight away.

In terms of education, a close eye must be placed on Muslim faith schools. You can make a strong case for banning them outright. At the very minimum, where there are practices which are unacceptable, such as the non-teaching of curricula[351] (eg evolution), segregation of the sexes[352], or any forms of radicalisation[353], then the school must be closed down immediately, and criminal prosecutions brought against those flouting the law.

So too in the mosques, must an even weightier eye be lent. Any mosque with extremist preachers or material must be closed without warning, and the perpetrators deported or interred. The foreign funding of future mosques must also be banned. Likewise, the 23,000 jihadis wandering the streets of Britain must be removed or interned, no ifs no buts. They are an unnecessary risk, and whatever the price we pay keeping them under lock and key, is a price well paid.

Our prisons too are out of control. Some have become prisons within prisons, where Muslims effectively run extremism schools and have hardly any contact with guards[354]. Again, this must no longer be tolerated.

Britain has always been an immensely tolerant society[355], perhaps too much so. It is now paying the price. Anyone who is already here and wishes to integrate fully into British society should of course be as welcome as any other. But those who wish to divide us must no longer be handled with kid gloves. Outside the EU, as the UK will soon be, a healthy, rigorous and sensible points-based immigration system must be implemented without delay. Many other countries have suffered the ignominy of such a policy, and we can too.

In terms of what Britain must do more readily, there must be a healthy reassertion of Britishness and British values. Traditions, festivals and the like must never be foregone under the pretext of not wishing to offend minorities. Immigrants need to integrate to the UK, not the other way around. That means learning English, and if not practicing English customs, then at least not complaining as they continue.

The answer to absolutely anyone who does not approve of this should be a firm handshake, and an unbarred path to the door, as it would be in any quintessentially British pub when a drunk has had one too many. The landlord would respectfully refuse to serve them. Islam has had a skinful; appeasement has not worked. A firm attitude is the one we now must start cultivating.

The biggest lie of our time

The citizen needs to keep his eyes sharply peeled for what is unquestionably the biggest lie of our time. Banalysis: the abolition of variance, masquerading as the noble ideal of equality. Whatever the topic, you can guarantee that the banalysis advocate can weave it into the fabric of the conversation.

The egalitarian thinker cannot understand why Greek and German unemployment rates are so different; the realist knows that Germans work harder. The egalitarian searches for male privilege; the realist accepts that men are superior. The egalitarian thinks that John from Milton Keynes can be seamlessly replaced by Mohammed from Syria; the realist now knows this is not the case.

At the precise moment this book is due for publication, the UK has its knickers firmly in a twist over the jihadi bride, Shamima Begum. Begum left the UK in 2015, aged 15, to join the Islamic State. Four years later, having had a good time at the camp[356], and suffering no pangs of remorse[357], she wishes to return, so that her new-born son can enjoy the benefits of the NHS. The same UK that denied asylum to the genuinely deserving Asia Bibi, for fear of its restive Muslim population, is now seriously considering allowing Begum back into the country. The egalitarian is wrong at every turn. His lie surrounds us, it is tedious, and it is killing us.

Pareidolia is the tendency to see faces in everything. Humans often mistakenly perceive patterns they do not exist. Now however, we are openly being banned from interpreting patterns where they *do* exist, even when our assailants scream the evidence at us. We have been taught to ignore reality. We can do this no longer.

It is worth revisiting the oft-quoted dictum of Edmund Burke: '*The only thing necessary for the triumph of evil is for good men to do nothing.*'

In just the same way that moderate Germans did not stop the Nazis, and moderate Muslims do not deter their extremist coreligionists, so too are we are implicitly guilty when we allow more courageous fellows than ourselves to be ostracised, imprisoned and even murdered for daring to say what we know to be true, but are too frightened to speak up about.

There are times in history when we have had the luxury of inaction. This is no longer one of those times. The position is now clear. It is not so much a question of left and right anymore, but rather a question of those who embrace reality versus those who refuse it at all costs. The current debate distils to realists versus fantasists, whatever other names they may give themselves.

Patriots vs globalists, free marketeers vs big government, Brexiteers vs Remainers, Conservatives vs Liberals, common sense vs political correctness. The people who wish to deny reality can no longer be allowed to remain unchallenged.

War is coming, I'm sorry to say it but it is undeniable. Never have I more hoped to be wrong, but I fear we are currently taking the deep-breath before the plunge. The west is poised, currently stymied between polarised arguments and beliefs so strong, and so evenly split, that it makes an ultimate conflict inevitable.

In the UK, the Brexit vote, a clash between realism and globalist fantasy, came down to the wire. All across Europe, the same debate is currently raging: elites who wish to radically alter the constitution of their nations or abolish them altogether, set against the simple wishes of their people who want their borders enforced and their children safe. The Yellow Vest movement currently taking Europe by storm is, I believe, a prelude of things to come.

According to a recent Pew Research Center study[358], at least a million sub-Saharan Africans have moved to Europe since 2010. Furthermore, it estimates that up to two-thirds of sub-Saharan Africa's 1.1 billion people want to migrate to the west, with millions intending to do so in the next five years. This has to be stopped, or there won't be a recognisable west left to migrate to.

The argument is going to have to be resolved, because the opposing camps could not be more diametrically-opposed, more mutually exclusive, or most important of all, more loathed by the other side. This situation is unsustainable: you can have the multi-cultural dream, or you can have the west; you can't have both. Let us pray that it can come down to a battle of ideas alone, and that the ballot box rather than the fist may provide a resolution.

On a personal note, I have absolutely no problem with other people's fantasies, I think they are charming. I just don't see why the rest of us have to play along. If you want a gender-neutral mother's day, a hamster for a fish, or an open door for a country, that's beautiful – but could you do it somewhere else without foisting it on the rest of us?

Our future beckons

For the United Kingdom at least, such drastic measures may not be necessary. Over the past few decades, we have been sailing our ship through stormy waters. Our skipper not only drunk, but also asleep at the helm. The navigator blindfolded and shackled by the EU; the crew sulky and ill-informed, having neither knowledge nor any say in where they were headed. That is all about to change.

Upon breaking political union with Europe and completing Brexit (making the huge assumption that our leaders do not manage to scupper it), we will once again be on the high seas, charting our own course, sinking or floating on the quality of our own decisions, and those decisions alone. It is at once a beautiful and scary prospect.

In order for the good ship Britain to be once again a proud, great nation it must have a long, hard look in the mirror and decide which game it wishes to play. If we choose to continue playing banalysis, Britain will likely not succeed. If, on the other hand, we decide once again to build a society based on reality, a society with open, honest dialogue, and a society grounded on facts rather than emotions, there really will be no stopping us.

Assuming that you have made it all the way through this book without vomiting, burning it or ripping its pages apart (which you are still, more than welcome to do), I thank you sincerely. I also ask you to do one last thing. Please think about the future that you want and act accordingly.

What is your version of the happy ending here? Sailing off into the sunset with our multicultural allies and coexist bumper stickers ain't gonna happen. There are precious few options left on the table. Inaction is a coward's resignation. If that genuinely is your move, then at least make it honestly.

The future we are sleepwalking into is a terrifying one: a totally anodyne, androgynous world where opinions are state-mandated. Procreation will likely be state-run too, since individuals are much too easily influenced by the dangerous variance thrown up by evolution. It is not inconceivable that foetuses will be terminated for being too masculine or feminine, and eugenics programs will be introduced not for the mentally inferior or criminal, but for those at the other end of the scale – those too intelligent, too healthy or simply too curious to accept the equality lie. We are going to have to stand up for variance now.

If resignation is not to your taste, then it is really getting a little late in the day to choose a course of action. The clock is ticking, so I say to you in the inimitable words of Don Logan[359], 'It's your move'.

BIBLIOGRAPHY & REFERENCES

1. Oxfam (2016). *An economy for the 1%*. Oxfam Briefing Paper.

2. While there is widespread evidence of deception, and sometimes fairly complex deception throughout the animal kingdom, the extent to which human lying has evolved and diversified may allow us to consider it a unique domain.

3. Evans, A. D., & Lee, K. (2013). Emergence of lying in very young children. *Developmental psychology, 49*(10), 1958-63.

4. Lee, K. (2013). Little liars: Development of verbal deception in children. *Child Development Perspectives, 7*(2), 91-96.

5. Talwar V., Lee K. (2008). Social and cognitive correlates of children's lying behavior. *Child Development, 79*, 866–881.

6. *Lying*, Sam Harris (Four Elephants Press, 2013).

7. Arthur Daley is a fictional character from the popular British comedy-drama 'Minder' (1979-1994). Daley is a loveable rogue; a small-time conman, and perpetual schemer. He will do anything for a pound note, especially if someone else can be made to face the consequences.

8. *The Selfish Gene.* Richard Dawkins (Oxford University Press, 1976).

9. Clutton-Brock, T.H., O'Riain, M.J., Brotherton, P.N.M., Gaynor, D., Kansky, R., Griffin, A.S. & Manser, M. (1999b) Selfish sentinels in cooperative mammals. *Science* 284:1640-1644.

10. Batson, C.D., Duncan, B.D., Ackerman, P., Bucldey, T., Birch, K. (1981). Is empathetic emotion a source of altruistic

motivation? *Journal of Personality and Social Psychology, 40,* 290-30.

11. Stephens, C. (1996). 'Modelling Reciprocal Altruism'. *British Journal for the Philosophy of Science. 47 (4): 533–551*

12. Kahneman, D, and A Deaton. 2010. 'High income improves evaluation of life but not emotional well-being.' *Proceedings of the National Academy of Sciences* 107 (38): 16489-16493.

13. Shigetomi, Carol C.; Hartmann, Donald P.; Gelfand, Donna M. (1981). Sex differences in children's altruistic behavior and reputations for helpfulness. *Developmental Psychology,* Vol 17(4), 434-437.

14. Goldberg, T. L. (1995). Altruism towards panhandlers: Who gives? *Human Nature, 6,* 79- 89.

15. West, Stephen G., Glayde Whitney, & Robert Schnedler. (1975) ⮚Helping a Motorist in Distress: The effects of Sex, Race and Neighbourhood. *Journal of personality and Social Psychology* 31:691-98.

16. Charities Aid Foundation. (2015). UK Giving 2014.

17. De Paulo, B.M., Lindsay, J.J., Malone, B.E., Muhlenbruck, L., Charlton, K. and Cooper, H. (2003) Cues to Deception. *Psychological Bulletin, 129,* 74-118.

18. Keila, P. S., & Skillicorn, D. B. (2005). Detecting unusual and deceptive communication in email. *IBM Centers for Advanced Studies Conference.*

19. Derrick, Douglas C., Thomas O. Meservy, Jeffrey L. Jenkins, Judee K. Burgoon, and Jay F. Nunamaker Jr. (2013). Detecting Deceptive Chat-Based Communication Using Typing Behavior and Message Cues. *ACM Transactions on Management Information Systems (TMIS)* 4 (2): 9.

20. Gregg, A. P. (2007). When vying reveals lying: The timed antagonistic response alethiometer. *Applied Cognitive Psychology, 21,* 621–647.

21. Caso, L., Gnisci, A., Vrij, A., & Mann, S. (2005). Processes underlying

deception: An empirical analysis of truth and lies when manipulating the stakes. *Journal of Investigative Psychology and Offender Profiling*, 2(3), 195–202.

22. *Why Your Five Year Old Could Not Have Done That: Modern Art Explained*, Susie Hodge (Prestel Publishing, 2012).

23. Spy Magazine: *My Kid Could Do That*.

24. Hawley-Dolan, A., & Winner, E. (2011). Seeing the Mind Behind the Art: People Can Distinguish Abstract Expressionist Paintings From Highly Similar Paintings by Children, Chimps, Monkeys, and Elephants. *Psychological Science, 22*(4), 435–441.

25. *Revolution*, Russell Brand (Ballantine Books, 2014).

26. Gamel, J.W. (2008). Hokum on the Rise: The 70-Percent Solution. *The Antioch Review. 66* (1): 130.

27. Womack, Sarah (7 January 2002). 'Gay past hit Portillo's leadership bid, says Clarke'. The Daily Telegraph. Retrieved 17 December 2012.

28. Annual Survey of Hours and Earnings (ASHE) - Office for National Statistics (2015).

29. Uniform Crime Reports [United States]: Supplementary Homicide Reports, 2009-2012.

30. United States Department of Justice. Office of Justice Programs. Bureau of Justice Statistics. National Crime Victimization Survey, 2009. Ann Arbor

31. Fachner, George and Steven Carter. 2015. Collaborative Reform Initiative. *An Assessment of Deadly Force in the Philadelphia Police Department.*

32. Roland G. Fryer, Jr, 2016.'An Empirical Analysis of Racial Differences in Police Use of Force,' NBER Working Papers 22399, National Bureau of Economic Research, Inc.

33. Greg Ridgeway (2016) Officer Risk Factors Associated with Police Shootings: A Matched Case–Control Study, Statistics

and Public Policy, 3:1, 1-6.

34. Shane JM, Lawton B, Swenson Z: The prevalence of fatal police shootings by US police, 2015–2016: patterns and answers from a new dataset. Journal of Criminal Justice.

35. United States Department of Justice. Federal Bureau of Investigation. Uniform Crime Reporting Program Data: Hate Crime Data, 2015 [Record-Type Files]. Ann Arbor, MI: Inter-university Consortium for Political and Social Research [distributor], 2017-07-28.

36. John E. Stewart II (1985) Appearance and Punishment: The Attraction-Leniency Effect in the Courtroom, *The Journal of Social Psychology*, 125:3, 373-378.

37. Rey Hernández-Julián and Christina Peters, 'Student Appearance and Academic Performance,' *Journal of Human Capital* 11, no. 2 (Summer 2017): 247-262.

38. Hosoda, Megumi, Eugene, F, Stone-Romero, & Gwen Coats. The effects of physical attractiveness on job-related outcomes: A meta-analysis of experimental studies. *Personell Psychology* 56(2003): 431-62.

39. Dion, K., Berscheid, E., & Walster, E. (1972). What is beautiful is good. Journal of Personality and Social Psychology, 24(3), 285-290.

40. Wilson, M., Crocker, J., Brown, C. E., Johnson, D., Liotta, R., & Konat, J. (1985). The attractive executive: Effects of sex of business associates on attributions of competence and social skills. *Basic and Applied Social Psychology*, 6(1), 13-23.

41. Li, Peggy (2014) 'Physical Attractiveness and Femininity: Helpful or Hurtful for Female Attorneys,' Akron Law Review: Vol. 47 : Iss. 4 , Article 4.

42. Debra Umberson and Michael Hughes (1987). The Impact of Physical Attractiveness on Achievement and Psychological Well-Being, *Social Psychology Quarterly* Vol. 50, No. 3, pp 227-236.

43. Willis, J., & Todorov, A. (2006). First Impressions: Making up your mind after a 100-Ms Exposure to a Face. *Psychological Science*, 17(7), 592–598.

44. Rushton, J. P. (1995). *Race, evolution, and behavior: a life history perspective*. New Brunswick, NJ: Transaction

45. *IQ and the wealth of nations*. Richard Lynn & Tatu Vanhanen (Praeger, 2002).

46. *IQ and Global Inequality*. Richard Lynn & Tatu Vanhanen (Washington Summit Publishers, 2006).

47. *A Troublesome Inheritance: Genes, Race and Human History.* Nicholas Wade (Penguin Books, 2014).

48. Gur, R. C., Turetsky, B. I., Matsui, M., Yan, M., Bilker, W., Hughett, P., & Gur, R. E. (1999). Sex differences in brain gray and white matter in healthy young adults: Correlations with cognitive performance. *The Journal of Neuroscience*, 19, 4065–4072.

49. Allen, J. S., Damasio, H., Grawboski, T. J., Buss, J., & Zhang, W. (2003). Sexual dimorphism and asymmetries in the gray-white composition of the human cerebrum. NeuroImage, 18, 880–894.

50. Van der Linden, D., Dunkel, C. S., & Madison, G. (2017). Sex differences inbrain size and general intelligence (g). *Intelligence,*63 (Supplement C),78–88.

51. *Lynn, Richard; Irwing, Paul (2004). 'Sex differences on the progressive matrices: A meta-analysis'. Intelligence. 32 (5): 481–498.*

52. Johnson, W., Carothers, A., & Deary, I. J. (2008). Sex Differences in Variability in General Intelligence: A New Look at the Old Question. *Perspectives on Psychological Science*, 3(6), 518–531.

53. Tamas Hajdu & Gabor Hajdu, 2013.'Are more equal societies happier? Subjective well-being, income inequality, and redistribution', IEHAS Discussion Papers 1320, Institute of Economics, Centre for Economic and Regional Studies, Hungarian Academy of Sciences.

54. Frank J. Elgar, Nicole Aitken; Income inequality, trust and homicide in 33 countries, *European Journal of Public Health*, Volume 21, Issue 2, 1 April 2011, Pages 241–246,

55. Cunningham, M. R., Roberts, A. R., Barbee, A. P., Druen, P. B., & Wu, C.-H. (1995). 'Their ideas of beauty are, on the whole, the same as ours': Consistency and variability in the cross-cultural perception of female physical attractiveness. Journal of Personality and Social Psychology, 68(2), 261-279.

56. Schmitt, D. P., Alcalay, L., Allik, J., Ault, L., Austers, I., Bennett, K. L., et al. (2003). Universal sex differences in the desire for sexual variety: Tests from 52 nations, 6 continents, and 13 islands. *Journal of Personality and Social Psychology*, 85, 85–104.

57. Wolf CC, Ocklenburg S, Oren B, et al. Sex differences in parking are affected by biological and social factors. *Psychol Res* 2010;74:429–35.

58. Gino, F., Wilmuth, C. A., & Brooks, A. W. (2015). Compared to men, women view professional advancement as equally attainable, but less desirable. Proceedings of the National Academy of Sciences of the United States of America (PNAS), 112(40), 12354-12359.

59. Ondish, P & Stern, C. (2017). Liberals Possess More National Consensus on Political Attitudes in the United States: An Examination Across 40 Years Social Psychological and Personality Science 1-9

60. Jones, Robert P., and Daniel Cox. "Merry Christmas' vs. 'Happy Holidays': Republicans and Democrats are Polar Opposites." PRRI. 2016.

61. Hiscox, M. (2017) Going blind to see more clearly: unconscious bias in Australian Public Services shortlisting processes.

62. Rotherham Metropolitan Borough Council, Independent Inquiry into Child Sexual Exploitation in Rotherham 1997 - 2013, (the 'Jay Report')

63. *Talking about Terrorism*, Alison Jamieson (Brilliant Publications, 2017).

64. *Enquête sur le complotisme,* Ifop pour la Fondation Jean-Jaurès et Conspiracy Watch (December, 2017).

65. Golby, J. (2015, May 27). 'Tea is a national disgrace'. *The Guardian.*

66. Harmon, A. (2017, October 17). 'Why White Supremacists Are Chugging Milk (and Why Geneticists Are Alarmed)'. *The New York Times.*

67. Takei, M. (2012). Racism and Global Warming: The Need for the Richer Countries to Make Concessions to China and India. Race, Gender & Class, 19(1/2), 131-149.

68. Eligon, J. (2017, July 19). 'Was that racist?' *The New York Times.*

69. Adewunmi, B. (2013, December 8). 'The everyday microaggressions I experience as a black woman in Berlin'. *The Guardian.*

70. Pells, R. (2017, April 24). 'Oxford University staff warned not looking a student in the eye is 'racist''. *The Independent.*

71. Snape, J. (2015, June 1). 'Manspreading arrests: the long arm of the law just invaded our personal space'. *The Telegraph.*

72. Bindley, K. (2012, September 21). 'Peanut Butter And Jelly Racist? Portland School Principal Ties Sandwich To White Privilege'. *Huffpost.*

73. Allen, C. (2014, April 4). 'Class, race and classical music'. *The Guardian.*

74. Timpf, K. (2017, October 25). 'Professor: 'Mathematics Itself Operates as Whiteness''. *National Review.*

75. Timpf, K. (2017, April 10). 'Clemson Diversity Training: Expecting People to Arrive on Time Is Culturally Insensitive'. *National Review.*

76. Sanghani, R. (2018, March 12). 'Is online dating racist?' *The Evening Standard.*

77. Kelbert, A.W. (2016, September 6). 'Climate change is a racist crisis: that's why Black Lives Matter closed an airport'. *The Guardian.*

78. Dennis, R. (1995). Social Darwinism, Scientific Racism, and the Metaphysics of Race. The Journal of Negro Education, 64(3), 243-252.

79. Chasen, R. (2017, September 28). 'Racist propaganda': Librarian rejects Melania Trump's gift of Dr. Seuss books.' *The Washington Post.*

80. Wootson Jr., C. R. (2016 October 21). 'To be white is to be racist, period,' a high school teacher told his class'. *The Washington Post.*

81. 'Having 'white nuclear family' promotes white supremacy, says New York professor, report says'. (2017, October 31). *Fox News.*

82. Prince, R. (2008, July 7). 'Toddlers who dislike spicy food 'racist''. *The Telegraph.*

83. Gander, K. (2017, September 20). 'Gentrification of food: why we need to stop calling immigrant cuisine 'ethnic''. *The Independent.*

84. Orr, D. (2013, August 28). 'Is having to pay for tomato ketchup racist?' *The Guardian.*

85. Morris, W. (2019, January 23). 'Why Do the Oscars Keep Falling for Racial Reconciliation Fantasies?' *The New York Times.*

86. Singh, A. (2018, February 27). 'Munroe Bergdorf: Model who said 'all white people' are racist appointed to LGBT+ board by Labour MP'. *The Independent.*

87. Elan, P. (2016, February 2). 'Is 'streetwear' a dismissive term?' *The Guardian.*

88. *Of Black Servitude Without Slavery: The Unspoken Politics of the English Language*, Agwu Ukiwe Okali (BookBaby, 2016).

89. Way, K. (2017, December 1). 'Sorry white people, but trying too hard not to be racist is low-key kind of racist'. *Babe.*

90. Citizenship and Immigration Canada. (2011). Discover

Canada: the rights and responsibilities of citizenship: study guide. Ottawa: Citizenship and Immigration Canada.

91. Human Rights Watch (Organization). (2001). Human Rights Watch world report. New York, NY: Human Rights Watch.

92. Crime in the United States 1996: Uniform Crime Statistics, 'Section II: Crime Index Offenses Reported.' FBI, 1997.

93. Vetterling-Braggin, Mary (1982). 'Femininity, Masculinity, and Androgyny: a modern philosophical discussion.' Totowa, N.J: Littlefield, Adams.

94. Oppenheim, M. (2017, November 14). 'Teacher suspended for referring to a transgender pupil as a girl rather than a boy'. *The Independent.*

95. Driessen, G. & van Langen, A. (2013) Gender differences in primary and secondary education: Are girls really outperforming boys? International Review of Education, 59, 67–86.

96. OECD (2015), The ABC of Gender Equality in Education: Aptitude, Behaviour, Confidence, PISA, OECD Publishing.

97. Pells, R. (2017, August 17). 'A-level results 2017: Boys overtake girls in top grades for first time in years'. *The Independent.*

98. Turner, D. (2011, February 26). 'Gender divide: Exam change may boost boys'. *Financial Times.*

99. Joint Council for Qualifications (2016). 'Entry Trends, Gender and Regional Charts GCE 2016'

100. Diver, T. (2018, February 1). 'Oxford University extends exam times for women's benefit'. *The Telegraph.*

101. Cantwell D (1996) Attention deficit disorder: a review of the past 10 years. J Am Acad Child Adolesc Psychiatry 35: 978-87.

102. Department for Education. (2017, July). 'Permanent and Fixed Period Exclusions in England: 2015 to 2016'.

103. Higher Education Policy Institute. (2016). 'Boys to Men: The underachievement of young men in higher education – and

how to start tackling it'.

104. Su, R., Rounds, J., Armstrong, P. I. (2009). Men and things, women and people: A meta-analysis of sex differences in interest. Psychological Bulletin, 135, 859–884.

105. Tzovaras, B.G. (2017, October 10). 'How Men Can Help Women in STEM: Shut Up, Sit Back and Listen'. *Scientific American.*

106. Williams, W. M., & Ceci, S. J. (2015). National hiring experiments reveal 2: 1 faculty preference for women on STEM tenure track. Journal of Multicultural Counseling and Development, 34(1), 38–49.

107. Wilkens, R. and Wooden, M. (2011) Gender differences in rates of job dismissals: Why are men more likely to lose their jobs? IZA Discussion Paper 6225.

108. Health and Safety Executive (2018, July 4). 'Workplace fatal injuries in Great Britain 2018'.

109. Obermeyer Z, Murray CJL, Gakidou E. (2008). Fifty years of violent war deaths from Vietnam to Bosnia: Analysis of data from the World Health Survey programme. British Medical Journal. 336:1482.

110. Flatley, J. (2018) Homicide in England and Wales: year ending March 2017, *Office for National Statistics.*

111. Grall, T. S. (2007). Custodial mothers and fathers and their child support: 2005. *Current Population Reports, P60 (234),* 1–12.

112. Starr, Sonja B., Estimating Gender Disparities in Federal Criminal Cases (August 29, 2012). University of Michigan Law and Economics Research Paper, No. 12-018.

113. O'Brien, P. (2014, November 6). 'We should stop putting women in jail. For anything.' The Washington Post.

114. Homeless Link (2017) Support for single homeless people in England: Annual review 2017.

115. Murphy, A. (2014, March 7). 'Why homeless services are

failing women'. *The Guardian.*

116. Murphy GE. Why women are less likely than men to commit suicide. Comprehensive psychiatry. 1998;39(4):165–75.

117. Archer, J. (2000). Sex differences in aggression between heterosexual partners: A meta-analytic review. Psychological Bulletin, 126(5), 651-680.

118. Parity (2010). 'Domestic Violence: The Male Perspective'.

119. Stemple L., Flores A., Meyer I. H. (2017). Sexual victimization perpetrated by women: federal data reveal surprising prevalence. Aggression and Violent Behavior. 34, 302–311.

120. National Center for Injury Prevention and Control. The National Inmate Partner And Sexual Violence Survey. 2011.

121. Denov MS. The myth of innocence: sexual scripts and the recognition of child sexual abuse by female perpetrators. J Sex Res. 2003;40(3):303–314.

122. Weiss KG. Male sexual victimization: examining men's experiences of rape and sexual assault. Men Masc. 2010;12(3):275–298.

123. Beck AJ, Berzofsky M, Caspar R, Krebs C. Sexual victimization in prisons and jails reported by inmates, 2011–12. 2013.

124. Smith BV. Uncomfortable places, close spaces: female correctional workers' sexual interactions with men and boys in custody. UCLA Law Rev. 2012;59(6):1690–1745.

125. Scarce M. The Spectacle of Male Rape. Male on Male Rape: The Hidden Toll of Stigma and Shame. New York, NY: Insight Books; 1997.

126. Ford, H. (2006) Women who Sexually Abuse Children. Chichester: John Wiley and Sons.

127. Omar Aziz, Norman Gemmell, and Athene Laws, Income and Fiscal Incidence by Age and Gender: Some Evidence from New Zealand, *The Review of Income and Wealth*, Vol. 62, Issue 3, pages 534-558, September 2016.

128. Haines, N. (2018). 'Divorces in England and Wales: 2017'. *Office for National Statistics.*

129. Solomon-Fears, C. (2013). Child support: An overview of Census Bureau data on recipients. Congressional Research Service RS22499.

130. OECD (2017), Life expectancy at birth, in Health at a Glance 2017: OECD Indicators, OECD Publishing, Paris.

131. 'The decline of the manly man'. (2016). YouGov.

132. *The Dangerous Book for Boys,* Conn Iggulden (William Morrow, 2006).

133. Levine et al (2017). Temporal trends in sperm count: a systematic review and meta-regression analysis, *Human Reproduction Update,* Volume 23, Issue 6, 1 November 2017, Pages 646–659.

134. Stein B. (2017, July 31). 'Sperm Counts Plummet In Western Men, Study Finds.' *NPR.*

135. Delassio-Parson, A (2017). Doing vegetarianism to destabilize the meat-masculinity nexus in La Plata, Argentina. Gender, Place & Culture (Online: 14 November 2017).

136. Chivers ML, Reiger G, latty E, Bailey JM. A sex difference in the specificity of sexual arousal. *Psychological Science.* 2004; 15:736-744.

137. Wright, M. (2017, November 23). 'Mother calls for Sleeping Beauty to be banned from primary school as it promotes 'inappropriate behaviour". *The Telegraph.*

138. Culbertson, A. (2017, September 20). 'End of macho culture: Macron to make wolf-whistling and asking for woman's phone number illegal'. *Daily Express.*

139. Bodkin, H. (2017, December 3). 'Ridicule as police say kissing under the mistletoe without consent is 'rape". *The Telegraph.*

140. Crowley, M. (2017, December 18). 'Lisa Bloom's infusion of 'dark money' into world of sexual assault is a tragedy'. *The Hill.*

141. That's Life magazine: 'The National Scruples and Lies Survey' (2004).

142. Bellis M. A., Hughes K., Hughes S., and Ashton J. R. (2005). Measuring paternal discrepancy and its public health consequences. *Journal of Epidemiology & Community Health* 59 (9):749–54.

143. Byers, E. S. (1996). How well does the traditional sexual script explain sexual coercion? Review of a program of research. *Journal of Psychology and Human Sexuality*, 8(1–2), 6–26.

144. DiCanio, M. (1993). The encyclopedia of violence: origins, attitudes, consequences. New York: Facts on File.

145. Kanin, Eugene J., 'False Rape Allegations', Archives of Sexual Behavior, Vol. 23, No. 1, Feb 1994, p. 81.

146. O'Connor, R. (2017, December 16). 'Matt Damon slammed for 'tone-deaf' comments on sexual assault'. *The Independent*.

147. Isabelle Chopin, Lilla Farkas, and Catharina Germaine, Equality Data Initiative, Ethnic origin and disability data collection in Europe: Measuring inequality – Combating discrimination MPG for the Open Society Foundations, (November 2014).

148. Murphy, M. (2017, April 27). 'Sex robots epitomize patriarchy and offer men a solution to the threat of female independence'. *Feminist Current*.

149. Weston, P. (2018, January 5). 'Sex robots could make MEN obsolete as women of the future get wooed by 'dashing menbots' who will also do the housework, Harvard mathematician claims'. *Daily Mail*.

150. Havas Global Comms (2017, December 7). 'Would you date a robot?'

151. Mazza, E. (2018, August 6). 'Counsellor, 30, who claims to only 'have sex with GHOSTS' reveals she's in a 'serious' relationship with a spirit she met in Australia - and she plans to have a 'baby' with him'. *Daily Mail*.

152. *Are Men Obsolete? The Munk Debate on Gender*, Camille Paglia

(House of Anansi Press, 2014).

153. *Why There Are No Good Men Left: The Romantic Plight of the New Single Woman*, Barbara Whitehead (Broadway Books, 2003).

154. *The End of Men and the Rise of Women*, Hanna Rosin (Riverhead Books, 2012).

155. Demetriou, D. (2017, April 11). 'Japan's population to shrink by a third by *2065*'. *The Telegraph*.

156. Rani, A. (2013, October 24). 'The Japanese men who prefer virtual girlfriends to sex'. *BBC News*.

157. Phillips, K. (2018, January 9). 'A 'White Racism' class just started at a Florida university. Police were on standby'. *The Washington Post*.

158. Daily Mail Reporter (2017, November 18). 'Oxford college introduces compulsory 'race awareness' course for all new students to make undergraduates 'more sensitive to the needs of ethnic minorities'. *Daily Mail*.

159. Richardon, B. (2018, January 18). 'Students quizzed on 'Pyramid of White Supremacy' at Salisbury University in Maryland'. *The Washington Times*.

160. Michael, A. (2017, December 6). 'I Sometimes Don't Want to Be White Either'. *Huffpost*.

161. The Washington Times. (2002, September 4). 'Harvard professor argues for 'abolishing' white race'. *The Washington Times*.

162. Zimmerman, J. (2015, February 25). 'We tend to empathize with our online avatars. So let's get rid of white emojis'. *The Guardian*.

163. Yankah, E.N. (2017, November 11). 'Can my children be friends with white people?' *The New York Times*.

164. Noor, P. (2017, December 6). 'White people need to learn how to integrate'. *Vice*.

165. Joyce, F. (2015, December 22). 'White men must be stopped:

The very future of mankind depends on it'. *Salon.*

166. *Stupid White Men*, Michael Moore (Harper, 2001).

167. Whitaker, M. (2013, August 28). 'Oprah: old racists 'have to die' to achieve racial progress'. *MSNBC.*

168. Stein, J. (2018, February 6). 'Trump immigration plan could keep whites in U.S. majority for up to five more years'. *The Washington Post.*

169. Hogan, M. (2016, January 14). 'The Oscars Are Way Too White, Again'. *Vanity Fair.*

170. Hale, V. (2017, November 14). 'UK Government Blasts Charities for Being 'Too White''. *Breitbart.*

171. Gladney, J. (2015, July 2). 'My 'colorblind' college campus is still racist. My white peers just don't see it'. *The Guardian.*

172. Salam, M. (2018, August 2). 'Hollywood Is as White, Straight and Male as Ever'. *The New York Times.*

173. Moss, V. (2018, March 21). 'Why we need to talk about the fact that the catwalks are still too white'. *The Telegraph.*

174. Ruiz, M. (2018, November 9). 'Why Do White Women Keep Voting for the GOP and Against Their Own Interests?' *Vogue.*

175. Daniels, J. (2018, March 13). 'White Families Are Engines Of Inequality'. *Huffpost.*

176. Singh, A. (2018, February 27). 'Munroe Bergdorf: Model who said 'all white people' are racist appointed to LGBT+ board by Labour MP'. *The Independent.*

177. Emba, C. (2016, September 2). 'Why not being a 'racist' isn't enough''. *The Washington Post.*

178. Eddo-Lodge, R. (2017, May 30). 'Why I'm no longer talking to white people about race'. *The Guardian.*

179. Evin (2017, May 21). 'You don't have to be racist to be racist'. *Affinity Magazine.*

180. Peck, P. (2017, December 28). '37 things white people need to

stop ruining in 2018'. *Buzzfeed.*

181. Young, D. (2017, January 30). 'White people need to be better'. *GQ.*

182. Labour Party Leadership (2010, June 9). 'Last call for Labour leader support'. *The Guardian.*

183. Hill, A. (2001, January 7). 'Dyke: BBC is hideously white'. *The Guardian.*

184. Mansfield, K. (2016, December 2). 'It's hideously white' Andrew Lloyd Webber blasts UK theatre for lack of ethnic minorities'. *The Express.*

185. Moore, G. (2016, February 11). 'Greg Dyke: Why the departing chairman is attacking the FA's 'old, white men''. *The Independent.*

186. Coates, S. (2018, January 23). 'Labour subsidy for non-white members 'divisive and illegal''. *The Times.*

187. Killalea, D. (2017, August 7). 'Handsome Her cafe in Brunswick, Melbourne charges men 18% 'gender gap' surcharge'. *News.Com.Au.*

188. Richardon, B. (2018, march 12). 'Restaurant charged white customers more to combat 'racial wealth disparity''. *The Washington Times.*

189. Randall, A. (2017, February 27). 'White Men Should Pay 5% Extra In Taxes Because They're Privileged'. *The Daily Caller.*

190. Parris, M. (2015, October 21). 'If I had a choice, I wouldn't be a whitey'. *The Times.*

191. Hitchcock, J. (1998). *Decentering whiteness.*

192. Ruiz-Grossman, S. (2017, September 19). 'These White People Will Respond To Your Racist Trolls So You Don't Have To'. *Huffpost.*

193. International migration: Key findings from the U.S., Europe and the world, Connor, Phillip (2016). Fact Tank, Pew Research Center.

194. *Building Support for Scholarly Practices in Mathematics,* Signe E.

Kastberg (Information Age Publishing, 2017).

195. Case, A., & Deaton, A. (2017). Mortality and morbidity in the 21st century. *Brookings papers on economic activity*, 2017, 397-476.

196. Weale, S. (2016, November 10). 'Schools must focus on struggling white working-class pupils, says UK charity'. *The Guardian*.

197. Schuessler, J. (2017, December 14). "'Youthquake' Is Oxford's Word of the Year. Sorry, Broflake.". *The New York Times*.

198. Cohen, C. J., Fowler, M., Medenica, V. E., Rogowski, J. C. (2017). The 'woke' generation? Millennial attitudes on race in the US.

199. Barnes, T. (2017, December 14). 'UCL forced to apologise for 'dreaming of a white campus' tweet'. *The Independent*.

200. Kaati, L. et al. (2017). 'Det vita hatet: radikal nationalism i digitala miljöer'. *FOI*.

201. Riddell, K. (2017, March 17). 'Milk: The new symbol of racism in Donald Trump's America'. *The Washington Times*.

202. Youngs, I. (2016, October 20). 'Classical music 'excludes' composers from minorities'. *BBC News*.

203. Allen, C. (2014, April 4). 'Class, race and classical music'. *The Guardian*.

204. Kosman, J. (2017). 'Classical so white and male: Time is overdue for diversity'. *San Francisco Chronicle*.

205. Bennett, A. (2017, November 11). 'Taylor Swift's Persona Is Not Built For 2017'. *Buzzfeed*.

206. Timpf, K. (2017, June 9). 'Professor: White-Marble Sculpture Contributes to 'White Supremacy''. *National Review*.

207. Rosenbaum, R. (2010, November 23). 'The Unbearable Whiteness of White Meat'. *Slate*.

208. BBC News (2018, March 13). 'David Lammy on the image of Africa shown by Comic Relief'.

209. McVeigh, K. (2018, March 23). 'Comic Relief to ditch white saviour stereotype appeals'. *The Guardian.*

210. Hirsch, A. (2017, December 5). 'Ed Sheeran means well but this poverty porn has to stop'. *The Guardian.*

211. Rannard, G. (2018, March 27). 'Never Again: Is gun control movement too white?' *BBC News.*

212. Goldenberg, S. (2014, May 8). 'Why are so many white men trying to save the planet without the rest of us?' *The Guardian.*

213. Thomas, D. (2015, April 14). 'Why white people aren't as cool as black people'. *The Guardian.*

214. Noor, P. (2017, December 6). 'White People Need to Learn How to Integrate'. *Vice.*

215. Eileen (2018, February 6). 'Dear White People: no melanin, no opinion.' *The Beaver.*

216. Office for National Statistics ; National Records of Scotland; Northern Ireland Statistics and Research Agency (2016): 2011 Census aggregate data. UK Data Service (Edition: June 2016).

217. 'Christmas shopping in the United Kingdom (UK)'. (2017). *Statista.*

218. *Santa's Husband*, Daniel Kibblesmith (Harper Design, 2017).

219. Frost, V. (2017, October 7). 'Should we be having fewer children for the sake of the planet?' *The Guardian.*

220. Saletan, W. (2012, March 12). 'After-birth abortion. The pro-choice case for infanticide'. *Slate.*

221. Valentine, N. (2017, June 21). 'Beyond Pro-Choice: The Solution to White Supremacy is White Abortion'. *Medusa Magazine.*

222. Kingston, A. (2017, February 21). 'Mothers who regret having children are speaking up like never before'. *Macleans.*

223. Norman, G. (2017, November 30). 'Texas student newspaper blasted over anti-white 'Your DNA is an abomination'

column'. *Fox News.*

224. McKie, R. (2018, February 10). 'Cheddar Man changes the way we think about our ancestors'. *The Guardian.*

225. Collins, T. (2018, March 2). 'Was Cheddar man white after all? There's no way to know that the first Briton had 'dark to black skin' says scientist who helped reconstruct his 10,000-year-old face'. *Daily Mail.*

226. Workneh, L. (2017, May 22). "Dear White People' Director And Star Break Down Why Black People Can't Be Racist'. *Huffpost.*

227. DeVilliers, J. (2017, July 5). "F**k White People' artwork not hate speech, court rules'. *News24.*

228. Mortimer, C. (2015, November 3). 'Bahar Mustafa: Charges dropped against student officer 'who tweeted #killallwhitemen''. *The Independent.*

229. BBC News. (2017, September 7). 'Wrexham man jailed over 'kill every Muslim' Facebook post'.

230. Crepeau, M. (2018, July 12). "Is that what a life is worth?' Last of 4 defendants pleads guilty to recorded beating of teen with disability'. *Chicago Tribune.*

231. Margan, M. (2018, March 23). 'Inside the 'most dangerous job in the world': White farmers in South Africa are FOUR times more likely to be murdered than anyone else - as Peter Dutton vows to 'fast-track' them into Australia as refugees'. *Daily Mail.*

232. News24 (2018, March 16). 'Human Rights Watch slams Australian minister over immigration offer to white SA farmers'.

233. Gaggero, S.C. (2016, September 16). 'Preserving My Children's Innocence Is An Act Of Preserving White Supremacy'. *Huffpost.*

234. Blow, C.M. (2018, June 24). 'White Extinction Anxiety'. *The New York Times.*

235. Warmington, J. (2018, March 3). 'WARMINGTON: UOIT

campus posters aim to shame straight, white, Christian men?' *Toronto Sun.*

236. Stolworthy, J. (2017, June 12). 'Katy Perry apologises for cultural appropriation in past music video'. *The Independent.*

237. Trendell, A. (2017, June 13). 'Katy Perry apologises for 'cultural appropriation''. *NME.*

238. Lawrence, R. (2018, February 20). ''There is nothing positive about culture appropriation': Jesy Nelson comes under fire from Little Mix fans after wearing her hair in dreadlocks'. *Mail Online.*

239. Carroll, R. (2016, June 27). 'Justin Timberlake on Jesse Williams's BET speech wasn't woke, just white'. *The Guardian.*

240. Andrews, T.M. (2018, March 12). 'Bruno Mars was accused of cultural appropriation. Charlie Wilson, among others, defended him'. *The Washington Post.*

241. Centers for Disease Control and Prevention. Estimated HIV incidence and prevalence in the United States, 2010–2015. HIV Surveillance Supplemental Report 2018;23(1).

242. Evans, M. (2017, December 10). 'Porn star Jaxton Wheeler releases statement refuting claims he 'caused August Ames' suicide''. *The Mirror.*

243. Steinberg, J. (2018, February 1). 'West Ham crisis: Tony Henry suspended after report over African players'. *The Guardian.*

244. *Mein Kampf (James Murphy Nazi Authorized Translation)*, James Murphy (Imperial Collegiate Publishing, 2010).

245. Vanderhart, D. (2017, November 3). 'Someone Created a (Now-Defunct) Website to Mock City Commissioner Candidate Spencer Raymond'. *Portland Mercury.*

246. Walters, S. (2018, February 17). 'Jo Cox's husband Brendan confesses to inappropriate behaviour amid new allegation that he drunkenly 'grabbed a woman by the throat' as he is forced to quit the murdered MP's charities'. *Mail Online.*

247. Platell, A. (2018, February 18). 'My friend Brendan Cox is not some Weinstein-like sex fiend - if anyone deserves a second chance he does'. *Mail Online.*

248. Ross, C. (2015, July 21). 'Leading Ferguson Activist's Hate Crime Claim Disputed By Police Report, Detective'. *The Daily Caller.*

249. *In Full Color: Finding My Place in a Black and White World,* Rachel Dolezal (BenBella Books, 2017).

250. Griffin, J. (2018, January 12). 'Is it discriminatory to refuse to date a transwoman?' *BBC News.*

251. *The Demon Lover: On the Sexuality of Terrorism,* Robin Morgan (W W Norton & Co Inc, 1990).

252. Warren, L. (2012, September 19). 'Monica's revenge: Lewinsky 'to publish secret love letters to Clinton revealing his insatiable desire for threesomes and how he trashed Hillary''. *Mail Online.*

253. Lewinsky, M. (2018, February 25). 'Emerging from 'the House of Gaslight' in the Age of #MeToo'. *Vanity Fair.*

254. Wrack, M. (2018, July 18). 'The real Grenfell scandal: over a year on, nothing has changed'. *The Guardian.*

255. Allen, K. (2017, August 12). 'A tale of two housing markets: booming Burnley and stagnant Kensington'. *The Guardian.*

256. Hughes, L. (2017, July 2). 'Grenfell row as Labour MP suggests 'white, upper-middle class man' should not have been hired to lead inquiry'. *The Telegraph.*

257. Lawless, J. (2018, June 4). 'Grenfell Tower Residents Wrongly Told to Stay Put As Fire Raged, Report Finds'. *Bloomberg.*

258. Walker, P. (2017, June 22). 'Tests on 600 tower blocks find seven with Grenfell Tower-style cladding'. *The Guardian.*

259. Baker-Jordan, S. (2017, June 15). ''Racism and classism killed the residents of Grenfell Tower'. *Huffpost.*

260. Spillett, R. (2017, June 21). 'Relief at last for Grenfell Tower families as 250 homeless residents are rehoused in a £2billion

luxury block in Kensington after authorities buy up 68 flats in £10million deal'. *Mail Online*.

261. Tomlinson, C. (2017, June 21). 'Amnesty for Illegal Immigrants Displaced by Grenfell Fire Whilst 7,000 Veterans Remain Homeless'. *Breitbart*.

262. Siddique, H. (2017, July 2). 'Grenfell Tower: illegal subletters will not be prosecuted'. *The Guardian*.

263. Hale, B. (2018, December 14). 'Pictured: The 14 Grenfell ghouls who stole £670,000 from the disaster's relief fund through lies and deceit'. *Mail Online*.

264. Boyd, C. (2018, March 6). 'Grenfell Tower resident whose cannabis oil factory was discovered when investigators searched his flat avoids jail'. *Mail Online*.

265. Britton, P. (2017, November 15). 'Prime Minister says Manchester will get 'the majority' of £17m promised after Arena bomb'. *Manchester Evening News*.

266. Owens, E. (2017, July 29). 'UPDATE: Not Being Stupid Is 'Cognitive Privilege' Now, Which Is Just Like White Privilege'. *The Daily Caller*.

267. Timpf, K. (2017, April 10). 'Clemson Diversity Training: Expecting People to Arrive on Time Is Culturally Insensitive'. *National Review*.

268. Gelonesi, J. (2015, May 1). 'Is having a loving family an unfair advantage?' *ABC*.

269. Ellis-Petersen, H. (2017, Mar 2). 'Riz Ahmed warns lack of diversity on TV will drive young people to Isis.

270. Airaksinen, T. (2017, July 14). 'NYU librarian laments 'fatigue' from 'presence of white people''. *Campus Reform*.

271. Chasmar, J. (2018, August 29). 'LeBron James: 'Took me a little while' to accept white people'. *The Washington Times*.

272. Chumley, C.K. (2018, May 17). 'Evergreen College students back at it with 'no white people' day'. *The Washington Times*.

273. Sopan, D. (2019, February 20). 'Jussie Smollett Faces Felony Charge, Accused of Faking Own Assault'. The New York Times.

274. Turner, C. (2017, March 2). 'Eight in ten British university lecturers are 'Left-wing', survey finds '. *The Telegraph.*

275. Blanden, J, P. Gregg and S. Machin (2005) 'Educational Inequality and Intergenerational Mobility' in What's the Good of Education? The Economics of Education in the United Kingdom, eds. S. Machin and A. Vignoles, Princeton University Press.

276. Hope, C. (2010, December 2). 'Britain embraces 'positive action' to abolish workplace discrimination'. *The Telegraph.*

277. Dodd, V. (2015, October 22). 'Theresa May: police forces are 'too white''. *The Guardian.*

278. Hodges, D. (2015, September 14). 'No women in top jobs? Welcome to the hypocrisy of the Jeremy Corbyn era'. *The Telegraph.*

279. Doyle, J. (2016, February 19). 'Sadiq Khan defends his legal work representing a man who described white people as 'devils' by insisting 'even the worst people need a defence''. *Mail Online.*

280. Wilkinson, M. (2016, May 4). 'Sadiq Khan says 'I'm sorry' after using 'Uncle Toms' slur against moderate Muslims'. *The Telegraph.*

281. *Challenging Racism: A Handbook on the Human Rights Act,* Barry Clarke (Lawrence & Wishart Ltd, 2002).

282. Nawaz, M. (2016, August 5). 'The Secret Life of Sadiq Khan, London's First Muslim Mayor'. *Daily Beast.*

283. Humphries, W. (2018, April 12). 'Police defend family's shrine to dead burglar Henry Vincent'. *The Times.*

284. White, S. (2018, April 9). ''They won't rest till they get revenge': Traveller makes chilling warning to hero pensioner as dead burglar's fugitive 'accomplice' is identified and a SHRINE to fallen criminal grows at OAP's home'. *Mail Online.*

285. Robinson, B. (2018, January 18). 'Lee Rigby memorial taken down for looking 'unsightly' after requests from local residents'. *The Express.*

286. Davis, C. (2018, April 12). 'Police chief warns you could be ARRESTED if you remove shrine to Hither Green burglar'. *The Express.*

287. Flower, P. (2018, October 31). 'It's criminal that the Met Police is giving up on burglars - but has 900 'anti-hate experts', writes former Scotland Yard chief PHILIP FLOWER'. *Mail Online.*

288. Parker, C. (2017, October 12). 'Police arresting nine people a day in fight against web trolls'. *The Times.*

289. Gov.uk. (2016). Lammy Review of Black, Asian and Minority Ethnic (BAME) representation in the Criminal Justice System: call for evidence - GOV.UK.

290. Morris, A. (2018, April 9). 'It's a Theyby! Is it possible to raise your child entirely without gender from birth?' *SBS.*

291. 'Transgender wrestler Mack Beggs wins Texas girls title again''. (2018, February 25). *The Guardian.*

292. Payne, M. (2017, March 23). 'Transgender woman wins international weightlifting title amid controversy over fairness'. *Chicago Tribune.*

293. Brown, M. (2018, April 11). 'When a Man Sets the Record for the Fastest Marathon Run by a Woman'. *LifeSite News.*

294. Henderson, B. (2015, September 30). 'Eight of Iran's women's football team 'are men''.

295. Petter, O. (2018, January 1). 'Transgender women face angry reaction for using Hampstead ladies' pond'. *The Independent.*

296. Joseph, A. (2017, September 6). 'Transgender rapist who was moved to women-only jail despite still having a penis is segregated after 'making unwanted sexual advances on female inmates''. *Mail Online.*

297. Rayner, G. (2017, December 24). 'Defence Secretary blocks

plans to drop Army's 'Be the Best' slogan'. *The Telegraph*.

298. Stickings, T. (2018, January 14). 'Prayer time on patrol: British Army defies critics of politically correct campaign as it releases new recruitment video showing Muslim soldier praying in front of his colleagues'. *Mail Online*.

299. Batchelor, T. (2016, September 25). 'UK forces fail to hire ethnic minorities: Not a single senior officer is black or Asian'. *The Express*.

300. Schaefer, A. G., Wenger, J. W., Kavanagh, J., Wong, J. P., Oak, G. S., Trail, T. E., & Nichols, T. (2015). Implications of integrating women into the Marine Corps infantry (RR-1103-USMC).

301. Bannister, C. (2017, May 30). 'Professors Claim Marine Corps Suffers from 'Toxic Masculinity,' 'Fraternity' Culture'. *CNS News*.

302. O'Hagan, E.M. (2018, March 6). 'Voter ID is just the latest Tory ruse to deplete the Labour vote'. *The Guardian*.

303. Helm, T. (2018, April 22). 'Tories in new race row over identity checks for elections'. *The Guardian*.

304. Kennedy, D. (2015, April 23). 'Tower Hamlets mayor Lutfur Rahman found guilty and removed from office'. *The Times*.

305. Connor, P. (2016, December 15). 'International migration: Key findings from the U.S., Europe and the world'. *Pew Research Center*.

306. Pearson, A. (2016, April 12). 'Why the ICM poll of British Muslims shows we need to defend our values more than ever'. *The Telegraph*.

307. Gov.uk. (2017, September). 'The Social Mobility Challenges Faced by Young Muslims'. *Social Mobility Commission*.

308. Corner, N. (2017, March 2). 'The moment a Muslim mother is forced to ask the permission of Islamic clerics in a BRITISH Sharia court to divorce her drug dealer husband'. *Mail Online*.

309. O'Neill, S. (2017, May 27). 'Huge scale of terror threat

revealed: UK home to 23,000 jihadists'. *The Times.*

310. Barnes, T. (2017, December 10). 'British-Pakistani researchers say 84% of grooming gang members are Asian: 'It's very important we talk about it''. *The Independent.*

311. Goodwin, M., Raines, T., and Cutts, D. (2017) What Do Europeans Think About Muslim Immigration? London: Chatham House.

312. Delingpole, J. (2016, April 16). 'Trevor Phillips's documentary on Muslims was shocking - but not surprising'. *The Spectator.*

313. Talwar, D. (2016, May 23). 'UK attitudes towards Islam 'concerning' after survey of 2,000 people'. *BBC Newsbeat.*

314. 'Ahmadi Muslims – Perceptions of the Caliphate'. (2016, April). *ComRes.*

315. Davis, N. (2017, July 5). 'NHS attended to 9,000 FGM cases in England last year, report reveals'. *The Guardian.*

316. Dearden, L. (2019, February 1). 'FGM conviction: Mother of girl, 3, becomes first person found guilty of female genital mutilation in UK'. *The Independent.*

317. Kay, B. (2018, January 17). 'Barbara Kay: Canadians don't need a 'National Day' scolding us for being Islamophobic'. *National Post.*

318. Malcolm, C. (2018, October 10). 'Canada's weak ISIS message is on display once again'. *Toronto Sun.*

319. Trinko, K. (2012, September 25). 'Obama: 'The Future Must Not Belong To Those Who Slander the Prophet of Islam''. *National Review.*

320. Matthews, A. (2016, March 18). 'Earth hour cancelled due to migrant rape: Swedish town refuses to turn lights off to protect women from attacks'. *Mail Online.*

321. O'Connor, R. (2017, July 4). 'Swedish music festival cancelled after multiple rapes and sexual assaults reported'. *The Independent.*

322. (2017, April 24). 'UN 'utterly horrified' by video appearing to show murder of two experts in Congo'. *The Guardian.*

323. Vulliamy, E. (2016, January 31). 'Angela Merkel says most refugees should go home - after Isis has been defeated'. *The Independent.*

324. Noack, R. (2015, December 14). 'Multiculturalism is a sham, says Angela Merkel'. *The Washington Post.*

325. Kerr, C. (2017, January 19). "the market of deterrence' German designer creates 'anti-rape pants' after spate of sexual assaults in Cologne at New Year'. *The Sun.*

326. Davies, G. (2017, June 28). 'Paris gets an app warning people if they are in a 'no-go' zone and giving live alerts of sexual assaults'. *Mail Online.*

327. Orange, R. (2016, march 8). 'Police warn women not to go out alone in Swedish town after spate of sex attacks'. *The Telegraph.*

328. Malm, S. (2017, September 5). 'Fury as German police tell women to 'jog in pairs' after runner was brutally raped in a park'. *Mail Online.*

329. Nussbaum, D. (2017, July 6). 'Report: Open Borders Advocate George Clooney Moving Family Back to Trump's America for 'Security Reasons''. *Breitbart.*

330. Maddox, D. (2018, September 14). "Labour CANNOT be trusted!' Diana Abbott immigration speech sparks FURIOUS response'. *The Express.*

331. Deacon, L. (2018, March 19). 'Claim: Police Dropped Cases Against 20 Telford Groomers Because They Were 'Too Much Trouble''. *Breitbart.*

332. Osborne, S. (2017, June 23). 'Refugee reality: Germany admits 75% face long-term unemployment and life on benefits'. *The Express.*

333. OECD (2017), 'Finding their Way. Labour Market Integration of Refugees in Germany', OECD Publishing, Paris.

334. Global Terrorism Index 2014: Measuring and Understanding the Impact of Terrorism (2014), IEP, Sydney–New York–Oxford.

335. Kern, S. (2017, January 17). 'The Islamization of France in 2016 'France has a problem with Islam''. *Gatestone Institute.*

336. Scarborough, R. (2017, September 26). 'New World Order: Muslims to be majority in Europe within two generations'. *The Washington Times.*

337. Mills, J. (2018, May 24). 'Extremist who left bacon at mosque 'died in prison after drug overdose''. *The Metro.*

338. Dearden, L. (2017, November 7). 'Mother who spread Isis propaganda on Facebook spared jail for terror offences due to children's 'suffering''. *The Independent.*

339. Ciccotta, T. (2018, June 5). 'The Atlantic: Is It Possible for Two People to Simultaneously Sexually Assault Each Other?' *Breitbart.*

340. Pells, R. (2017, August 9). 'Professor says students should choose own grades to help reduce stress'. *The Independent.*

341. Jolly, B. (2018, July 12). 'Families told to remove community paddling pool so 'burglars don't drown''. *The Metro.*

342. Jenkins, J. (2018, September 7). 'Pedophiles Believe They Should Be A Part Of The LGBT Community'. *The Daily Caller.*

343. Worley, W. (2016, April 8). 'Norwegian rape survivor 'feels guilty' the man who assaulted him was deported'. *The Independent.*

344. Travis, A. (2017, October 3). 'Amber Rudd: viewers of online terrorist material face 15 years in jail'. *The Guardian.*

345. 'Man guilty of hate crime for filming pug's 'Nazi salutes''. (2018, March 30). *BBC News.*

346. White, N. (2018, March 12). 'Far-right Austrian activist and his American girlfriend say they have been deported from Britain over plans to speak in Hyde Park'. *Mail Online.*

347. Graham, C. (2018, April 6). 'Who is Nasim Aghdam? Everything we know about the YouTube HQ shooter'. *The Telegraph*.

348. Mendick, R. (2018, September 11). 'Hate preacher Anjem Choudary to be freed from jail despite remaining 'genuinely dangerous''. *The Telegraph*.

349. Heffer, S. (2015, January 15). 'Why it's time to debunk the Churchill myth'. *The New Statesman America*.

350. Patient, D. (2016, May 5). 'Sir Winston Churchill named most influential Briton of the last century'. *The Express*.

351. Gurney-Read, J. (2016, January 28). 'Creationist views 'risk going unchallenged in schools''. *The Telegraph*.

352. Agerholm, H. (2017, November 11). 'Government allows faith school to split in two to avoid gender segregation law'. *The Independent*.

353. Evans, M. (2018, March 2). 'Teacher tried to raise army of jihadist children at school rated as outstanding'. *The Telegraph*.

354. Dearden, L. (2018, September 25). 'How British prisons became a breeding ground for Islamist extremism'. *The Independent*.

355. Berggren, N. & Nilsson, T. (2013). 'Does economic freedom foster tolerance?' *Kyklos*, 66 (2).

356. Wyatt, T. (2019, February 17). 'Shamima Begum: Isis child bride says she had 'good time' in Syria but wants to bring baby home'. *The Independent*.

357. Russell, R. (2019, February 17). 'Shamima Begum: ISIS bride gives shock interview - 'I don't regret it''. *The Express*.

358. Pew Research Center, (2018, March). 'At Least a Million Sub-Saharan Africans Moved to Europe Since 2010.'

359. Don Logan is a villain from the 2000 film *Sexy Beast*.

Milton Keynes UK
Ingram Content Group UK Ltd.
UKHW030721051124
450766UK00006B/643